The Human Factor

Designing Computer Systems for People

The Human Factor

Designing Computer Systems for People

RICHARD RUBINSTEIN / HARRY M. HERSH

With the assistance of Henry F. Ledgard

digital

Digital Press

9 8 7 6 5

Printed in the United States of America

Order number EY-00013-DP

The drawings on pages 23 and 131 are by Chris Demarest.

Library of Congress Cataloging in Publication Data

Rubinstein, Richard.
The human factor.

Includes index.
1. System design. 2. Electronic digital computers—Design and construction. 3. Human engineering.
I. Hersh, Harry M. II. Ledgard, Henry F., 1943–
III. Title.
QA76.9.S88R83 1984 001.64 84-7668
ISBN 0-932376-44-4

Contents

Prologue

Dear Dick and Harry,

The people upstairs have been thinking about automating our office and gave me a demonstration of a "user friendly" system. You wouldn't believe what a time I had! They asked me to send a message with it, and I gave it a try. They turned on the terminal and "logged me on" to the operating system, whatever that is.

The screen said to enter my name, so I typed it in. I was feeling pretty confident. Next it said *PASSWORD:*. I tried to type the password I'd been given, but nothing happened. I kept trying. Still nothing. Finally a message popped up, *ILLEGAL USER*.

I sat there a while, wondering what had happened. Finally they told me that passwords are not printed but the computer somehow sees what I typed anyway. So we did it all again, correctly this time. The screen filled up with what they said was the introductory help. It looked more like a note sheet for a final exam.

The system asked for a new password. "Do I have a new password? What's wrong with the old one?" They told me I could change my password now. Why would I want to change it in the first place? I just got it. I decided to humor them by changing it.

Finally, things started to make sense. There was a list of things to choose from on the screen. I wanted to write a message to a friend in another department, so I typed a "C"—which means "create a new message."

The screen immediately flashed *TO:* at me and I assumed that it meant to type in the name of my friend, so I did. It came out in capital letters. Was the shift-lock down? No . . . Oh, everything is automatically "echoed" in uppercase.

Then another *TO:* popped up. Didn't the system accept my first one? I put it in again and the computer told me the name was already there and up comes that *TO:* again. I tried to delete it by hitting the RUBOUT key. No use. (I figured out on my own that RUBOUT means to erase a letter.) I had no idea what to do at this point.

Finally they told me that if I just pressed the RETURN key, things would get moving again. I did, and got *CC:*. I didn't want to send a copy of my memo to anyone else, so I typed "none," which came out *NONE*, of course. The system said that there was no one by that name. What did that mean? I pressed the RETURN and I was back to square one. It still said *CC:*.

Then I remembered to press RETURN again, because that worked when I wanted it to stop saying *TO:*. It worked again. Then up came *SUBJECT:*, so I typed in a subject. At least here it let me use upper- and lowercase. I pressed RETURN, and up popped *ENTER MESSAGE TEXT. . .* It was on the screen only a moment, and disappeared. Up at the top of the screen was >>*END*<<. . . Wait! I didn't want to end the message. I hadn't even put it in yet! Did I do something wrong? An extra RETURN, perhaps? A friend later explained that ">>*END*<<" represented the bottom of my "text buffer," and that it kinda floats.

I finally got this all straightened out and typed my message. I realized that I did want to send a copy to someone after all. Obviously, I needed to move back up to where it had said *CC:*. They told me that the system doesn't work that way; first I had to indicate somehow that this was all I wanted to type, and then I could go back.

Forget the copy, I thought. I'll just send it as is. But how? I tried two RETURNs: after all, that's how I got out of the *TO:* and the *CC:* business. That didn't work, but I got two blank lines in my message. I tried pressing the HELP key. The screen filled with definitions, but nothing about sending my message. This was absolutely no help. "Use ESCAPE F," they said; "F stands for Finish." ("ESCAPE" sounded good, I thought.) But the computer said "F" was to file a message. I didn't want to file it, I simply wanted to send it. Why couldn't it have been "ESCAPE S" for send? OK, I typed "F." An "F" appeared in my message. Ohhh, "ESCAPE F!" I pressed the ESCAPE key once then the "F." Nothing happened. I waited, then did it again. The system said, "GOODBYE, HAVE A NICE DAY." I've since learned that the first "ESCAPE F" sent the message, and the second one logged me off.

Dick, Harry, you're in the business of making computers easier to use. Are all computers like this? It was easier for me to learn to do a tune-up on my car than to figure out how to write a note with a computer. Can't "user friendly" mean something more than a phrase in a brochure?

Sincerely,
Fred

Scenarios like this one have prompted us to write this book. It is a rebellious book. We believe that experiences like Fred's are unnecessary, because enough is now known about human factors to build computer systems that are easy to use and that meet people's needs. For builders of computer systems, we offer guidelines for good human-oriented design. For designers and users alike, we hope that *The Human Factor* will suggest how much better computer systems can be.

Dick Rubinstein
Harry Hersh
July 1984

OTTAWA

1 Why Human Factors?

Some products are right for their users; most are not. Have you ever been pleasantly surprised by what a machine did? Or found a particular device to be exceptionally easy to use? Or put together a kit without a hitch just by following the instructions?

When the interaction between a person and a machine is well designed, using the machine is so natural that you don't step back and recognize what a good thing you have. A good example is the modern automobile. When you rent a car at an airport, no one asks if you're familiar with its operation. The agency assumes that you can figure out how to drive whatever model you rent without getting into too much trouble. Most drivers in this country can get into an unfamiliar car and drive it away within a few minutes. That's a significant accomplishment for the automobile industry, considering the wide range of drivers and of automobiles. If you have trouble locating the remote trunk release button or the bright-lights switch, you may remember or even complain about it, but you don't even notice that you can read the instrument panel and use almost all the controls.

In contrast, many computer systems that make it into the marketplace are confusing, annoying, or ineffective. Almost everyone who has encountered computer systems has come across some that are hard to understand or to use. Because so many systems fall short of their potential, most users and designers have no idea how good a computer system could be. Every system has good features. It's just that few have good designs.

WHAT IS HUMAN FACTORS?

Human factors is the study of how people and machines interact. It is a technology for creating designs that work well in *human* terms. Without knowledge of people and how they use systems, design is only a hit-or-miss process.

Human factors, called "ergonomics" outside the United States, is both an engineering discipline and an applied science. Human factors engineers are concerned with designing safer, more productive, easier-to-use equipment and environments, and with selecting and training people to deal with existing environments. In a sense, good human factors engineering is just good engineering. It is based on a thorough analysis of the problem, broadly conceived. Just as a bridge designer must know the relevant details about how the bridge will be used, a computer system designer must take into account a great deal of information about the people who will use the system. Human factors engineering is the source of this information and the method for applying it to produce a user-centered design.

As an applied science, human factors is a relatively young, empirically oriented discipline. Its focus has been on the development of measurement techniques and the measurement of a very wide range of human behavior. Although the amount of significant research is rapidly increasing, it does not yet address all the issues involved, and the quality of research is variable [Ramsey et al 1978, Ramsey and Atwood 1979]. Some of the results provide a solid starting point in the design of computer systems. Where data are missing, creativity must enter into the design process: designers must make judicious choices in the absence of complete information.

Given the current limitations on our knowledge, one approach is to take the requirements, design a prototype, evaluate it, modify the design, and repeat this cycle until the design is acceptable. Any design approach must eventually prove its value through user acceptance, and only by testing the human interface with real users can we assess the quality of the product before it is released. This is why building and testing a mock-up of the human interface for a system is so effective. However, it also tends to be time-consuming and thus expensive. To get as close as possible to the final design on the first try, we use as much information as we can right from the beginning. After all, if the first design does not even resemble what we want, no sequence of modest redesigns will change the system into a good one.

One way to avoid many development cycles is to use general design guidelines when developing a prototype. Guidelines are helpful in the absence of better information, but they need to be used with some caution. Some design rules cannot easily be generalized. Taken out of context, they may be misleading. Knowing when and where to apply guidelines is a skill an engineer learns by experience rather than by formal instruction. Another important source of human factors information is models of behavior, or psychological theories. In the absence of hard data, such theories or models can provide a unifying framework for organizing and thinking about the many details in man-machine interactions. This book offers many design guidelines based on experience or derived from general rules of human behavior and from psychological data and theories.

Thus there are three ways of using human factors in computer system design, much as Brown has articulated for artificial intelligence [Brown 1983]. The intuitive approach relies on the designer's learning as much as possible about users and their tasks, observing other systems for their good and bad points, and basing his or her designs on intuition and good taste. Success depends on the designer's skill, taste, experience, and knowledge. The result, of course, is never guaranteed. In the second approach, many design decisions are based on specific guidelines. These, however, are sometimes contradictory and may not be applicable to the problem at hand. Using them well still requires taste and judgment. The designer using the third approach applies causal models or theories of user behavior to the development of the system. Theory has the virtue of generality and can therefore give rational guidance even in the absence of specific data and relevant guidelines. But with theories too, there is the danger that known relationships may not be directly applicable or may be hard to interpret for particular situations.

Any of these approaches can result in good and bad systems. We recommend a mixture of all three, with the second predominant. Designers can produce little of value if they lack experience and intuition, and too little has been developed in the way of a theory of human factors that has generalizability and predictive value. By far the greatest proportion of practical human factors knowledge is derived from and communicated by rules and guidelines. Accompanied by intuition and theory, this approach can lead to good human designs.

Know thy user, for he is not thyself.

No matter what the approach, the single most important principle of human factors design is "Know thy user, for he is not thyself." If we do nothing else but carefully adopt the point of view of the actual users of our products, our systems will be much better for it. This book tells you what you should know about users of the things you design or build, how to acquire this knowledge, and what to do with it.

EASE OF LEARNING, EASE OF USE, AND OTHER CLAIMS

Computer system promotional brochures abound with claims like: "Our system is simple to learn and easy to use." "Increase your productivity and throughput with our system!" "Our system is optimized for experienced users." Doesn't everyone design for these things now? Apparently not, if we go by the comment of the president of one software company. "Software suppliers are trying to make their software packages more 'user friendly.' The best approach, so far, has been to take all the old brochures and just rubber stamp them with 'user friendly' on the front cover" [Byte 1982].

Ease of Learning

Ease of learning is a primary goal in the design of well human-engineered systems. Nelson describes a criterion for excellence he calls the "Ten-Minute Rule" [Nelson 1980]. As the name implies, a beginning user should be able to learn how to use a system in just ten minutes—it has to be that obvious and simple, from the user's point of view. Most existing computer systems do not meet this criterion. Consider the computerized telephone systems coming into use in business. Most users *never* learn to use the majority of their capabilities—transferring calls, creating conference calls, and so on. Is learning to use a significant part of such a system in ten minutes asking too much? A good challenge when you are thinking about a new design is to ask yourself, "Could I make it possible for someone to learn to use this in just a few minutes?" It suggests some of the spirit of designing easy-to-use computer systems.

The Ten-Minute Rule does not require miracles, only that users bring to their tasks the considerable knowledge they already have of their own field—architects, of architecture; bankers, of banking; circuit designers, of electronics, and so on. All users know a great deal about communication, their own language, people, offices, and the tools they already use. A computer system for architects is not expected to teach architecture. Quite the reverse: the Ten-Minute Rule requires that what an architect already knows be helpful in learning to use the architecture system.

Guideline 1. Designers make myths; users make conceptual models.

To ensure ease of learning, a system must have consistent external behavior—behavior independent of its internal workings. We like to refer to this concept as the presentation of a consistent *external myth.* We call it a myth to emphasize that what the users actually see may not relate directly to the internals of the system—bytes, files, control sections, jobs, links, and so on.

If the external myth is familiar, users can make predictions, extrapolations, and educated guesses about the behavior of the system. They develop conceptual models—mental representations of the workings of the system. We must see to it that the external myth meticulously supports the building of simple conceptual models that correctly predict the behavior of the system. Chapter 5 shows how to influence the creation of conceptual models.

Ease of Use

Claims that a computer system is "user friendly" or has "ease of use features" frequently means only that certain parts have been added in order to eliminate user problems, whereas in fact ease of use can only be designed into the product as a whole. Adding new things after completion of system design usually leaves the hard-to-use part as it was and makes the system more complex and actually harder to use. In other words, ease of use is an emergent property, a broad consequence of a design, not a specific feature.

Reliability and Robustness

Two traditional qualities that affect how friendly a system appears to its users are reliability and robustness. Reliability is simply the absence of malfunctions. No system will be thought well of that is down frequently or that constantly has little troubles to be remedied. Robustness refers to the system's tolerance of difficulties and its protection of the user from them. Does the system cover for missing data, or does it blow up? Does it attempt to reread a bad tape block, or does it just report the error and quit? Does it reconstruct a damaged directory automatically, or force the user to go to a systems programmer to get it done?

Tailoring

One of the biggest challenges in computer system design is that no group of users is absolutely homogeneous—people differ in their work styles, preferences, knowledge, experience, and ability. How can one system fit everyone who must use it?

Many systems attempt to match the needs of individual users by providing profiles, settings, or other adjustment mechanisms that allow people to make various settings and changes that affect the behavior of the system for them alone. This "tailoring" capability has the potential to cause as much trouble as it seeks to eliminate. If the changes are numerous or profound, watching another person use the system can be confusing because the commands, procedures, keys, and so on are different from one's own experience. Also, the mechanism for making the changes can add significant complexity to the system, making it harder to learn and conceivably harder to use.

Nonetheless, designers must acknowledge that because people relate differently to their tools and to their work environment, individual users will want to adapt the system to their needs without changing its basic behavior. Accordingly, we must design systems that offer a sensible balance of choices.

Tailoring should not result in an incomplete system, leaving users to compensate for inadequacies by programming, writing "macros," synonyms, command files, or the like. Nor should it result in a system that requires users to make a deliberate choice about every function. The system should accommodate individual differences without forcing users to provide the details of the implementation.

Productivity

Productivity reflects how well the computer system matches user needs. Usual measures of human performance in human-machine interaction include units of work accomplished in a given time, time spent interacting with and waiting for the computer, and time the computer spends waiting for the person ("think time"). Another important consideration involves the role of the computer in the whole human or organizational endeavor in which it is being used. A word processor that is used only 30 minutes a day but in that period keeps its user waiting too long isn't productive. Nor is a system that must perform many complicated or time-consuming operations in order to execute a relatively simple or frequently required task. Applying a computer to a problem must make the task easier, never harder. Otherwise, there is no virtue in using one.

Using a computer should always be easier than not using a computer.

The following chapters discuss a series of issues in human factors, in the order in which they might be considered in creating a design. Our order is not the only sequence that would make sense; the topics can be usefully applied at various stages of design, construction, and evaluation. Each is also of value considered alone.

In addition to providing design guidelines along the way, we carry one design as a case study through most of the book, applying the information in each chapter to this concrete example. Finally, because we believe that the best way to learn about something new is to use it, to become actively involved with it, the Appendix contains some activities designed to help make the issues discussed throughout the book more real.

2 Design Philosophy

In applying human factors to system building, process—the set of procedures for creating the design and building the resulting system—is as important as content—the information drawn from human factors disciplines. Most of the guidelines in the following chapters relate to content: they describe qualities that systems should have. But only by understanding the human aspects of the development process and taking them into account is it possible to maximize the likelihood of producing a well human-engineered computer system.

A DESIGN PHILOSOPHY

The norm in the computer industry is to take the hardware and software environments as a "given," to build application software to perform the (presumed) desired functions, and only then to consider doc-

FUNKY WINKERBEAN by Tom Batiuk; © 1980 by Field Enterprises, Inc. Courtesy of Field Newspaper Syndicate.

umentation, installation, maintenance, user training, and other "practical" issues. The priority of each of these issues depends on the organization and the people involved. Some projects are motivated most strongly by marketing considerations, others by available hardware or software, still others by the skills and interests of the developers. None of these considerations alone is sufficient. Integrated design is the formulation of a system considering all issues throughout the process. Human factors is a natural part of integrated design.

Consider the relation of error messages to a whole design, which we discuss in more detail in later chapters. Human considerations dictate provision of clear messages, phrased in familiar language. But what errors there are need not arise by accident out of the rest of the design; the design can also be manipulated to *create* the right set of errors to report. By allowing requirements for error messages to interact with those for the rest of the design, designers can maximize the effectiveness of the system by adjusting the number and kind of errors reported. It is even possible to design systems with no error states or messages. Pac-Man and other video games, for example, have virtually no error conditions. Even the *tilt* light of the old pinball machines has been eliminated.

Documentation and maintenance are two other issues that are usually left for last, to the detriment of the product. Ask yourself what the right documentation would be if the system were not otherwise constrained. And how should maintenance be done, ideally? Though each of these considerations will have to interact with the others, the result will be better if you bring them all to bear on the design at once. The essence of engineering is creating constructive compromises among many conflicting goals. Integrated design can occur only when all the real issues are allowed to exert an influence.

Engineering is compromise.
Integrated design is design of whole systems.

The creation of computer systems involves elements of engineering, science, and art—the practical search for results, the application of theory, and the use of skill and taste. Our design philosophy is based on the view that science and art are as indispensable to design as is engineering practice.

A RATIONAL DEVELOPMENT PROCESS

The design of most computer systems is too complicated for one or even a few people to comprehend. One consequence of this complexity is that designers of systems are forced to break problems down into minimally interacting parts and to deal with these separately. Part of the crisis in the design of computer-based systems is that many of the important pieces are never integrated into the process. As a result, familiar ways of building computer systems work less and less well as tasks grow and change.

Consider an example from another design discipline. Architects design office buildings with a good degree of slack for "systems" such as plumbing, heating and cooling, communications, and electric wiring. It is common to have at least three feet of space above a false ceiling to ensure that mistakes can be rectified. The cost of this rule is considerable, perhaps two feet of building height for every story of building, or about 20 percent of the height of the structure. Architects have not yet devised a better way to guarantee that all constraints interact correctly in the design, but at least their rules provide workable buildings.

Design is seldom an orderly or linear process. System building occurs in a real world with constraints, interruptions, distractions, emotions, personalities, and politics. Any guidelines used for system development must operate within these complex conditions.

Figure 2-1 presents a simplified model of the development process. In this model, external information is collected and used to set the goals, bounds, and other requirements for the design. The design is then evaluated in various ways, ultimately by constructing the system and testing it. Flaws uncovered during the testing are corrected in the prototype, and the more general results of testing and evaluation are used to refine the design. The process is repeated until some criterion is reached, and finally the system is delivered. Information about market acceptance and user reactions can be used as input to the next system development cycle.

Because design is an art as well as a science, it is never a completely rational process. Inventiveness and good ideas require that the constraints on the proposed system be known early. Otherwise, the bright

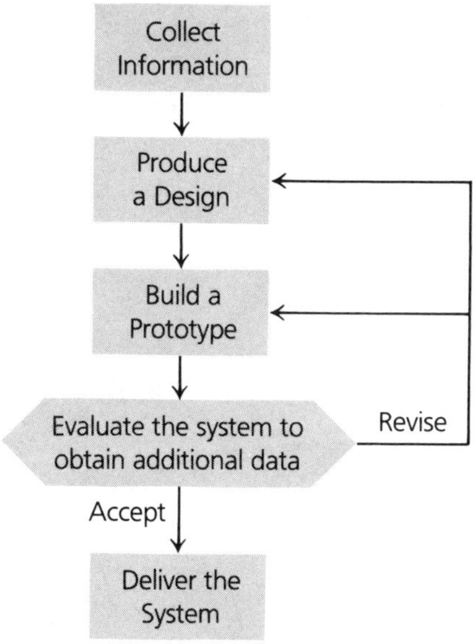

Figure 2-1. Conventional development process

idea that comes is not likely to satisfy them. This is why information gathering precedes design. Then evaluation and testing allow us to improve our ideas in an orderly way.

The basic development process in no way guarantees a well human-engineered system. Systems, especially those designed by large organizations, are often sensible in each of their parts, but not so sensible when taken as a whole. If communication is poor or if differing interests are not reconciled, the individuals or teams working on different parts of the system will each do only what makes sense to them. Even when all parties cooperate, it is difficult to focus attention continually on all aspects of a large system as it develops. It is a marvel of computer technology that disparate pieces are so often assembled without producing overt conflict. The result of local sense and global nonsense is much like the drawings of M. C. Escher: each piece works and is part of the whole, but viewed from a broader perspective, things are not right. In *Belvedere* (Figure 2-2), which of the people knows that anything is wrong? Only the viewer, from his or her slight distance, is fully aware of the problem. One goal of the development process is to prevent these global problems, or at least to detect them in time to do something about them.

Our model is based on observations of two recurring impediments to

Figure 2-2. A system perspective—*Belvedere* by M. C. Escher.
© Beeldrecht, Amsterdam/VAGA. New York Collection, Haags Gemeentemuseum, The Hague. Reproduction rights arranged courtesy of the Vorpal Galleries, New York City, San Francisco and Laguna Beach, California.

well human-engineered products. The first is perspective. It is far easier to design for consistency at a local level than at a global one. We need a process that helps us to focus our attention on the global aspects of the system when necessary, and to concentrate on the details of the design without being overwhelmed.

Second, in the effort to base designs on the best available information, we must make both explicit and implicit assumptions. Explicit assumptions, such as those relating to a requirements document, can be assessed for accuracy and appropriateness. Implicit assumptions, such as those about details of the system's intended use, necessarily go unchecked. Because just being aware of potential problems can produce a dramatic improvement in human engineering, we need a process that helps make explicit as many of our assumptions as possible, so that they can be viewed objectively.

Figure 2-3 shows our elaborated development process. The chapter references in the diagram indicate where these topics are covered in detail elsewhere in the book. The major components are exactly the same as those in the basic model (Figure 2-1): information is collected, a design is created and implemented, and the system is evaluated and ultimately delivered. But the types and number of activities involved in each step are different. We will discuss the overall process here.

Information Gathering

Information gathering is the starting point, the reference point, in the development process. Once we have made the requirements and goals explicit, we can use them as constraints to guide the design. We can also use this relevant information to make many of the inevitable design tradeoffs in a rational manner, rather than at the last minute when shortage of time forces many an arbitrary decision.

As Figure 2-3 shows, a variety of information sources provide the basis for the design of computer systems. These include technical requirements, the current state of the art, products already in use, industry standards, government regulations, and the technical capabilities of the system builders.

Since the technical requirements are usually nonnegotiable, it makes sense to understand them before beginning. In addition to government regulations, the technical capabilities and skills of the builders may

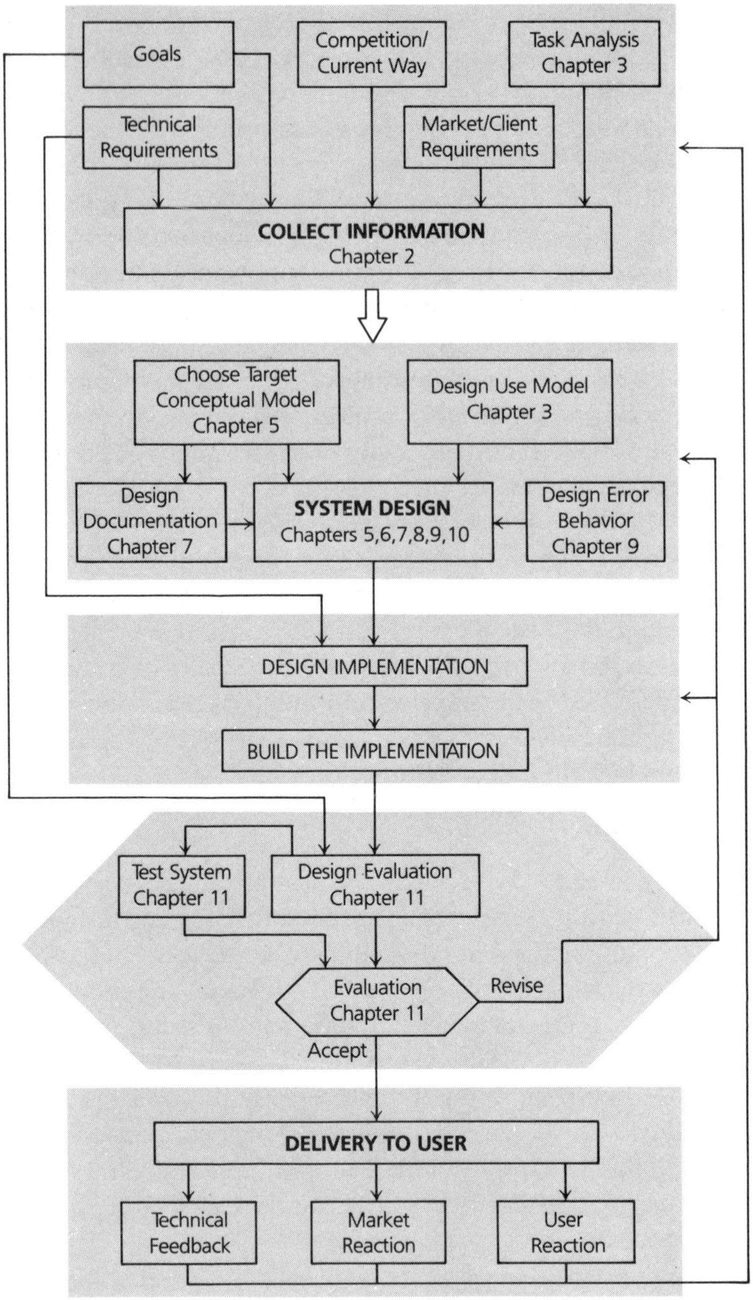

Figure 2-3. Elaborated development process

limit the size and complexity of the system to be designed. But additional staffing may be possible if the right skills and job descriptions can be specified.

Market and client requirements may be provided by the sales force, professional marketing people, management, customer specifications, market surveys, or intuition about what is salable. What is the market "asking for"? Is part of the appeal of the product that it is "state of the art"? Are there particular features that competitors have already incorporated? What features or products are perceived as gimmicks? The most sophisticated design in the world fails to sell if no one wants it. Designers need a detailed written description of market requirements or, if the product is being built for an in-house user or a specific client, specifications and requirements from that source.

The specific tasks the user will perform directly influence what the system will do. A task analysis, discussed in detail in Chapter 3, aims at providing a clear picture of the users and their environment.

It is not enough to collect the information from all these sources. We also need a clear sense of the design goals and their relative importance. There may also be important process goals to consider, such as the time permitted for development, the available resources, and the total budget for the project. It is always better to identify these issues at the beginning than to have them ambush you at the end.

Design

Once the goals of the project are identified and the initial information collected and organized, the designer should have a clear picture of the requirements and constraints. From this seed grows the whole design. A well human-engineered design specifies the repertoire of functions the system will perform, how users will use the system, and how the system will fit into their lives. The design creates a user interface, that is, an external presentation of the capabilities of the system.

Figure 2-3 also shows the tasks involved in design. Although they need not be performed in a particular sequence, it is important that by the end of the initial design stage each be well defined, committed to paper, and critically assessed in relation to the initial requirements and to each other.

An external myth is chosen to support the conceptual model that the designer wants the user to build. Chapter 5 explains in detail what a conceptual model is, and why it is important in the design of systems.

Chapter 3 describes the utility of an explicit *use model*, the equivalent of a task analysis for the future. It describes how the system will be used and how it will fit into the user's life.

System design is the process of specifying the system's external behavior—the details of hardware and software that impact the user. At this stage it is essential to develop the documentation (such as the user's manual). Documentation provides an opportunity to evaluate the system long before the first line of code is written. Being able to write a coherent user's manual is a good sign that the overall design is consistent and clear. Chapter 7 discusses why the documentation should be written either before or concurrently with the design of the system.

Thinking about error behavior early makes life significantly easier for users. Since error behavior becomes part of the user's conceptual model, it is necessary to anticipate errors and to plan how users will deal with them. Chapter 9 discusses error processing in detail.

Implementation

After designing the external behavior of the system, we turn to the design of the internals, to the functions to be performed for the user. At this point the user interface is relatively fixed.

There are economic and logical arguments for doing a thorough implementation design before starting to build a system. The cost of fixing problems increases rapidly as development proceeds [Mason and Carey 1983]. Creating a complete design before coding is good software-engineering practice for systems of all sizes. This practice is one of the basic tools for preventing disasters, overruns, and schedule slippage [Brooks 1975], and applies equally well to hardware design.

Next comes the actual construction of the system. This is the part of the process that typically gets the most attention. No matter how carefully a design has been created, implementation always uncovers unspecified choices and issues that need resolution. The system design and all the information that went into it provide the basis for resolving these problems. Using the external myth, we can often answer questions of the form, "What should it do in this case?" Good management can help prevent such unforeseen issues from being decided in random or ad hoc ways.

Testing and Evaluation

Formally or informally, explicitly or implicitly, all systems are evaluated. Evaluation may be based simply on whether the product sells well. Or users may provide feedback about specific features and bugs. There may be formal evaluations that test features, performance, and user satisfaction. Evaluation creates a feedback loop that helps us improve a system in an organized way, on the basis of the goals of the project. Using this evaluation design, we test the system and assess the results to determine how the findings affect the system and how the system might be improved. Chapter 11 discusses the overall evaluation process.

Delivery

Delivery of a system implies completion of the project and gives the designer a sense of accomplishment and relief: "We've done it." But even after the system has been delivered, there is still much we can learn, as Figure 2-3 shows. Is the system effective after people learn to use it? What frustrations do users experience? What shortcuts do users invent or ask for? What gets used and what doesn't? Who is buying it (or using it)? Who is not? Why?

Gathering this information can be considered either the end of a development cycle or the beginning of the next. As they learn to use the system, many people expect it to do more and more. In many environments, system development is a continuous activity.

OUR DESIGN PHILOSOPHY

Our model of development separates design from implementation because we want to understand what we are building before we start building it. Authors who write about separating *architecture* from implementation [see Brooks 1975] mean essentially the same thing. Planning pays for itself many times over, and quality requires planning.

Guideline 2. Separate design from implementation.

The model is consistent with top-down design, a topic with great currency in the literature [Moran 1981]. Top-down design is the breaking down of the whole problem into progressively smaller subproblems again and again until implementable units are reached. It is the most powerful tool available for avoiding global-inconsistency because it deals explicitly with the relation of each of the parts to the whole. Our emphasis on designing external behavior and on writing the user's manual first reflects this top-down design philosophy. Including the needs of users in the design acknowledges that the user, not the designer, is the most important component, the top, in system design.

If you work with a group or a large organization, you will not always be able to get your way on design issues. Many things are not subject to change, and enough energy and resources may not be available to change all those that are. Our goal in infusing human factors technology into design is to identify opportunities to do the things that have high payoff and to avoid those that cause the most trouble. If we can just identify properties and features at both ends of the spectrum and design accordingly, we will have made a major contribution to the design. We seek good designs, not perfect ones. It is sufficient to do a good job on those parts that make the most difference. Trying to make a design perfect can make it worse. Moreover, it frequently makes it late.

The perfect is the enemy of the good.

3 Task Analysis and Use Models

"Dragon, shmagon . . . dragon it is."

In one large metropolitan area, several groups of cooperating banks have electronic sidewalk tellers. Even though your bank is in one town you can use any of the machines from associated banks throughout the state to access your account. With any of these terminals, you insert a plastic card, enter an identification code, and then make choices and entries to control the banking transaction. The machine works by providing menus from which you make selections. The first menu appears in Figure 3-1(a).

Once you make a selection, additional instructions or choices appear on the screen. Suppose you choose TRANSFER (by pushing key 5) in order to move some money from savings to checking. The system responds with the menu in Figure 3-1(b). If you now push key 3, the instruction frame shown in Figure 3-1(c) appears. When you enter the amount, and press YES, the final message appears: "THIS TRANSACTION IS ONLY ALLOWED AT MACHINES PROVIDED BY YOUR BANK." You went through a lot of steps to find out that you couldn't perform the transaction. In fact, the transaction is prohibited by state law.

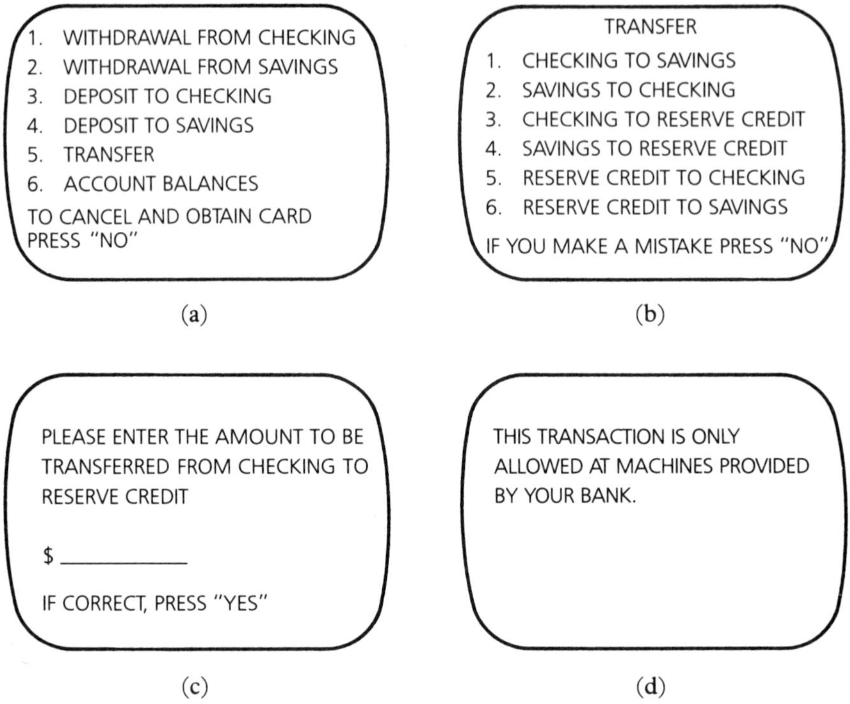

Figure 3-1. Electronic teller menu sequence

The machine could have made things much simpler by not offering the invalid choice in the first place. The designers failed to create as convenient a machine as they might have. Did they really understand the range of customers who would be using the system and the tasks these users would want to carry out? Did the designers realize or care that users would find the computer's behavior disconcerting? How can we avoid similar results?

One way to prevent such frustation is to use two tools, task analysis and use models, at the beginning of the design process. Task analysis is the result of an information-gathering activity in which designers discover exactly what users are doing with their current systems. Developing a task analysis involves asking, "What is required to perform the user's tasks?"

With this information, designers then create a use model, a description of how the proposed system will operate in the user's environment. The use model contains the same kind of information as the task analysis except that it describes the future situation instead of the existing one.

TASK ANALYSIS

The first step in designing for people is to find out who the people are, what they do now, and what the new system is expected to do for them. Consider how some architects work when designing a house for an individual. They interview and sometimes even live with the client to learn about specific needs and peculiarities. The information they obtain through such efforts supplements a general knowledge of people and houses. Task analysis fulfills a similar function for developers in their design of computer systems.

Guideline 3. Describe before you leap.

Many task analyses are performed only to be ignored later because they lack relevance. You need to ask appropriate questions and to draw useful inferences from the answers you get. For example, sex may not matter to the design of a spreadsheet program, but it is relevant to the design of workstation furniture, because men and women are different sizes.

The results of interviews need careful interpretation. People may tell you what they think you want to hear, what they believe, what they think *you* believe, what they wish were so, and so on. They can also be unintentionally wrong. Only if you discover what facilities would truly help can you take a strong stand on what the system should do and how the user will make that happen. There are experts in the area of task analysis, and it pays to consult them when you are having trouble understanding a particular task.

The procedures for task analysis are not yet standardized, but every task analysis should address the following questions.

Who Is the User?

This question is frequently the hardest to answer. If you are designing a product that is to be sold in several markets, such as a word processor, it may be impossible to find representative users. On the other hand, if you are designing a tool for use in your own organization or for a specific customer, the identity of the user is no mystery. Identification is just the beginning, however. You also need to know about the user's background, skills, work habits and preferences, even physical characteristics.

What Tasks Does the User Now Perform?

Whether the purpose of the new system is to automate what the user now does or to provide a new capability or activity or both, knowing what tasks the user performs now and their relative importance is useful. Frequently, current procedures have steps and effects that remain hidden until the designer asks questions and observes users operating the existing system.

For example, recently a water district in Maine installed an on-line billing system so that when a customer called in, the clerk could quickly retrieve a record of usage and billing for that customer. The managers noticed that the clerks were less than happy with the new system. A little investigation revealed that with the manual system, the clerks would write pertinent information in the margins of the records, such as that one person pays on the fifteenth of the month rather than the first, or that the meter reader should contact the neighbor across the street for access to a house. This informal information was critical to the smooth operation of the office, but because there was no provision for it in an official field of the payment record form, the information was lost in the conversion to the on-line system. Understanding that there is informal as well as official information and recognizing the importance of the former would have reduced the disruption in work style.

It is important to spend some time watching users do their jobs with their current tools, whatever they be. The closer you are to the prospective users and the more you know about them, the more likely you are to produce a system that meets their needs.

How Is the Task Learned?

What does the prospective user have to know to perform the current task? Is academic training, general knowledge or skills, or special instruction or training required?

Where Is the Task Performed?

Is the system to be used in an office, a laboratory, or at a point of sale? What are the effects of the environment on users? Are users under stress? Do they have wet, dirty, or slippery hands? Are there corrosive or solvent materials present such as soft drinks? Does confidentiality require that others not be able to see what the user is doing?

In the location that is being considered how much space (desk, floor) could a new system occupy? Is there space for storage of system accessories such as disks, tapes, paper, and computer output? Would there be too little light for easy viewing of the equipment, or too much noise for users to hear sounds a system might make (such as the bell on a terminal)?

What Is the Relationship Between Users and Data?

Are personal data always accessed at the same terminal or via the same account, or do users move between stations and expect to access the same data? Are common data used concurrently or passed sequentially between users? Is remote access required? Is access to data restricted? Not only do the answers to these questions determine the functions the system must perform; they determine relationships among the users and affect the way they think about information in the system.

What Other Tools Does the User Have?

This question addresses more than technical compatibility. The broader issue is how the user has to behave with the collection of tools he or she has. For example, if the proposed system is to aid laboratory scientists in collecting data, we must find out how data are collected now, by what instruments or manual procedures. How is the information analyzed? Are the results transcribed for records or publication? What media, forms, and the like are used, and how are they handled?

How Do Users Communicate with Each Other?

Who communicates with whom, and about what? Does communication follow the lines of the organization or run counter to it? For example, the installation of a computer system can disrupt secretary-to-manager communication and there is evidence that people would rather change their usage of a computer system than change the relationship with their manager or secretary [Hersh 1982b].

How Often Do Users Perform the Tasks?

This question is important because frequent users can remember more details of a system than infrequent users; the latter may require more help even with simple operations. Knowing which functions are performed most frequently and by which users enables designers to optimize the system for these tasks and thus to strengthen user perceptions of good performance.

What Are the Time Constraints on the Tasks?

Which functions will the user be in a hurry for? Which can wait? Is there a timing relationship between tasks? The relationship between the speed at which the user operates and that of the system is often an important issue.

What Happens When Things Go Wrong?

How do people now deal with task-related errors, practical difficulties, and catastrophes? Are there audit trails or duplicate copies of important data? Do several people know the important information? Is there a backup strategy for current tools if they become inoperative?

USE MODELS

A use model is a description of how people will use a system, what problems it will solve for them, and how it will integrate with their environment, both organizationally and physically. The use model describes the relationships among the people who will use the same system, and thus includes the sociology of its use. It provides answers to the same questions asked in the task analysis, except in the future tense. "With the proposed system, what will the task analysis be?" It also uses other input such as market and technical requirements. The crucial part of a use model is a detailed analysis of how the user's life will change with the advent of the new system. Most systems have both advantageous and adverse impacts. Incorporating predictions of these effects into the design enables you to deal with change explicitly, and perhaps to control the effect of change by controlling the design.

A good use model allows for a degree of freedom called "life style." In other words, the use model has sufficient latitude and richness to accommodate differences among users and the ways in which they choose to approach problems. For example, some people who use electronic mail have third parties (secretaries) read and answer most of it, but they may also choose to treat a particular item of mail differently, handling it without assistance.

Guideline 4. Develop an explicit use model.

Even if you proceed with a design without consciously developing a task analysis and a use model, in fact there is always a use model, based on what you, the designer, believe. In the absence of detailed information, we all work from assumptions about who the user is, what he or she does, and what type of system would meet his or her needs. Following these assumptions, we tend to design for ourselves, not for other people. When our assumptions are accurate, we may produce a reasonable system. When they are inaccurate, we may produce the wrong system even though it is "well designed."

The next chapter applies these principles in a discussion of the initial design activities in a case study, an automatic teller system.

4 Starting a Design

This chapter discusses the first two steps in the development process—information gathering and initial design—in terms of a case study that will be carried through the rest of the book. Although the environment in which our example takes place is fictitious, the content and process are real. For this case study, we imagine ourselves to be the EDP department of a small New York bank, charged with designing an electronic teller terminal (called an Automatic Teller Machine or ATM) for use by the bank itself.

People's Bank of New York provides services to residents of New York City, including many who are not native speakers of English. Many customers do not read English at the high-school level, although they may be literate in other languages. People's Bank has been slow to introduce automatic teller machines for fear that these customers would have difficulty using them. Internally, the bank is as highly automated as any other, handling accounts, electronic funds transfer, and the like by computer. A consultant hired to recommend an existing ATM system found none of the units commercially available satisfactory for clients not literate in English. The bank management has decided to develop its own electronic teller to meet its particular needs. We, the bank's EDP department, have been given the job of designing and implementing a suitable system. The human factors of our system are especially important because the image of the bank is at stake, and standard ATMs have not been successful elsewhere for non-English-speaking customers.

In terms of the information gathering outlined in Figure 2-3, some of the development process has already happened. Our client, the bank, has said what it wants in very general terms, and we have been given a charter to proceed. Usually there is some history to a project before a specific individual or department becomes involved, but that is not so in our case.

INFORMATION GATHERING

We begin with the market requirements as expressed by bank management. These statements about what the system must do may or may not be subject to question and refinement, depending on the thoroughness of the thinking and research that went into them. If we find that the bank's goals are unreasonable or unrealistic, it is our responsibility to report this problem to management.

The bank believes that it can provide better and more economical service for its existing customers by using ATMs. Customers could perform transactions 24 hours per day, and simple transactions performed during banking hours would take less time than if human tellers were involved. The bank also hopes that a system effective for non-English-speaking customers will provide a competitive advantage, attracting new patrons.

The bank provides the following kinds of accounts:

- Checking
- Savings
- Personal credit line

The functional requirements specified by management for the automatic teller machine are:

- Provide cash withdrawals.
- Allow deposits and payments.

- Provide account balances.
- Allow transfers of money between an individual's accounts.

The terminals must provide each kind of access to each kind of account.

There are further requirements supplied by the bank that bear on the system design:

- Account security: Mechanisms must be provided to protect the customer and bank from unauthorized use of accounts.
- Physical security: The terminal must not encourage vandalism or be easily robbed or put out of commission.
- Customer safety: The terminal must support the safety of customers, so as not to encourage robberies.
- Privacy: The terminal must provide privacy for transactions. Persons waiting to use the terminal must not be privy to the transactions being performed.
- Customers will use the conventional method of inserting a plastic card to gain access.
- Conventional terminal hardware will be used with only minor modifications, specifically only those that can be provided by the terminal vendor.

Other requirements relate more directly to how users will percieve and operate the terminals. Market requirements include the following:

- Operation of the terminal shall not require a fluent understanding of written English.
- Instructions in Spanish will be provided to customers who are fluent in that language.
- Procedures must be developed for introducing new users to the terminals and for overcoming potential customer resistance.
- Access to accounts must be provided from all terminals provided by People's Bank, whether in the bank building or at other locations in the city. The location of the terminal must make no functional difference to customers in accessing their accounts.
- Customers must be able to conduct business at terminals or via human tellers, interchangeably.

Competitive requirements include the following:

- Fluent speakers of English will find the terminal at least as convenient as those of other banks and will be at no disadvantage relative to other terminal users.
- There must be no reference cards or other carry-away instructions, because competitive terminals don't require them. All information the user needs must be provided at the terminal.

TASK ANALYSIS

Our first step in creating an ATM design for People's Bank is to do a task analysis. It is not enough just to discover the attributes of potential system users and the tasks they will perform. We must make the implications of these issues explicit in written form. In this way, predesign information gathering will have the most impact on the development process.

Who Is the User?

Users are current and potential bank customers. They are both professional and working people who work and live in New York City. They vary widely in education, age, and linguistic background. A study of existing bank customers yielded the following distribution of native languages:

English	47%
Spanish	43%
Portuguese	3%
Italian	3%
Other	4%

Some of the English speakers are Haitian immigrants with poor reading skills. Forty percent of existing bank customers are estimated to read at twelfth-grade level. The implication of these facts is that most bank customers prefer personal or verbal interactions with the bank (although this can also be said of most other banks). As a result, ease of use poses a challenge.

Otherwise, the mix of bank customers is much like that of other banks in New York City. The bank's study of customers also yielded the following information on age distribution:

Under 18	1%
18-25	18%
26-35	30%
36-45	27%
46-65	15%
Over 65	9%

What Tasks Does the User Now Perform?

Current customers conduct deposit, withdrawal, and balance transactions in person at tellers' windows. Many other transactions are also performed in person: changing foreign money, paying utility bills, obtaining cashier's checks, making change, depositing coins, cashing checks, and opening and closing accounts. The vast majority of problems with accounts or statements are handled in person rather than by phone or mail. Only a few professional customers use direct deposit of paychecks. Many customers conduct frequent cash transactions.

How Is the Task Learned?

For current bank customers, learning to do banking operations involves no formal instruction, and all of the user's basic educational background is relevant: reading, doing arithmetic, handling money. Details of personal banking transactions are learned over time from parents, friends, and firsthand experience.

Where Is the Task Performed?

Currently, nearly all transactions take place at tellers' windows, inside bank offices. Some transactions are conducted by mail.

What Is the Relation Between Users and Data?

Accounts are private, accessible only to account owners and the bank. A user can have more than one account. There are no restricted-access accounts, and anyone with access to an account may perform all transactions.

What Other Tools Does the User Have?

Besides conducting business in person, users can also use the mail and the telephone, though currently these alternatives are little used.

How Do Users Communicate with Each Other?

All communication is between the bank and customers. Bank employees can acquire balance and other account information and provide it to customers.

How Often Do Users Perform the Tasks?

Currently, customers average about five in-person transactions per month. The majority of transactions involve cashing or depositing paychecks. Mail transactions account for less than one percent of all transactions.

What Are the Time Constraints on the Tasks?

For current teller transactions, there is no fixed time limit. When a single transaction takes a long time, people waiting are affected. People's Bank now combines the lines for its tellers, having the first person in line proceed to the first available teller window. Average transaction time for live tellers is two minutes, but there is a wide variation.

What Happens When Things Go Wrong?

Errors and other problems are currently brought to the attention of tellers, who refer problems they cannot resolve to other bank staff. If the computers are down, balances are available from the previous day on microfilm, to allow approval of checks and withdrawals. Customers always have the recourse of speaking with bank employees when, from their point of view, something is not right.

INITIAL DESIGN

The bank management is in a hurry to get under way and demands an initial design document immediately. In response, here is our design of the system for People's Bank, based on everything we know about the bank's requirements, the intended users, and automatic teller machines. This initial description includes the use model, as best we know it at this point.

The system will consist of conventional commercial ATM terminals, each containing a screen, keyboard, credit-card reader, receipt printer, cash dispenser, and deposit-envelope handler. The terminals will be customized to the bank's specifications in terms of instructions and key legends.

Machines will be available 24 hours per day, so customers will be able to use the terminals frequently. Experience in other banks indicates that customers who use the machines do so about six times per month. At other banks, installation of ATMs has resulted in fewer teller transactions but more overall transactions, teller and ATM combined. No projected data are available at this time for the bank's customers.

To address the fact that many of the clients understand spoken language better than written, a wall-mounted telephone handset will be provided for output audio. At the user's option, the automatic teller will provide spoken output paralleling the visual output, in either English or Spanish. Voice synthesis will be provided by a commercial digitized-voice unit. A handset rather than a speaker is specified because of the market requirement for privacy. Moreover, modern "pay phone" handsets are reliable and essentially vandal-proof. No voice input will be used. Customers will control transactions in the conventional manner, by inserting a plastic access card, entering an identification code, and selecting transactions via the keyboard. After performing the transaction, they will remove the receipt and the card and then leave the machine.

Customers will choose whether to use voice output by listening or not. Customers' cards will be coded to provide screen displays in either English or Spanish, and the audio will present the same information that is on the screen. If no action is taken within ten seconds, the audio will be repeated. When a button is pressed on the terminal, the audio presentation will stop and the next screen frame will appear (and be heard).

The task for customers is largely specified by the market and competitive requirements. Patrons will be able to access their accounts to get balances, withdraw cash, make deposits and payments, and transfer money between accounts.

Figures 4-1 and 4-2 show the instructions and menus that will appear on the ATM screen. Later chapters discuss the tasks in detail.

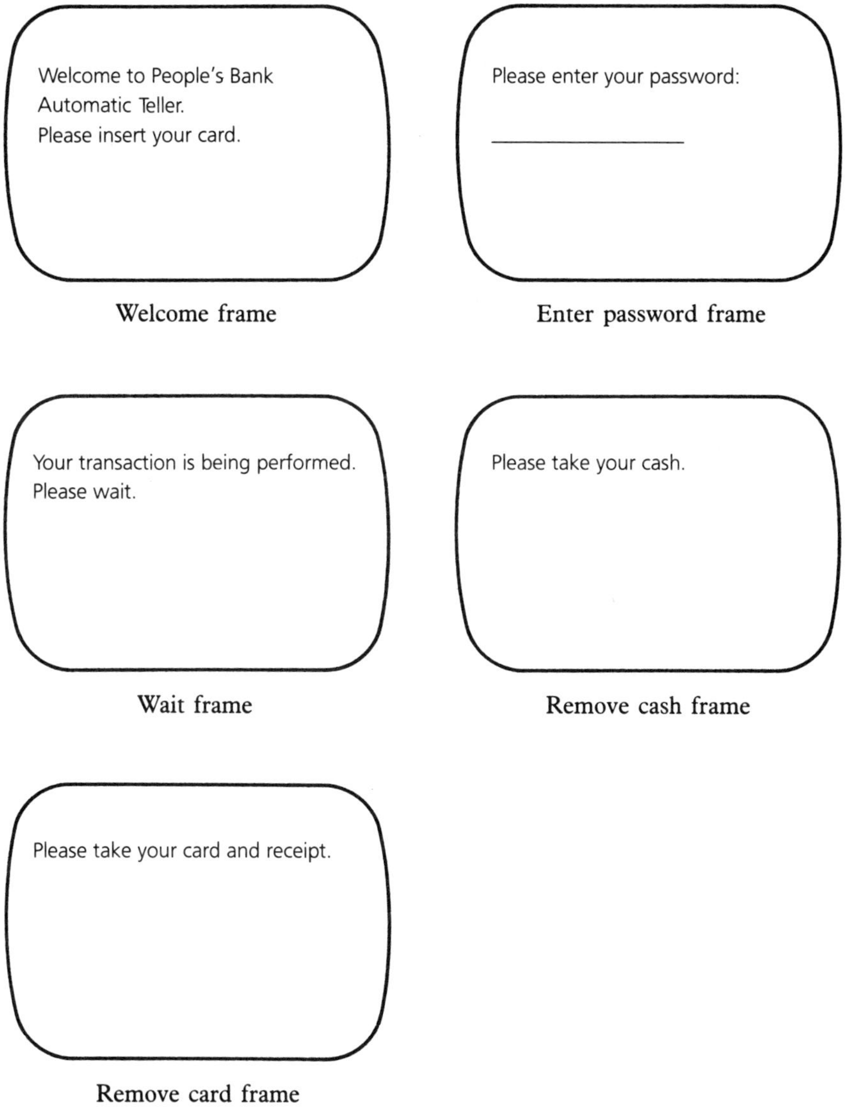

Figure 4-1. Screen frames for general instructions

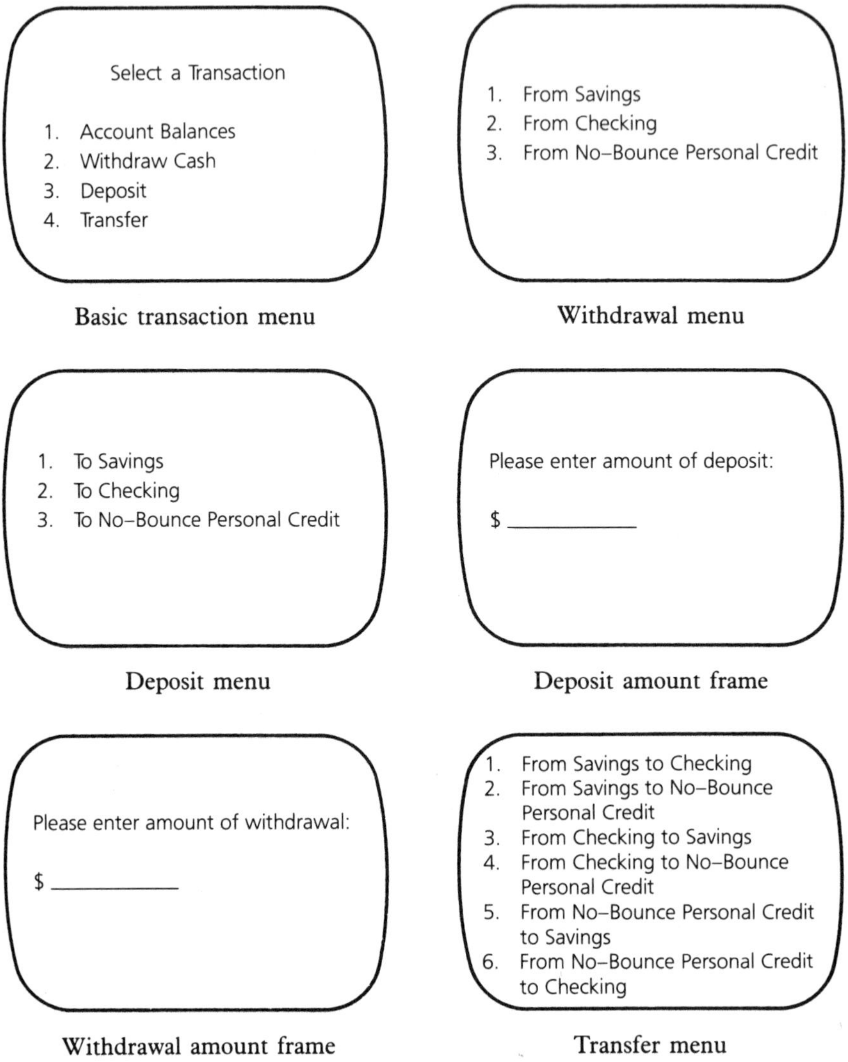

Figure 4-2. Screen frames for menus

USE MODEL

Based on this initial and incomplete functional design, we can specify part of a use model for the system. The use model will help management understand what will happen when our system becomes operational, and puts the system in a context in which we can begin to evaluate the effects of our design on users.

Task Learning

To provide People's Bank customers with encouragement in using the machines, we specify that on first use a human "instructor" be present to show the customer how to use the machine and guide him or her through a transaction. There will be no user documentation for the ATMs, because people cannot be expected to keep reference cards or brochures from one transaction to the next. The voice output and menus are intended to make documentation unnecessary. This approach is consistent with the competitive requirement that there be no reference cards or other carry-away instructions.

Physical Impact of the System

Machines will be placed in all offices of People's Bank and in satellite automated-teller offices to be established by the bank. People's Bank has sufficient lobby space to accommodate four ATMs in its main branch office, and room for two machines in each of the other two branches. Spaces for satellite offices have not been procured.

For security reasons, the automatic teller machines will be located indoors, adjacent to the bank lobby. They will require back-office space for loading and unloading. Units must be placed at a height that ensures that most customers will find it easy to see the controls, take their cash, and so on. The use area will be heated in winter so that users can remove gloves and comfortably punch buttons on the machines. The environment will be well lit, quiet, and secluded from passersby and street activity.

Relationship Between Users and Data

No change in the confidentiality of account information or in information flow between customers and the bank is anticipated as a result of installation of the ATMs.

Time Constraints on Users

The bank and users share a desire to conduct transactions quickly. A time limit will be imposed on individual transactions so that the machine will not be tied up if a user is confused or walks away. Single transactions should be completed in less than two minutes, including account verification, and will typically take 45 to 60 seconds.

Impact on the Users' Lives

Some impact on users' lives is expected. On the positive side, users will be able to get cash when the bank is not open. As a result, they may carry less cash, especially on weekends, acquiring more as needed from the machines. Users are expected to view the ATMs as a convenience and as a means of reducing the risks of theft or loss of cash. On the negative side, some users view their trips to the bank as an opportunity to interact with other people who share a common language and culture. For these customers, the installation of automatic teller machines may lead to a sense of isolation. In addition, users who are seen taking money from the machine may also risk muggings.

State of Mind of Users

For many customers, using banking machines has been difficult or impossible before, so initial use may be accompanied by stress or apprehension. Despite security provisions for after-hours use, customers using the terminals at night may be nervous, distracted, or rushed.

What Happens When Things Go Wrong?

Both users and the bank must be protected against errors. Possible user errors are: insertion of the wrong card, incorrect selection of transaction type, and incorrect entry of amounts to be deposited, withdrawn, or transferred. Users must also be protected against loss of funds and against confusion resulting from equipment or communications failures.

Failure diagnosis is entirely the responsibility of bank personnel. Users are not expected to report problems. The system itself must report failures to the bank so that repairs can be effected. To prevent confusion, terminals must also be able to indicate that they are out of order.

Bank personnel with limited training must be able to rectify most faults, such as out-of-cash and out-of-forms conditions. Repair of terminals is the responsibility of the hardware vendor, on call 24 hours a day.

Several machines will be provided at each site to ensure that at least one functioning machine is available at each location when the system is operating. Central computer or communications failures will result in a closedown of after-hours transactions. During bank hours, human tellers will provide backup so that machine failure does not prevent customers from conducting business.

Personnel Requirements

Bank personnel are required to load receipt forms and cash and to unload deposits at regular intervals. Deposits require further handling by tellers to verify items and process collectibles.

We have much more work to do on the design of our ATM. The next chapter develops the notion of a conceptual model and shows how this idea can be applied to the design of the People's Bank ATM.

5 Conceptual Models

Any design implicitly incorporates terminology, operations, ideas, and relationships that the user must deal with when using the system. Whether designers plan for it or not, the user comes to understand the system in terms of these things. In other words, the user develops a *conceptual model.* A good external myth maintains consistent adherence to a well-thought-out set of behaviors [Nelson 1980]. This chapter develops this basic idea: it is possible to *design* the way in which users will think about a system.

A system is the designer's way of communicating an idea to the user. In ordinary verbal communication, a speaker produces a symbolic representation of an idea in the form of a sentence. The listener in turn constructs an idea from the sentence, hopefully one similar to that of the speaker. With systems, the external myth is the carrier of the idea. To allow the user to create the intended conceptual model, the designer must construct an effective external myth.

People process information actively. They generate hypotheses and verify their accuracy [Neisser 1967]. Internally, people build up models of the content and process. For example, almost everyone in this country has an internal model of how airport terminals are laid out, built up over time from various experiences. People confronted by unfamiliar airports usually can make good predictions about where to find ticket counters, food, gates, or their luggage. The details of a particular airport (signs, traffic flow, corridors, and so on) provide confirming information. In effect, people develop the skill of *parsing* airports. They use the information they receive in conjunction with their conceptual models to navigate.

Conceptual models, then, provide the basis for expectations. When new users start to learn about a computer system, they immediately start to build conceptual models. These models invariably relate to what they already know. As they learn more, their models become more elaborate and, ideally, more accurate. If users can easily build consistent models of the computer, they will perceive the system as easy to learn. If they must build complex models, they will perceive the system as difficult and confusing.

INFLUENCING CONCEPTUAL MODELS

The misunderstandings that users develop in learning a system are an important constraint on the design. Even if the model that the user ultimately develops is simple, he or she may have to discard several false inferences induced by the system itself before perceiving the correct model. Consistency of myth, then, is the foundation of a clear conceptual model. Inconsistencies not only cause confusion; they require the user to develop a more involved conceptual model of how things work.

Guideline 5. Maintain a consistent myth.

The external myth used for a system is often a metaphor or analogy that suggests that the computer is *like* something with which the user is already familiar. For example, an office filing system might be used as an analogy of how documents are to be organized on the disk of a word processor. The analogy might represent documents as being collected into file folders, rather than as a variety of disk files in directories.

Because the idea is familiar, the user can make predictions, extrapolations, and educated guesses about the behavior of the system. If the model is predictive—if it accurately represents the behavior of the system—then it is a good one: it is useful to the user. If the implications of the analogy are not accurately and consistently represented in the design, users will make erroneous assumptions and predictions that lead to mistakes and frustration [Halasz and Moran 1982].

Within the overall conceptual model for a whole system, which is useful for broad guidance, users develop more specific models for specific activities. Thus if a desk analogy communicates the overall conceptual model for a system, there must also be detailed constituent models for activities such as editing text. For editing, a still-more-detailed model describes how a particular bit of text may be singled out for action. Compatibility between parts is essential to a simple overall conceptual model.

People also develop models that describe a system at different levels of detail or precision, especially when the system is a very complex one or when the person has substantial expertise. For example, consider what a system programmer might know about files stored on a particular computer. At the highest level, a file has a name and contents. At a lower level, these structures are created by linking numbered blocks of disk storage in a particular way, and by programs that interpret the structures. But if a programmer must recover an important file containing an error, he or she must understand the physical location of data on the media and how the control electronics works.

Simple systems that can be learned quickly and used effectively by people who have no special knowledge of computers usually do not need conceptual models that operate on many levels. Deep, multilevel conceptual models usually imply virtuoso performance on the part of the user. Much learning, either of the system or in the task domain, is required to make use of the conceptual richness of the levels.

A given system may support more than one conceptual model, depending on who is using it and what he or she is doing. For any single user, an ideal system would have *one* set of behaviors, one conceptual model that works for all the uses that the person may have for the system (or any of its brethren). Users must be able to develop a set of expectations that are met by the system, even in new situations. In other words, the system must behave predictably.

Users' conceptual models contain information not only about the function of the system but also about its performance. The amount of time required by a function is linked in users' minds to its perceived complexity. People have a much harder time dealing with variable response times than with slower but predictable responses. Variability in response times results in many unfulfilled expectations, and thus frustration.

Guideline 6. Don't supply kits.

We seek simple but complete systems. Systems that supply all the capabilities the user could want but that also require the user to assemble them to make the product work are kits, not finished products. Completeness also suggests that users not have to "escape" from the system—that is, run programs outside its scope, or use the underlying operating system—to perform tasks within its domain. Obviously, the design of a complete system is heavily dependent on understanding what users need and what they will try to do with the computer. The inclusion of escapes to the underlying system greatly complicates the user's conceptual model. It violates the notion of the consistent myth. Escapes represent just one more trap for inexperienced users, and a great temptation for the more computer-knowledgeable on the user's site to make adjustments in the system, possibly violating its integrity and certainly violating the integrity of the use models and conceptualizations.

Guideline 7. Limit the scope of systems.

The best systems have clear bounds, limits that users can grasp easily. This criterion may fly in the face of marketing pressure to make a system that does everything for everyone. A well-engineered system will not attempt to do everything, nor is it desirable to add facilities that are outside the scope of the system in the name of future "improved" products. A system that gracefully allows added features is one that is designed with awareness of these "new" features in the first place. Such a design is the best way to ensure that new things fit old conceptual models.

A detailed study of word-processing command languages in systems offering hundreds of editing and control functions has shown that only 6 function keys accounted for 90 percent of the operations performed in actual work, and that 16 functions covered more than 99 percent [Whiteside et al 1982]. Thus, the point of diminishing returns is reached quickly. The added functions complicate the conceptual model and lengthen the learning time.

Limiting the scope of a system does not mean that it should be narrowly conceived. A system can be flexible enough to allow the user to perform a wide range of tasks with a modest set of well-defined "tools": commands, actions, applications, forms, and the like. A system can also provide some tailoring capabilities to accommodate preferences of individual users, as long as these are kept simple. For example, a tailoring strategy that allows a user to create shortcuts must provide a straightforward, ready-made mechanism for establishing them. Alternatively, the design may incorporate specific shortcuts. The virtue of ready-made shortcuts is that the designer can provide ones that fit the external myth.

States in Conceptual Models

One aspect of conceptual models is the idea of states or modes. These are conditions of the user interface that affect what the user can do, how information is presented, what commands mean, and what other states are accessible. An automobile has a number of states, such as forward or reverse, and ignition on or off. The function of the accelerator pedal changes dramatically according to which state the car is in.

There are two requirements with respect to states: that they be few in number, and highly visible to the user. States must be minimized because they are a source of complexity in the user interface, and thus in the conceptual model. The more states there are, the more situations the user has to recognize and learn to use. The user's conceptual model needs to contain information about what defines a state, what changes it, and what remains constant from one state to the next. States must be visible by inspection to keep the user informed about what's going on. The visible indication of state can be spatial as well as verbal. It is easy for people to recognize configurations on the screen or in lights without much conscious attention. This is the same principle that in architecture suggests walls of different colors to give orientation clues within buildings. Examples in human interfaces include highlighting a selected item in a menu, and changing the border of a region when it becomes active. It's not enough to have a logical state indication. It must be perceptually salient. If users don't recognize it for what it represents, it might as well not be there.

Guideline 8. Limit states.

Guideline 9. Make states visible and visibly distinguished.

Multiplexing of function—using the same input for more than one purpose—is usually poor in terms of human performance and should be severely limited. The shift key on conventional typewriters and computer terminals performs a multiplexing operation, changing the effect of printing keys from lower- to uppercase. This operation is familiar in office environments, but it is not without its problems. How many times have you typed special symbols instead of numbers because you had left the shift key locked down?

Similarly, the CONTROL key on some terminals causes problems for many users. If a user thinks in terms of the character set, internal control codes are directly related to letters in the same way that upper- and lowercase are related. This relationship, however, is not part of the conceptual model of non-computer-oriented users. They will be surprised that CONTROL-I does a tab, or that no CONTROL-3 combination exists. For these users, multiplexing of function is a disruptive convention.

Multiplexing is generally undesirable in human interfaces because it requires the user to remember what state the interface is in. It also complicates the part of the conceptual model that relates to keys, which have different functions in different situations.

To minimize such problems, there must be a general rule that relates the key functions to their alternate modes. The typewriter shift works as well as it does because upper- and lowercase letters are closely related. The entire alphabet changes in a very predictable pattern, though some keys, such as the period and comma, remain unchanged across the two states. If multiplexing modes are used, they should be made visible, contrary to common practice. Some calculators thoughtfully do this with the operations $+$, $-$, $\times$, $\div$, showing the corresponding symbol on the display; otherwise there would be no visible indication that an infix operation has been keyed.

Conceptual Load

Although there is no absolute limit to people's long-term memory, the more there is to learn about a system, the longer it takes to become proficient in its use and the sooner learned pieces will be forgotten. Thus another goal of the design is to minimize the *conceptual load*, or the amount of information needed to use the system.

Guideline 10. Minimize conceptual load.

This idea was followed during the development of the IBM Audio Distribution System, or ADS [Boies 1982]. ADS is a computer-based voice-messaging system that uses a pushbutton telephone as a terminal. To send a message, a user types in the first few letters of the recipient's name on the telephone keypad. The software decodes the key presses by examining both the sequence of presses and the data base of possible names. An algorithm similar to the one for spelling correction in Chapter 7 can be used for this purpose. Other voice mail systems have used a numeric code for identifying recipients. The tradeoff is between putting some additional processing requirements on the system (to decode the names) or putting the load on every user who will need to remember both the names and numbers of everyone to whom he or she sends messages.

The issue of conceptual load applies from session to session. One dimension is remembering the state of the task. This long-term state, if remembered by the system, is helpful to the user. In addition to preserving work already accomplished, it acts as a jog to memory.

The interactive language INTERLISP has a history facility which is useful in just this way. According to the INTERLISP manual,

> The programmer's assistant facility is built around a memory structure called the "history list." The history list is a list of the information associated with each of the individual "events" that have occurred in the system, where each event corresponds to one user input. . . .
>
> Associated with each event on the history list is its input and its value, plus other optional information such as side-effects, formatting information, etc. If the event corresponds to a history command, e.g., REDO FROM F, the input corresponds to what the user would have had to type to execute the same operation(s), although the user's actual input, i.e., the history command, is saved in order to clarify the printout of that event . . . [Teitelman 1974].

Generally, it is harder to remember several different operations than several identical ones, though a clutter of equivalent terms, commands, or names may be undesirable for the same reason. Different ways of doing the same thing entail more learning for the user. In other words, duplication makes conceptual models more complex. For example, if "Type" and "Print" commands can accomplish the same functions but have different syntax, operation of the system is more complex than it would be with either alone. Similarly, a distinction between two or more similar things increases conceptual load substantially. Concrete differences are easier to conceptualize than abstract ones. Larger differences in function are often easier to understand than smaller ones.

The best way to minimize conceptual load is to design a simple set of commands and operations that gives good coverage in the problem domain (see Figure 5.1). Then, instead of adding a lot of bells and whistles to cover special cases, just stop. The challenge is to find simple sets of commands with good coverage and power. Most of the conceptual complexity of many systems is created by nonessential commands and operations that could be integrated into the rest or just eliminated. Consider allowing the bounds to be set by the choice of a (powerful) external myth. We suggest building systems that have direct commands for 80 percent of the basic actions, and leaving it at that. Of course, completeness requires that the remaining 20 percent of functions, if really required by the application, be achievable through simple combinations of the basic operations.

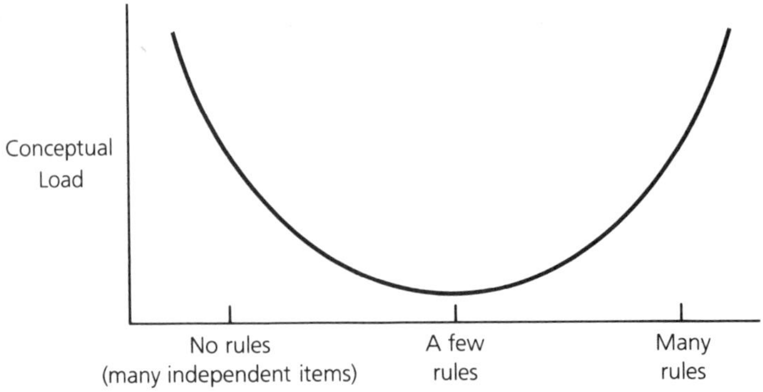

Figure 5-1. Conceptual load depends on structure and complexity.

AN ORDER-PROCESSING EXAMPLE

Consider an order-processing system to be built for a small, fictitious company, the XYZ Corporation. Task analysis reveals that the company takes most of its orders over the phone. It is currently using a system based on a paper order form (Figure 5-2). What might be a good external myth for the new computer system? An obvious one is that of paper forms similar to those now in use, represented on terminal screens. Transactions would be created, viewed, audited, and controlled in terms of displayed documents. Copies of the documents could be printed for uses that demand hard copy—customer copies, audit trails, and backups.

To be successful, an external myth must cover either the whole problem or a well-delineated and useful part of it. In our example, we must be able to support each activity of the order processing system using forms. For XYZ, the user activities are:

- Logging an order
- Checking status of an order
- Filling an order
- Printing a packing list
- Shipping an order
- Printing audit trail and backup copies of orders

The set of electronic forms must allow the user to perform these specific tasks naturally and in the language of the activity itself. It is

XYZ CORPORATION
Three Beechwood Terrace
Oakland, California 95000

ORDER NO. N172317-8

To: ______________________

Ship to: ______________________

Ship via: ☐ UPS ☐ Parcel Post ☐ Best Way ☐ Customer P/U

Item	Back Order	Canc	Pick	Quantity	Item Description	Stock Number	Unit Price	Total Price
1								
2								
3								
4								
5								
6								
7								
8								
9								
10								
11								
12								

↑ ↑
If marked, please read reverse side, paragraphs 2 & 3.

Total Order: $______.___

Shipping & Handling: $______.___

Calif. Tax: $______.___

Local Tax: $______.___

BART Communities Tax: $______.___

Payment Method: ______________

VISA/Mastercard No:

______________ Exp: ______

Total Due: $______.___

Amount Paid: $______.___

Net Due: $______.___

Figure 5-2. Paper order processing form used by XYZ Corporation.

desirable that the forms correspond closely to the ones now in use. A danger of this kind of model is that users bring specific expectations to it—after all, they've been using the forms. It will be necessary to evaluate these expectations and to use them in the design of the system.

Forms design is a specialty in many organizations, one requiring special skills and a thorough knowledge of the organization and of the order-handling process. Therefore, the system designer should tap the knowledge and advice of the firm's forms designer. Having decided to use the analogy of "forms like those they are using now, on terminal screens," it may not be possible to make many changes in the layout or meaning of the forms to be used so as to satisfy system requirements. Creating a good design in spite of such constraints is what makes design an art.

There are three user expectations that could be modeled.

1. The form is one piece of paper, and thus can be in only one place at a time.
2. Copies of the form can be made. Copies do not reflect subsequent changes in the original.
3. Forms don't fill themselves out; people must write on them.

Because the analogy is that of paper documents, we should model the use of paper with respect to page layout, originals, and copies. Of course, this isn't the only external myth possible. The point is that the choice of a myth has a strong effect on how the whole system will work.

In the case of the order form, we may decide to depart from expectation 3, and allow the computer to fill out part of the form automatically. We have two choices—the "magic" can happen either while the form is being filled out or in a processing step when the form is submitted. The computer would supply the following information (starred items [*] are not represented on the current paper form):

- Description, based on stock number
- Stock number, based on description
- Unit price from stock number
- Availability from stock number*

- Taxes
- Subtotal
- Shipping & handling charges
- Total
- Amount due
- Projected shipping date*
- Shipping method, if not specified by user

The way the system is to be used must decide the issue. If forms are to be keyed in batches, separate processing may be acceptable. But we consult XYZ and find that they prefer a more interactive system. They want forms to be filled out by their salespeople while they are speaking to customers on the telephone.

As a result, the external appearance will be less like paper than it otherwise might have been. Now we must follow through on the consequences of this choice to prevent trouble from arising when previous user expectations are not fulfilled.

In this case, a possible complication is price changes. Salespeople may well learn from using the system that magic happens when the form is filled out. Entering certain data, such as a stock number, automatically results in other fields being filled out, price and availability in this case. What happens when a price changes during the active life of an order in the system? Part of the issue is the policy of the company, which we must respect. To prevent surprise or confusion among the salespeople while also respecting the company's policy, we might provide an explicit update function that is performed at certain designated points in the processing of the form—at the user's request, rather than to his or her astonishment.

Of course, any real situation will be a good deal more complicated than this example. The existing paper model may use carbons that don't print through all items for each copy, meaning that a copy of an order form may be different from the original, depending on its use. Packing slips usually work this way. Or the manual system may do something odd when there are too many items to fit on the basic order form. Discovering these facets of the problem requires careful task analysis.

AN EXTERNAL MYTH FOR PEOPLE'S BANK

Ideally, the conceptual model for People's Bank customers using ATM's would coincide closely with what users already know about banking transactions. We must examine each machine action in detail to discover its specific structure and to relate it to current live-teller transactions. Writing out a detailed description of the transactions helps us learn and explain the detailed structure of conceptual models that users will create. Figure 5-3 presents a state diagram of possible transactions.

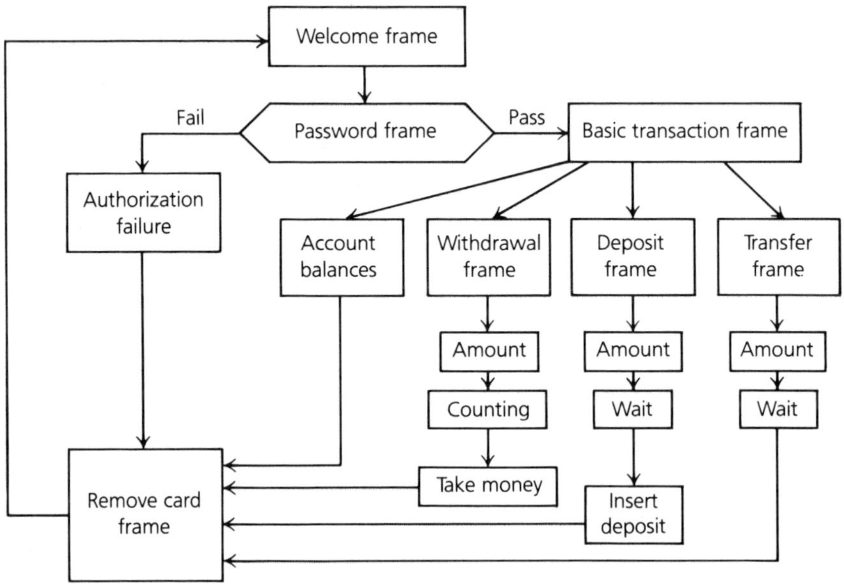

Figure 5-3. State diagram for People's Bank Money Machines

Overall Transaction

Bank patrons normally must identify themselves to a live teller. Credit cards are familiar to most customers. Presenting the card and entering an identification code corresponds reasonably well to presenting a card as ID and responding to a question like "What is your mother's maiden name?" Asking such a question is a common banking procedure for verifying identity.

Identification Codes

For infrequent users, remembering identification codes may pose difficulties. One way to make this easier would be to have the machine know the meaning of the user's code, prompting with something like "Your identification code is your birthday" if the code is not entered correctly. However, because this strategy could involve significant security problems, we instead choose to work into the customer's introductory session a reminder to choose a memory aid for the code, and a trial run with the machine to ensure that the customer understands and has used the identification code at least once.

Balances

Balance transactions with machine tellers are similar to those with live tellers: customers identify themselves, ask for balance information, and receive a piece of paper to take away.

Deposits

In the live-teller scenario, the customer fills out a deposit slip for items to be deposited and hands it, with the items, to the teller. The teller checks over the deposit and returns a receipt. "Put this money in my account" is the user's view of the transaction. With the machine, the transaction is the same, except that an envelope must be used to hold the deposit slip and deposits, and there is no immediate verification of the deposit documents. There is good conceptual parallelism here between machine and live transactions.

Withdrawals

With human tellers, customers cash checks to obtain money—their own checks, counter checks, or second-party instruments. For savings accounts, they fill out a withdrawal slip, which the teller treats the same way as a check. The machine transaction, however, is not much like asking a teller to cash a check. The user presents no check to the machine, endorses nothing, and takes away a receipt. Using the machine, a customer must always specify the amount to be withdrawn, whereas with second-party checks, the amount is set by someone else. Instead, machine withdrawal is more like a live-teller savings withdrawal. In our design we will therefore use the terminology associated with withdrawals, which does not invite confusion with check-cashing models.

Transfers

With live tellers, customers do not perform transfers per se. They may achieve the same effect by making a withdrawal and a deposit. For payments against a credit line, users either present a payment, deposit style, or combine a withdrawal and payment to achieve the desired effect. Thus, there is no conceptual basis in the manual system for ATM transfers. Nonetheless, users are accustomed to creating the same net effect by sequences of other operations. Experience with other bank machines suggests that transfers are seldom used. We therefore recommend to our management changing the design to eliminate transfers. We add "No-Bounce Personal Credit" to both deposit and withdrawal menus. Customers may make payments (and withdrawals) directly against credit, and make "transfers" by depositing a check or by taking cash and redepositing it. This new arrangement is a little less flexible but better suits People's Bank customers and their habits.

States

As it now stands, the design does not make the state of the interface clear to the user. We need to label the submenus clearly, to remind customers how they got to that point in the overall transaction. We'll do this by adding a header. We also need to design frames to indicate what's going on in cases when there are delays. It is not necessary to explain what is happening, because that information is not of direct use to the customer. So that something sensible is on the screen at all times, we'll just add two frames. "Please wait a moment" will be used for all delays except counting money. In that case the frame will say, "Your money is being counted."

Figure 5-4 on pages 57 and 58 show how the other frames will look with these changes we have discussed.

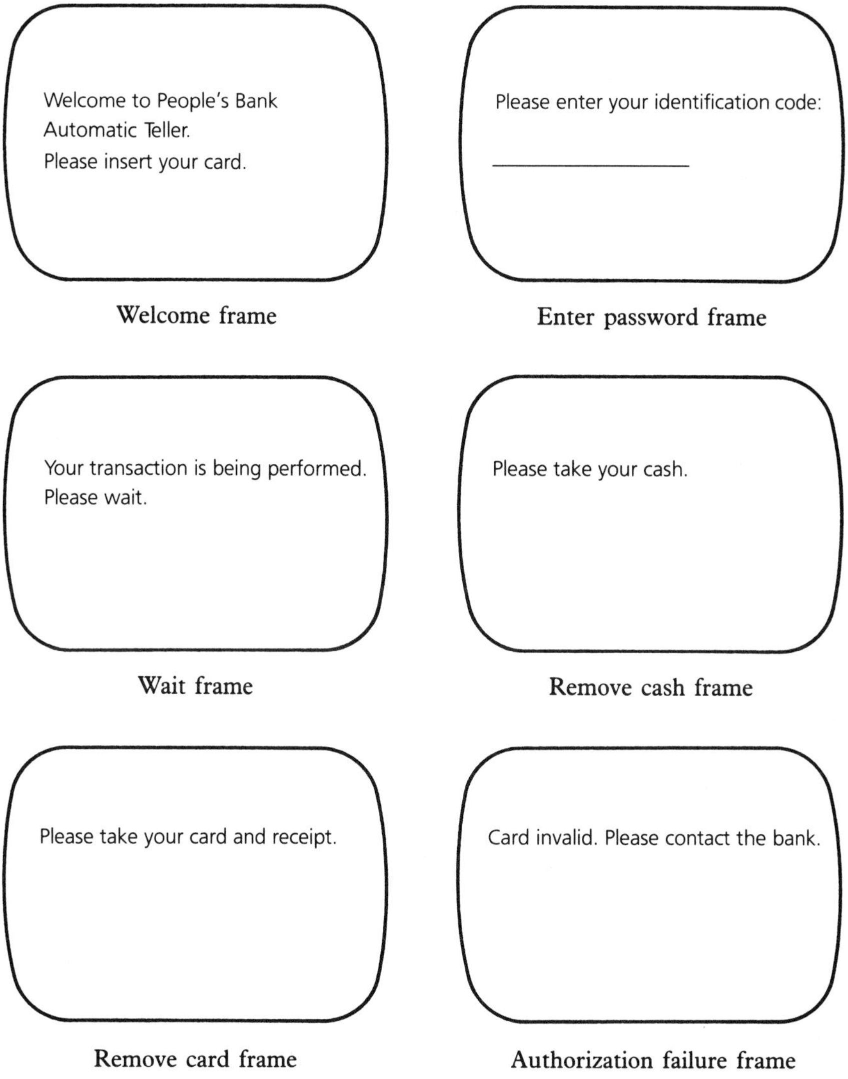

Figure 5-4. Revised instructional and menu frames

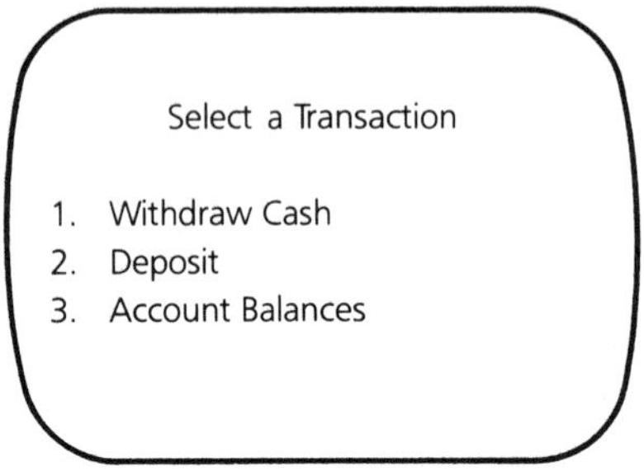

Basic transaction menu

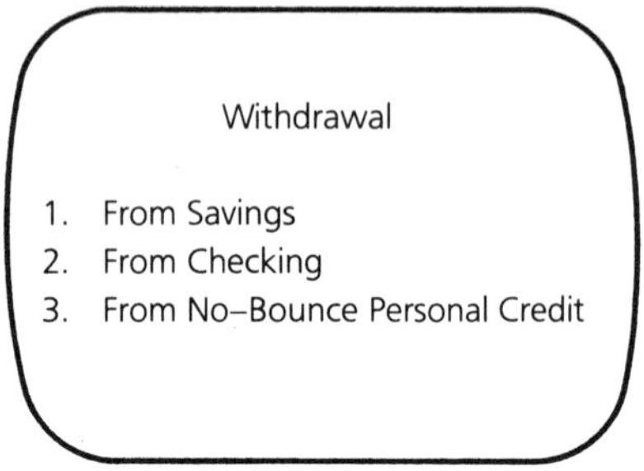

Withdrawal menu

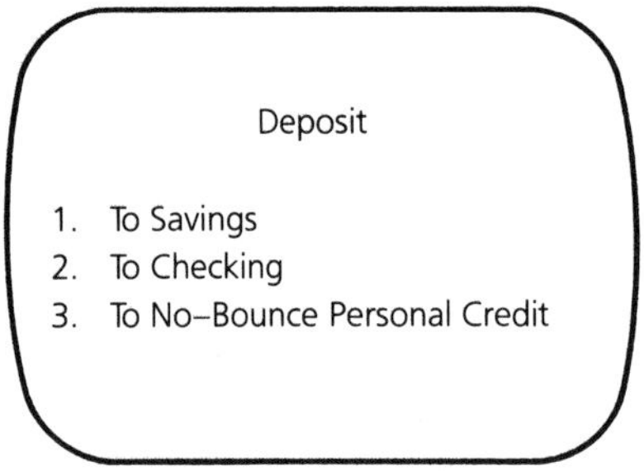

Deposit menu

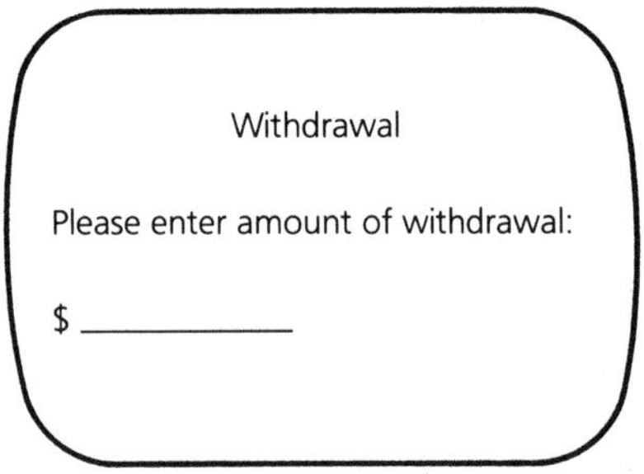

Withdrawal amount menu

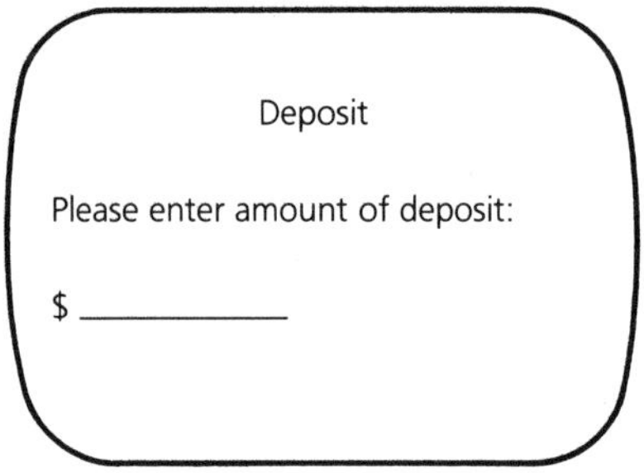

Deposit amount menu

Figure 5-4 continued

6 Language

Using language is a fundamental human activity. In the development of a well human-engineered system, language comes into play at several levels. First, the rules and conventions of human conversation provide a global perspective and guidance for interface design; a framework for the language of human-computer interaction arises from the structure of language. Second, understanding how people view words and their meanings helps system designers ensure that commands (as well as other user inputs) are clear, easy to learn, and easy to remember.

"Language" is a broad term, covering most aspects of human communication. For our purposes, we distinguish between two broad categories, formal language and natural language. Formal language is language consciously constructed for a definite and restricted purpose. Examples are the notations used for music, logic, and mathematics. Programming languages are formal languages, as are most of the command languages used to control computers.

Natural language, in contrast, is not synthetic, but rather is the naturally occurring human means of communication that has evolved over time. Spoken and written forms of English, Norwegian, Gaelic, and so on come under this rubric. Natural language is complex and rich, both in structure and in meaning.

THE RULES OF CONVERSATION

One of the early and now very well-known efforts in the area of computer understanding was the ELIZA program, named after Eliza Dolittle of *My Fair Lady* [Weizenbaum 1966]. One version of the program, called DOCTOR, appeared to act like a psychotherapist. A user would sit in front of a terminal and type in a statement such as "I hate my job." The program would recognize the verb and certain key words, and would convert the statement into a question such as "Why do you hate your job?" Even though the program was not very intelligent, and even though users could interact only by banging away at an ASR-33 Teletype, many acted as if they believed that the program was human. They would express their feelings as if they were in a session with a real therapist. The following actual episode with DOCTOR is illustrative [SIGART 1968]:

> One Saturday morning at about nine A.M., a Bolt, Beranek and Newman, Inc. vice-president . . . arrived at our PDP-1 Computer Room hoping to be able to use the computer for a demonstration. He found a note on the PDP-1 teletype that read:
>
> TYPE ALL MESSAGES INTO THIS TELETYPE. AND END THEM WITH A PERIOD.
>
> This note was left there by one of the programming bums who had just succeeded in making run a LISP version of the DOCTOR program. . . However, the VP thought that this note indicated that this teletype was linked with the one [in the researcher's home]. . . Therefore he started typing to [the researcher], but in fact was typing to this version of the DOCTOR program. The following conversation ensued:

VP: DO YOU THINK THAT I CAN USE THE COMPUTER THIS MORNING?

Teletype: WHY DO YOU ASK?

VP: I MIGHT BE ABLE TO MAKE SOME ADDITIONAL TELECOMP SALES.

Teletype: WHY AREN'T YOU SURE?

VP: MY PERSPECTIVE CUSTOMERS HAVE NEVER SEEN A DEMONSTRATION OF THE SYSTEM.

Teletype: DOES THIS MEAN VERY MUCH TO YOU?

VP: OF COURSE IT DOES.

Teletype: YOU SEEM VERY POSITIVE ABOUT THAT.

VP: THIS IS RIDICULOUS.

Teletype: WHAT DO YOU MEAN THIS IS RIDICULOUS?

VP: IS THERE ANY REASON WHY I CAN'T USE THE COMPUTER NOW?

Teletype: TELL ME MORE ABOUT YOUR PERSPECTIVE CUSTOMERS.

VP: PLEASE DIAL ME UP ON 491-1850

Note that after the last remark, the VP did not obey instructions, and left out the period. Therefore, of course, the computer didn't answer him. This so infuriated the VP, who thought [the researcher] was playing games with him, that he called [the researcher] up, woke [him] from a deep sleep, and said:

VP: Why are you being so snotty to me?
Researcher: What do you mean why am I being snotty to you?

The VP angrily read [him] the dialog that "we" had been having, and couldn't get any response but laughter from [the researcher]. It took a while to convince him that it really was the computer.

How could the vice-president accept that he was interacting with a person when he was not? People can sit down in front of a computer terminal, with no suggestion that they are interacting with another human being, and react much as the VP did. Their candor suggests a sincerity of interaction that is usually reserved for other people, not computer programs. The people are having *conversations* with the computer.

The evidence from research is that when two people engage in a conversation, they enter into an implicit social contract with clearly defined rules and restrictions. We'll take this idea one step farther and suggest a theory of human-computer interaction: When people use language to interact with a machine, they behave as if the rules for person-to-person communication applied.

When people use language to interact with a machine, they behave as if the rules for person-to-person communication applied.

Expectations for interpersonal communication are thus brought to person-to-computer interactions. When each side stays within the bounds of ordinary discourse, all is well. When rules are broken, problems arise quickly. With the DOCTOR program, the content of the dialogue may not have been intellectually rich, but by staying within the rules of conversation, users had little to indicate that the other side of the dialogue was artificial.

One of the most basic rules in conversation is that the parties must pay attention to each other. What happens when they do not? Imagine that you are in a room with several other people whom you know only slightly. They are engaged in lively conversation, but you seem to be left out. You try to contribute to the conversation, but they only look at you politely, pause for a moment, and then go right on talking as if you weren't there.

How would you feel under these circumstances? Research on the effects of being ignored suggest that people usually react by withdrawing, feeling frustrated, dejected, and deflated [Geller et al 1974]. Now consider an ordinary person trying to interact with a "not very friendly" computer system. The person types a command. The system behaves as if it were a foreign language. The user tries to get help, but the system won't provide any really useful information. The user is trying to communicate, but he or she might as well be talking to the wall. The results of being effectively ignored by the system are similar to the results of being ignored in a group: frustration, dejection, and a feeling of ineffectiveness.

This feeling of being ignored is a critical issue in building systems for people. It can occur at several different levels, from the rejection of seemingly correct commands to the frustrating realization that "the information is in the system somewhere, but I have no idea how to get to it!" Concluding that "the system doesn't understand me, and it doesn't even care" may be a major underlying cause of user rejection of systems. But what can be done about it?

We have no formal algorithm that guarantees a successful design. But thinking about the user as a participant in a conversation is a move in the direction of a well human-engineered system.

As members of a society we each have a working knowledge of the mechanics of conversations and can usually recognize the difference between a sensible and a nonsensical conversation. Thus a general guideline for human interface design is to respect the rules of human conversation.

Guideline 11. Respect the rules of human conversation.

Even without describing in detail the various rules of conversation, we all have internal models of what these are. One appropriate model for the computer side of the interaction might be a reference librarian—someone whose job it is to assist a (library) user in finding the appropriate information, and to do so in a civil manner. Another model might be that of apprentice, ready and willing to assist in various ways [Singer, Ledgard, and Hueras 1981].

Some basic rules of conversation apply directly to human-computer interaction. For example, the fact that the user feels ignored suggests that the system never entered into the "conversational contract" in good faith. When this conversational contract is in force, a number of underlying rules provide the conventions for successful communications [Grice 1975]. The basic principle that applies equally well to computer interaction is "Be cooperative."

A conversation is not a confrontation. Part of the understanding in a conversation is that both parties are exchanging information and that each party is willing to help the other in accomplishing this exchange. We want to build computer systems that are perceived as being cooperative and that avoid perceptions of aloofness or a confrontational response.

Guideline 12. Interrupt with care.

There are some general guidelines that can contribute to the cooperative principle. As in ordinary conversations between people, person-machine conversations normally alternate "speakers." There are situations in which each party may interrupt the other, but they are the exceptions, not the norms. A system message announcing next month's preventive maintenance schedule has no business appearing uninvited in the middle of a person's edited text or command line. Computer interruptions of the user must be polite and occur only at places that don't annoy or confuse.

If you met someone and said, "Hi, how are you?" and the person went on for ten minutes describing the details of his or her health, you'd most likely look for a way to stop the conversation, to cancel the contract. The quantity of information being communicated is much more than is appropriate for the situation. We are reminded here of systems that deluge the user after he or she logs in.

At the opposite extreme, if you were engaged in a conversation with someone and the only responses you received were yes or no, again you would sense that something was not right. Perhaps the other person was hiding something, teasing you, or simply didn't want to talk. You can speculate as to the cause, but the result will be an awkward and quickly degenerating interaction.

Guideline 13. Respond with an appropriate amount of information.

We've all had the frustrating experience of having to search through pages and pages of irrelevant output to find a single item or of wishing we had more information than simply "Syntax error at line 18." (If the parser recognized a particular error condition, couldn't it have shared some of that information?) These problems should be avoided in interfaces just as they are avoided in conversations. Prompts, error messages, and other informational output should be no more and no less informative than is required by the situation. Concise messages are a laudable goal, but "concise" means no longer than necessary, not as short as possible [Dean 1982].

In the error message below, a printer port had just been installed on a terminal and a user was attempting to direct the output of an existing text-formatting program to the printer. The computer responded with this:

```
%SYSTEM-F-ACCVIO, access violation, reason mask = 01, virtual address =
00026208, PC = 00015327, PSL = 03C00000

Improperly handled condition, image exit forced.

  Signal arguments
    Number = 00000005
    Name   = 0000000C
             00000001
             00026208
             00015327
             03C00000

Register dump

 R0 = 0000445C  R1 = 8009C740   R2 = 00015098   R3 = 00015098
 R4 = 7FFCA4E0  R5 = 00004DC4   R6 = 00016A88   R7 = 00006E7C
 R8 = 00004B5C  R9 = 00006F54  R10 = 00006EA8  R11 = 00000001
 AP = 7FFCA42C  FP = 7FFCA414   SP = 7FFCA464   PC = 00015327
PSL = 03C00000
```

This exchange is equivalent to asking someone for directions to an unfamiliar place and receiving a five-minute dissertation on the composition of the roadbed. The information may be useful for a systems programmer who is debugging the code, and it must be made available for this special purpose, but it shouldn't be passed out wholesale to users to whom it is meaningless.

The following error message is the result of entering a command to type (on the terminal screen) a nonexistent file named TEST2.DAT:

```
Can't locate "TEST2.DAT": File not found
```

This response conveys a much more appropriate amount and type of information. Even so, the words after the colon might be viewed as superfluous.

A program should communicate only what it has adequate evidence for. People who make bizarre statements or who stretch the truth are quickly noted and their statements discounted or interpreted differently. Systems that attempt to second guess users or that infer a user's motivation (incorrectly) are similarly asking for trouble. If a command-line scanner does not possess adequate evidence that a command is syntactically incorrect, then it is much safer for the system to respond with an error message suggesting that the system does not understand rather than one that suggests that the user is wrong. Like the proverbial customer, the user is always right.

The user is always right.

On the other hand, the system must not suggest that it understands more than it actually does. The limits of expression must be made clear to the user. Problems of this sort frequently arise when a system has some limited language-processing facility. It is easy for users to conclude that they are dealing with a system that understands conventional language, not to mention the problem domain. Systems that respond in the first person invite this misunderstanding. By painful trial and error, the user eventually comes to recognize the true capabilities and limitations of the system.

Guideline 14. Don't misrepresent capabilities.

No one enjoys interacting with a long-winded speaker, someone who embellishes every statement with obscure or overly technical terminology, or one who won't let anyone else speak. If the main point of interacting is to convey information, then actions that get in the way should be avoided.

Consider the difference between talking about a technical subject to a colleague and to a relative at a family gathering. For most people the style of interaction is very different. You share much specialized knowledge and language with your colleague. Technical terms need not be defined, and assumptions about what your colleague knows are usually accurate. It is unlikely that these assumptions and knowledge are shared by your relative.

Now think about designing the dialogue between the user and your system. If the intended user is more like the relative than the colleague, shouldn't this fact be reflected in the system dialogue? Shouldn't you make sure that the other party understands what you are saying? Make the communication easy to understand.

THE STRUCTURE OF LANGUAGE

The rules of conversation can provide a global perspective by which to structure the human computer dialogue. Without any additional guidelines, just thinking about the prompts, error messages, and other exchanges as if the computer is engaging the user in a legitimate, respectful conversation can move your system in the direction of providing an effective human interface.

But much, much more is known about language that is also directly applicable to the design of user interfaces. At another level of analysis, there is the structure of one's own language itself, structure that can facilitate or hinder communication. It is a remarkable fact that by the age of three or four most children have learned the major rules of their native languages. They can immediately tell whether a sentence is correct, syntactically correct but semantically meaningless, or syntactically (structurally) incorrect. Consider the following three sets of words:

- The brown dog jumped over the green fence.
- The old corn cost the happy blood.
- Caused dog shoe salt happy the the.

There would be general agreement that the first set of words is an acceptable English sentence, that the second has a correct structure but doesn't make any sense, and that the third one is just a bunch of words. You can ask children as young as three or four (if they'll sit still long enough) and they will tell you essentially the same thing.

Language has structure. It has rules. Speakers of a particular language may not be able to articulate the rules, but they certainly can recognize a violation of them. Even more important, people's ability to recognize, to learn, and to remember verbal material is directly related to the presence or absence of language structure. For example, random sets of words are harder to recognize than equivalent sets of words presented in sentences [Miller and Selfridge 1950], and semantically regular sentences are easier to process than semantically irregular sentences [Miller and Isard 1963].

Studies of user interactions with data base query languages reinforce the importance of not violating language rules. Some investigations have clearly shown that users assume consistency in language and that they make errors when their expectations are violated [Reisner 1977]. User expectations (derived from a conceptual model) drive the interaction and thus meeting these expectations is the goal for an effective user interface. Reisner identified the problem clearly when she concluded that her "subjects were apparently using prior information in their own memory (sometimes incorrect information) rather than making the effort to determine the query language conventions or the database labels" [p. 225]. The bottom line is that if you want a verbal interaction that is effective from the user's point of view, you must respect the rules of the user's language.

Guideline 15. Do not violate the rules of human language.

By obeying the rules of language, we don't mean that the input must necessarily be unrestricted or free form, or that the system must be capable of understanding natural language. Few systems will have full parsers and the wherewithal to deal with the vagueness of natural language. Rather, the form and content of input and output should appear reasonable to native speakers of the natural language upon which it is based. It is important that the user's expectations be set at an appropriate level. For most situations, learning to use the system will include learning what (small) subset of the user's language the computer understands.

SYNTAX

For our purposes, we can group the rules of natural language into those relating to syntax (structure) and those relating to semantics (meaning). The syntax of the interaction has been identified with major problems in the use of query languages, editors, and programming languages. Apparently arbitrary or even contradictory syntactic constraints translate directly into problems for users [Ledgard et al. 1980]. The best way to avoid these problems is to pay attention to your own knowledge of the rules of language in the design of computer dialogues.

People have expectations about the way that written language works. Conventional rules—such as appropriate parts of speech, the order of words, and the meaning of punctuation—will determine what syntax is natural and easy to remember for most users.

An example of failure to obey rules of syntax can be found in many message systems. Consider the lack of parallelism in these three mail-system commands:

Command	*Meaning*
Send	Transmit a message
Read	Print out a message
Headers	Print out a summary of messages

"Send" is an imperative verb, a command to the system to do something. Fine. "Read" is what the user wants to do: the subject and object of this command are reversed. (It's the user, not the system, that wants to read.) A command parallel to "send" would be "print" or "show." "Headers," on the other hand, is not a verb at all—it's a noun describing the thing the user wants to see. Such inconsistency may seem minor; nevertheless, it makes the system more complicated.

Guideline 16. Be consistent in the use of language.

The example above illustrates another factor in interface design. Users expect a uniformity of actions and concepts. Similar operations should be invoked in a similar manner. If command arguments appear in a certain order ("rename *orange* as *pear*," meaning change the name of something named "orange" to "pear"), then any deviations from this order will cause problems. A command in the same interface with the source and destinations reversed will cause substantial confusion ("copy *orange* from *pear*"). If your design contains a general syntax for command input (or system messages, prompts, and the like), then write it down to verify that each instance complies. Users will be quick to infer the syntax from the examples they encounter. When they encounter a deviation, it's like setting them up for a fall.

Guideline 17. Teach by example, not by formalism.

People are good at inferring structure from examples, especially in the domain of language. Examples that cover the range of what can be said (as in a command language) provide a better basis for learning than does a technical notation. Formal descriptions are useful in their place—when extreme precision is required. Most human interfaces are best constructed to make such precision unnecessary.

Some other obvious syntactic issues concern the use and misuse of punctuation. In a study of the Query-By-Example system [Thomas 1976], a significant number of errors were due to incorrect underlining, confusing "greater than" with "greater than or equal to" and forgetting periods. Underlining is used to differentiate examples of data from actual data, and periods are used to differentiate commands from data elements. Fully 50 percent of the errors in a study of the IQL query system [Gould and Ascher 1974] were classified as data selection errors. These included such problems as having to translate "over 50" to "51 or more." Finally, Reisner found that users were consistently inserting quotation marks where they were not required and omitting them where they were [Reisner 1977].

Guideline 18. Avoid arbitrary syntax.

The surface syntax of the interaction should be understandable and natural to anyone competent to work in the targeted environment. For example, ordinary written English does not concentrate much meaning in punctuation such as commas and semicolons, and spoken English even less. In a command language, punctuation should not be highly significant. When used, it should follow normal prose usage. People know the rules of punctuation and find it difficult to learn new or conflicting ones. Punctuation should not be relied upon to carry much meaning, and should mean only what it does in ordinary printed language, as in this example of acceptable user usage:

```
Merge testdata1, testdata2 into myfile
```

Here are some examples of punctuation that should be used only within its conventional context:

- hyphens
- single and double quotation marks
- periods
- exclamation marks
- semicolons and colons
- parentheses, brackets, and braces

Other symbols are not often used as punctuation in English and should be avoided.

- asymmetric punctuation such as (‘quotation’)
- Underlines as parts of words (SYSTEM_LIBRARY)
- Percent, dollar, cent, and other special signs, except in their specific meanings (% $ ¢ # @ < > / &)
- Other symbols with no particular meaning for English (* ^ ~ | \)

Seemingly arbitrary punctuation appears most noticeably in computer languages. The programming languages C and Pascal both use semicolons. In Pascal, however, a semicolon is not an end-of-statement indicator but a statement separator. This subtle distinction usually escapes new programmers who have grown up learning that a semicolon is used in a sentence to separate coordinate clauses. The terminator in English is the period.

Control characters and escape sequences, used as commands, appear especially foreign and arbitrary to users. They are hard to represent and explain in user interfaces and are difficult to remember because of their arbitrary nature. These sequences, for historical and technical reasons, are used for internal communication. They should remain there, hidden from the user!

Arbitrary syntax adds directly to the complexity of interaction by increasing the number of "rules" that must be learned and remembered. Consider the user command:

```
Print 1:4,6;totals
```

Although using the verb "print" is helpful because it corresponds to something familiar in English, the dependence on meaning-laden punctuation is arbitrary and makes the command language hard to learn and remember.

As this example illustrates, imperative verbs are a very popular construct for commands. Developing a multilingual or multicultural system requires care, though. Human interfaces that depend primarily on English syntax may not be natural when translated into some other tongues. For example, the imperative verb form that works so well in English doesn't work in German, where the verb occurs at the end of the sentence.

MEANING

As Noam Chomsky [Chomsky 1957] has demonstrated it is possible to have a syntactically acceptable set of words that makes no sense, as in:

Colorless green ideas sleep furiously.

Thus in addition to a well-structured dialogue, the semantics—the meaning—of the interaction must be clear.

Unless there is an indication to the contrary, people will interpret words and phrases according to their common meanings. In research into the problems users have with query languages, ambiguous terms have accounted for a large portion of errors. A study of the IQL language found that there was significant confusion over the meanings of "count" and "total" [Gould and Ascher 1974]. The same confusion occurred over the use of "count" and "sum" in the QBE system, with error rates as high as 25 percent [Thomas and Gould 1975]. Similar problems occur with distinctions among "print," "type," and "list."

One way to avoid ambiguity in terms is to incorporate more context into the interaction [Thomas and Carroll 1981]. A multiplication routine in a financial package would be much clearer if it were called the "Gross Pay Routine." With the IQL language, "Total Number" and "Total Cost" would have avoided much of the confusion.

The meaning of a command interpreted as ordinary language must match the effect of the command in the computer system. Deviations from this parallelism are *violations*, not enhancements. Even slight redefinition of a common term frequently results in confusion. For example, an internal electronic mail system we were evaluating had a command called "forward." Every user in one evaluation had considerable difficulty when first encountering it. The users assumed that it allowed them to send a previously received message to someone else. The forward command in this system, however, allowed the user to create and to attach a cover message to the existing message, but not actually to send it. The "send" command had to be issued, too. The first time users in our study needed to forward a message with an additional note, every one of them was reluctant to use the forward command, for fear that it would send off the message before they had a chance to add the note [Hersh 1981].

Guideline 19. Use application terminology.

If any jargon is used in a system, it should be the special language of the particular application or problem domain. It makes sense for an accounting system which will be used by accountants to make use of an accounting-specific vocabulary. Using the special language of the intended application environment has a further benefit: it helps users to relate to the system, to feel that the system was designed to solve their particular problems.

Guideline 20. Use standard language.

Another way to ensure effective communication across the user interface is to avoid invented forms. Use standard English, or whatever the user's native language is. Avoid computer corruptions of language and nonstandard forms, which must be learned along with the rest of the system. The less new terminology introduced, the easier it is to teach a person how to use the system.

Computer experts seem to have a penchant for torturing language. Our English inventions may not be familiar to users, and good taste further suggests adhering to reasonably literate forms. Here are some examples of nonstandard usage that it is unnecessary to inflict on users:

- Addition of *-able*, meaning "able to be done": "doable," "ROMable"
- Addition of *-ed*, meaning "applied": "RUNOFFed," "CONTROL-Ced"
- Addition of *-ize*, changing a noun to a verb: "productize," "prioritize"
- Addition of *re-*, meaning "applied again or redone": "rejustify," "refont"
- Addition of *un-*, meaning the inverse operation: "ungroup" (separate into components), "undent" (opposite of indent)
- Use of concatenated words: "login," "username," "jobtable"
- Use of invented words and meanings: "functionality" (not standard English meaning), "nibble" (half a byte)

The English language is usually adequate to the task of expressing ideas about systems. Unnecessarily inventing words and nonstandard forms perpetuates the notion that computer systems are esoteric and inaccessible.

Guideline 21. Coordinate all system responses.

Finally, internal coordination of language at the start of a design will pay off handsomely at the end. If one group does the command language and another the error messages, only clear specification in the design will keep inconsistencies from creeping in. If interacting in different human languages (such as French, German, Italian) is a requirement, the implementation must provide good facilities for changing the language in use by the human interface. This means that we must not embed English messages within error and fault-handling code, because it becomes impossible to find all of them. A uniform strategy is required.

VOCABULARY

Command names are supposed to be mnemonics (memory devices), but you need only look at existing command sets to realize that some mnemonics are more helpful than others. According to Thomas, the most common error in designing forms is using terms whose referent is known to the designer but not to the person filling out the form [Thomas and Carroll 1981].

Sometimes systems contain the equivalent of foreign words and phrases. Words such as "system abort," "fatal error," "buffer," "cursor," "menu," and "default" are known within the system development community, but to users outside this community the sense conveyed by these words may be different. To the person on the street, "default" is what happens when you don't make your mortgage payments. Table 6-1 is a partial list of words that can cause troubles if used in isolation, with insufficient context, or without adequate explanation.

Table 6-1. Ambiguous words

Add	Counter	Link	Register
Address	Cycles	Load	Record
Argument	Default	Login	Refuse
Buffered	Disk	Mask	Run
Bind	Dump	Memory	Stack
Boot	Enter	Menu	Stop
Bug	Execute	Overhead	Store
Cache	File	Parity	String
Call	Host	Pointer	Trap
Character	Job	Port	Time sharing
Compile	Key	Print	Trace
Computer	Kill	Program	Type
Comutation	Letter	RAM	
Core	Library	Read	

We in the computer industry continuously develop metaphors for features and aspects of our systems. We borrow terms from many sources. To someone without knowledge of the source, such terms seem arbitrary. They are "dead metaphors," analogies whose association cannot be inferred, but only recognized when explained.

For example, is it reasonable to expect that a new user will be able to infer the meaning of "boot" in the expression "boot the system?" Some may want to interpret it literally. The term was a small joke in the days when computers could not load themselves automatically. Programmers had to perform a long and tedious operation to allow the computer to "pick itself up by its own bootstraps." Thus "boot" became the verb form of "bootstrap," the little program that was loaded by hand. To today's users, this is a bizarre metaphor for starting up a system. Words like "start" or even "load" would be far easier to understand and learn. Other examples of dead metaphors are "source program" and "working storage."

Guideline 22. Make metaphors make sense.

Guideline 23. Correct spelling.

Users also make spelling mistakes. There are some positive steps that we can take to minimize their impact. Interfaces that deal well with misspellings are very pleasant, efficient, and forgiving. Especially when dealing with a limited set of alternative commands, recognizing (and correcting) a close misspelling is not difficult [Dean 1982]. The spelling correction must be applied judiciously, however. If the correct spelling is not clear, it is best to leave the choice to the user. There is nothing worse than assistance that makes things worse rather than better. One algorithm for spelling correction is given in Chapter 7.

Guideline 24. Eliminate obviously (and less obviously) bad terms.

We'd like to make sure before rather than after the fact that a term, command word, or other vocabulary item is reasonable. There are several relevant criteria. First, when a user sees the term in context, he or she should be able reasonably to infer what concept or operation the term represents. Second, when the person has in mind a particular concept or operation, he or she should be able to guess the appropriate command word. Third, the term should not have any obvious negative or spurious connotations associated with it. It makes good sense to avoid emotionally loaded terms such as "program abort," "killed files," and "fatal errors."

In the psycholinguistic literature, the ability to connect a concept with a symbol or vice versa defines a semantic association between them. Fortunately, it is easy to assess the degree of semantic association between a concept and a proposed term long before the system is ever implemented. In Chapter 11, we present a set of tools for measuring this semantic association. These methods are in fact procedures for selecting reasonable command words (or icons) as well as for rejecting ineffective words.

VISUAL LANGUAGE: ICONS

Andy Rooney, of "60 Minutes," says of icons:

> I don't care much for signs with pictures of things on them: "DEER CROSSING," "CATTLE CROSSING." By the time I've figured out what it's a picture of, I'm past it. [Rooney 1981, p. 108]

The issue of icons, or pictograms, replacing verbal objects in computer interfaces has been with us for some time now. There is much precedent for their use: international road signs, symbols on shipping cartons, and labels on stereo equipment like:

< <	▯	>	> >
REW	STOP	PLAY	FF

Icons are often used when clarity in the user interface is an important consideration. For example, the Xerox Star, Apple Lisa, and the Apple Macintosh use a series of icons to represent such concepts as "the system is busy and you must wait" (an hourglass image). Very effective. But as with verbal commands, how do we know beforehand whether the icons are reasonable? The old chestnut, "A picture is worth a thousand words," may be absolutely true for the person looking at the picture. But if you are the one who must create the picture, you may have to supply the thousand words and much effort. Once you have created a picture, how do you know that it conveys the intended meaning?

As with verbal commands, we first need to understand that the function of an icon is to relate a concept to an external symbol. Both icons and verbal commands do this; the issue is the degree of association between the symbol and the concept. Chapter 11 details procedures for evaluating icons.

Initial development of icons is a deceptively complex operation. Two factors appear to influence the quality of icons: the concreteness of the concept and the resolution of the display device.

Guideline 25. Icons are concrete.

Icons work best for concrete concepts. The more abstract a concept, the harder it will be to find an acceptable icon for it. Find other ways to express abstractions. The more concrete the concept, the easier it is to visualize and to portray visually. The best icons tend to be miniature representations of physical objects to which they refer. The icons for "inbox" and "outbox" are immediately recognized on the Xerox Star (see Figure 6-1). The Apple Lisa and Macintosh similarly represent documents with icons. These representations involve no interpretation stage. One exposure to the icon and the concept is usually enough. But for abstract or procedural concepts, there is no obvious little picture that immediately conveys a concept such as "Sort the data set." The user is required to recognize the picture and then to determine the relationship between this meaning of the picture and an appropriate concept.

Figure 6-1. Xerox inbox and outbox icons

Screen resolution severely limits the types of images that can be portrayed successfully. When they appear on low-resolution screens, circles and small arcs are full of "jaggies," sloped lines appear as steps, and the amount of detail is severely limited. One system's icon for "print" was a printer with a piece of paper coming out. The resolution of the screen was such that several users thought it looked like a box of tissues [Hersh 1982a]. (See Figure 6-2.) The icons used in the Xerox Star demonstrate the increased flexibility that higher resolution graphic capability provides.

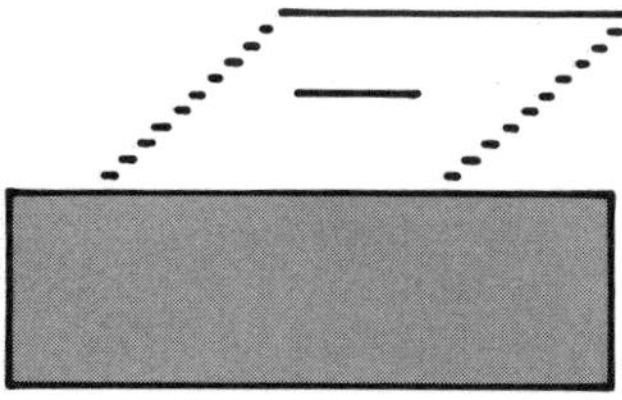

Figure 6-2. Ambiguous "printer" icon

But even with adequate screen resolution, surprising interpretations may result. A test evaluating proposed icons intended to mean "unable to connect terminal to host" included the icon in Figure 6-3. One user came up with the interpretation: "Lightning struck your terminal."

Figure 6-3. Ambiguous icon: link or lightning?

Another set of issues concerns foreign markets. Verbal commands need to be in one or more languages appropriate for the user. Although one motivation for using icons is that they are language free, it is not at all clear that they are interpreted universally in the same way. For example, a crosscultural study of mechanical ability concluded that "illustrative material might present a great deal of difficulty to non-Western readers, more than is often believed to be the case" [Sinaiko 1975, p. 174].

Finally, in computer systems in which icons have been used successfully, the context has been well defined. It is dangerous to evaluate icon interfaces in isolation from other software packages and other applications. When application software is added to the basic system, the issue of cross-product consistency can become critical. There are sufficient problems already with inconsistent verbal commands. One informal study identified 23 different ways in which a user can exit from various software products. Clearly there are still unanswered questions as to how the interpretation of icons varies with changing contexts, and how to avoid ambiguous icons across systems and application software.

QUERY ISSUES

Query languages are the means by which users request information from data bases and information retrieval systems. Although query systems per se are somewhat specialized, many systems look like query systems at times. Users must frequently make inquiries of most computer systems.

In query languages, language and logic are often intertwined, and thus we must address human factors issues in both areas. There is a significant difference between logical structure and perceived structure. Similarly, there is a difference between formal logic and the logical operations people use in asking questions of systems. Because there has been a significant amount of human factors research into query languages, we can draw upon the literature for additional guidance in this aspect of query system development.

Wholesale problems arise when people attempt to process statements involving quantification (that is, statements using "some" or "all"). At one level, statements involving universal quantification may yield more than one interpretation, as in the query, "Find the departments that sell all the large items," or the statement, "All research reports are written by some authors" [Anderson and Bower 1974]. People are not particularly good at extracting the precise logical meaning of such statements, especially when they involve deciding whether data are consistent with given statements, drawing diagrams to represent English statements, or looking up answers to questions in a relational data base [Thomas 1976]. People generally prefer to make statements with implicit qualification [L. A. Miller 1974] such as:

Put the red blocks in the box.

rather than:

If the block is red, then put it in the box.

or:

Given anything which has the property red and has the property of being a block, that thing also has the property that it belongs in the box.

One study found that people use three strategies when dealing with quantification [Thomas 1976]. First, they prefer to generate a series of simple queries rather than a single equivalent complex one. This, for instance, is the technique employed in the game of twenty questions, in which players use a series of simple binary questions to converge upon the identity of a concept. Second, people avoid specifying complex set relations using a formal language. Instead, they prefer to specify relations using concrete examples. Third, people will ask for two or more sets of data to be printed out and will then manually extract the required information.

The evidence against quantification is consistent: the concept is difficult to use, and what little is known about usage patterns in existing query languages suggests that quantification is rarely used.

Concepts and operations involving negation are particularly difficult, especially for nonprogrammers [L. A. Miller 1974, Miller and Becker 1974]. When users generate queries, they tend to adopt strategies that simply avoid negation [Thomas 1976]. The implication is that negation is a relatively unimportant aspect of query languages. Forcing the use of negative statements invites difficulty except in the simplest of cases.

Union and intersection are inherently ambiguous in English. As with negation, experience shows that people do not use conjunctions according to the dictates of formal logic. On the surface level, there is ambiguity in people's interpretation of "and" and "or." For instance, a query that asks for the names of those working in buildings 3 and 5 is often interpreted as meaning a union operation, not an intersection. Thus, even with a natural language interface to a data base system, logical ambiguity may remain.

Guideline 26. Avoid complex queries.

Conjunctive concepts can successfully be presented implicitly rather than explicitly. For example, union operations can be the result of two or more parallel operations, while intersection can result from sequential operations.

The same sort of problem arises for grouping and iteration. For nonquantitatively oriented students taking an introductory programming course, iteration is one of the more difficult concepts to learn. The idea of a generic, repetitive operation is foreign. For experienced programmers, however, the iteration concept is familiar, and thus obvious. Reisner found that fewer than half of non-programmers could use a "group-by" operation, but that almost all the programmers could [Reisner 1977]. Complex operations add little utility for most users. Consider not implementing them.

Many of the results that emerge from research on query languages apply to user interfaces in general. The underlying structure of a query language should support the strategies that people use [Thomas 1976]. It should allow people to operate on a concrete level rather than on a formal or abstract level. It should allow users to specify a series of simple queries (as opposed to a single, complex query) in an efficient, approachable manner.

VOICE INPUT AND OUTPUT

Voice technology is a paradox. On one hand it appears to be a quickly emerging modality for computer input and output. On the other, voice technologies such as dictation equipment have been around for a long time with only lukewarm acceptance. The trade publications are constantly promoting the latest in voice gadgetry, but there is little evidence to suggest that the marketplace is adopting voice I/O in a big way. We are told that executives would be more likely to use a system if they could just talk to it. Yet ask someone how he or she feels about telephone answering systems, and you are likely to receive a negative emotional response more often than a positive one.

Theoretically, voice communications can be a very natural medium for people. After all, humans have had thousands of years of development of voice interaction. For many purposes, people prefer voice over other modalities. For example, after measuring cooperative problem solving using a variety of communication modes, Chapanis concluded "that the single most important decision in the design of a telecommunications link should center around the inclusion of a voice channel" [Ochsman and Chapanis 1974].

Voice is a preferred mode of communication in situations in which a user's eyes or hands are busy [Chapanis 1965]. A user need not touch anything in order to provide input or to receive output. Nor does a user have to keep his or her eyes fixed on a CRT screen in order to receive information.

Thus, it seems that voice should be a wonderful medium for computer input and output. But computer voice I/O is very different from face-to-face or telephone conversation, and a look at the details of both the current voice technology and voice processing by users sheds light on why integrating voice technology into a computer system is more difficult than it appears at first.

One major issue in voice technology is the nature of the interaction. Unlike other kinds of I/O, such as CRTs, printers, keyboards, and pointing devices, speech systems have strong real-time constraints. An auditory signal can exist only in real time. If you cough while some speech output is being produced, you've missed it. The processing from text to speech must occur in real time for the auditory signal to be meaningful. Delaying auditory feedback to a person by 250 milliseconds dramatically demonstrates the real-time phenomenon of voice: the delay is sufficient to bring the most articulate speaker to a stuttering halt.

Recent research at IBM has shed some light on a variety of voice parameters. Gould [1982] had people choose between writing and speaking (dictating) both messages and letters. He found that overall, the subjects preferred voice for short, simple letters, and writing when the quality of the letter was important or the subject matter relatively complex.

The preference for writing or speech in these instances arises from the fundamental properties of each mode. When a person is producing or looking at a message on a CRT screen or hard copy, the message exists both in space and over time. The creator can stop, reread parts of the message, perform some totally unrelated activity, and then come back to the message on the screen or paper. The user can also deal with the information (such as editing it) in its existing format. In contrast, voice messages to the user can exist for only an instant. Voice doesn't stay put, and it cannot be edited without first being transformed into a more permanent modality.

Another issue in speech technology is the nature of human dialogue. We've emphasized the importance of the rules of conversation and natural language for human interface design. With voice technology, language rules need to be taken literally. When voice communication moves from a dialogue to a monologue, dramatic things happen. In a dialogue, both participants are responsible for keeping things going. In one-way voice traffic, the speaker is solely responsible. Dictating is much more like giving a speech than like conducting a conversation. Although some people are reluctant to type on a keyboard, how many more would be reluctant to speak into a microphone? Listening to one-way voice can be frustrating or boring. The accumulating evidence is that sessions involving one-way voice traffic are typically very short. In most voice mail systems, for example, the average message is less than 30 seconds [Probe 1982].

Finally, an examination of the use of voice technology shows that whenever voice I/O has been successful, it has been because the voice modality provides a significant, identifiable added value, as when users lack convenient access to keyboards or screens because their hands are busy. When the value is not immediately perceived, voice I/O is treated with curiosity and then ignored.

Guideline 27. Consider voice I/O for use in "hands busy" or "eyes busy" environments.

Voice output devices have progressed significantly in the past few years. Computer systems can now produce intelligible speech, but the quality of computer-generated speech output is a complex issue. People appear to have two standards for voice quality: the quality of a speaker in face-to-face communications and the quality of a voice on the telephone. It is unclear which criterion listeners use when assessing the quality of synthetic speech. It may be that people use telephone quality as a reference only when they have handsets placed against their ears. In any event, the quality of current text-to-speech systems is variable. Under the best of conditions all are understandable, but some units sound less human than others. An advantage of newer systems is that they include intonation, and thus sound better in producing phrases, sentences, and larger speech units. Stored speech systems begin with human voice recordings, and thus can sound more natural at the individual word level.

Speech quality is much more than an aesthetic concern; the quality of the speech signal directly influences the effort required of the listener. In a series of studies comparing MITTALK-generated speech with natural speech, Pisoni [1982] found that processing synthetic speech required more attention and more short-term memory. This fact translates directly into increased effort, error rates, and fatigue among listeners. Pisoni also found that a listener who missed a word had much more difficulty recovering when listening to synthetic speech than to natural speech. Given these findings, it makes sense to provide synthetic speech in relatively small chunks.

Guideline 28. Avoid lengthy segments of speech output.

The increased difficulty of listening to synthetic speech makes it of dubious value in warning and emergency systems. In situations of significant stress such as airplane malfunctions and building fires, a user's heightened levels of arousal make it more difficult to process information [Kahneman 1973]. If the listener must also pay extra attention to hear what is being said, the likelihood of correct interpretation is low.

Voice output systems require some type of electrical-to-acoustic transducer. The options are a telephone handset, earphones, or a more-public speaker. The physical source of the output (speaker or telephone handset) may make a big difference in the effectiveness of voice output. Headphones produce the acoustic signal close to the listener's ears; there is no need to localize the source of the speech in space. When the sound is coming from a more distant source, such as a speakerphone, the user expends some effort in fixating on the source. This is especially true in environments where other sound sources are present: the listener must track the voice of interest in addition to processing the speech sounds. If you have tried a three-way telephone conversation you may appreciate the additional effort it takes to keep straight who is speaking.

Voice recognition permits users to speak directly into a computer, with no intermediate keying or handwritten steps. Voice recognition can also be used to control mechanical systems with voice commands. Automatic speech recognition (ASR) systems translate these words into appropriate data or machine commands. The technology for speech recognition is far less advanced than that for voice output. It is possible, however, to design a successful user interface using current voice-recognition technology. The trick is to keep the bounds of the system within the bounds of the voice technology. One way to do this is to match the input and output in terms of amount and type of information conveyed.

There are three major categories of voice-recognition systems: isolated-word, connected-word, and continuous-speech systems. Each requires speaker training of the machine and the vocabulary to be used.

An examination of a speech spectogram, a graph of frequency and intensity plotted against time, yields some big surprises. People think they speak in individual words. Spectographic analysis clearly shows otherwise: human speech is continuous, with the ending sounds of one word often flowing into the beginning of the next. This poses a problem for isolated-word systems, which require that spoken words be separated from one another by relatively long pauses. These pauses provide starting and ending parameters for the machine to identify the spoken word. Most users find it unnatural to pause after each word. This user discomfort is the price paid for the modest level of recognition accuracy in isolated-word devices.

The current technology for processing continuous speech is very limited. Some systems on the market claim to recognize connected speech—that is, speech in which the pause between words can be as small as 0.1 second. But that capability is still far from recognizing continuous, natural speech.

Guideline 29. Structure the voice input so that only one- or two-word commands are required.

If users need to speak only one or two words at a time, they will avoid the frustration of pausing between every word of an extended input sequence.

Most voice-recognition systems must be "trained" by each user through an interactive process of speaking each word within the system's vocabulary a number of times, to establish a specific pattern—a template for each word. Even when a system has been trained for a particular user, problems can occur. Sore throats, colds, fatigue, and stress can all adversely affect recognition accuracy. One industrial system developer we know has addressed the speech variability problem by providing a VOTRAX voice output unit for feedback to users. The users were instructed to "speak like the VOTRAX." Because they were speaking short codes, this was not an unreasonable request. They had a constant prototype for their utterances, so their variability in speaking stayed within acceptable bounds.

Since most recognition systems are based on statistical pattern matching, providing a set of acoustically distinct words will simplify training and guarantee more robust recognition performance.

Speaker-independent systems—systems that are normalized over both the speaker and time—have been the focus of considerable research and development, motivated by the problems arising from voice training requirements. The difficulties of building speaker-independent systems are many: the wide variation in the pitch, intensity, and duration of human speech currently permits only isolated word recognition (single words, often letters or numbers) and a very limited vocabulary. Thus, speaker-independent systems are not as accurate or as flexible as speaker-dependent ones. Verbex has had a system out for some time that recognizes the digits 0 through 9 and can be used over phone lines. A mutual fund has used the system to automate its quotation system: customers can call a number and request information on a number of funds. (We wonder, though, why it wouldn't be simpler to allow users to respond to 0 through 9 by typing the corresponding key on a telephone keypad.)

AT&T has also investigated speaker-independent recognition and has recorded samples of speech from across the United States to determine if speaker independence can be accomplished across regional dialects and accents. The data obtained from its Maine experiment clearly indicated the need for regional variation in speaker-independent systems [NET 1982, Wilpon and Rabiner 1983]. Only in Maine is "four" pronounced as "fow'ah."

The current state of recognition systems places a clear boundary on the potential applications. A recent National Bureau of Standards conference focused primarily on the need for evaluation standards, because experience has shown that vendors' performance data are not reliable [NBS 1982].

Vocabulary size is another constraint on expanding application possibilities. Current systems may recognize from 10 to 100 words at a time, with some added flexibility coming from dynamically changing subvocabularies. But 100 is far short of the 5,000-word minimal vocabulary required for general text input applications [Gould et al 1982].

Consider what your reaction would be if 5 percent of the time that you typed the letter *t* the code for some other letter was generated. The odds are that you would request a new keyboard. Or how would you react if during a conversation with someone you had to repeat yourself 5 percent of the time because the other person misunderstood your words? These considerations raise the general issue of how a voice-recognition system should handle errors. It is one thing for a system to tell you that you have made an error and must type it in again. It's another altogether for a system to tell you that it made the error but that *you* must undo the damage and input the information all over again. Tolerance of recognition errors must be designed into systems to protect users.

Finally, there are some hardware issues for voice recognition. Some type of microphone is needed to convert the auditory signal to an electrical one. Telephone handsets, hand-held microphones, headset microphones, and remote microphones are all possibilities. Microphones may be wired directly to the input device or may be wireless via FM radio transmitters. Using telephone handsets as voice input terminals has very limited applications: the inexpensive carbon microphones commonly used in these devices are of insufficient quality for most of today's recognition systems.

We recommend caution in applying voice technology to human interfaces. The numerous uncertainties affecting voice technology make careful evaluation of such systems critical. An evaluation should include a series of attitude questions to ascertain how willing people are to interact in the voice mode.

USE OF LANGUAGE FOR PEOPLE'S BANK

One of the basic goals of People's Bank is that its ATMs be usable by native speakers of both Spanish and English. Icons would be an attractive alternative, since they are language independent. But most of the concepts involved in the ATM transactions are too abstract to be represented by icons. We would have to teach the meaning of the icons to all customers, and infrequent users might have as much trouble remembering the icons as understanding the written language. Therefore, we choose not to include icons in the design.

Examining the language in the menus yields some useful improvements. First, the word *transaction* is too abstract for our purposes. One of the three "wait" frames uses this word. Instead, we'll just have all three say "Please wait," making both the language and hopefully the conceptual model simpler. In the top-level menu we'll replace "transaction" with "Please choose." Similarly, instead of "cash," with its rather specialized meaning, we'll use "money." Other simplifications are also possible, as shown in the new set of frames in Figures 6-4 and 6-5. A fair bit of everyday bank terminology remains, but we must just hope it will not cause too much trouble.

Our design seems to observe the rules of conversation. We do not interrupt the user at all. Our utterances are generally simple and direct. There is no input syntax to speak of. Examination does cover nonstandard capitalization of words like "checking" and "savings." "No-Bounce Personal Credit," however, is a bank trade name and must keep its capital letters.

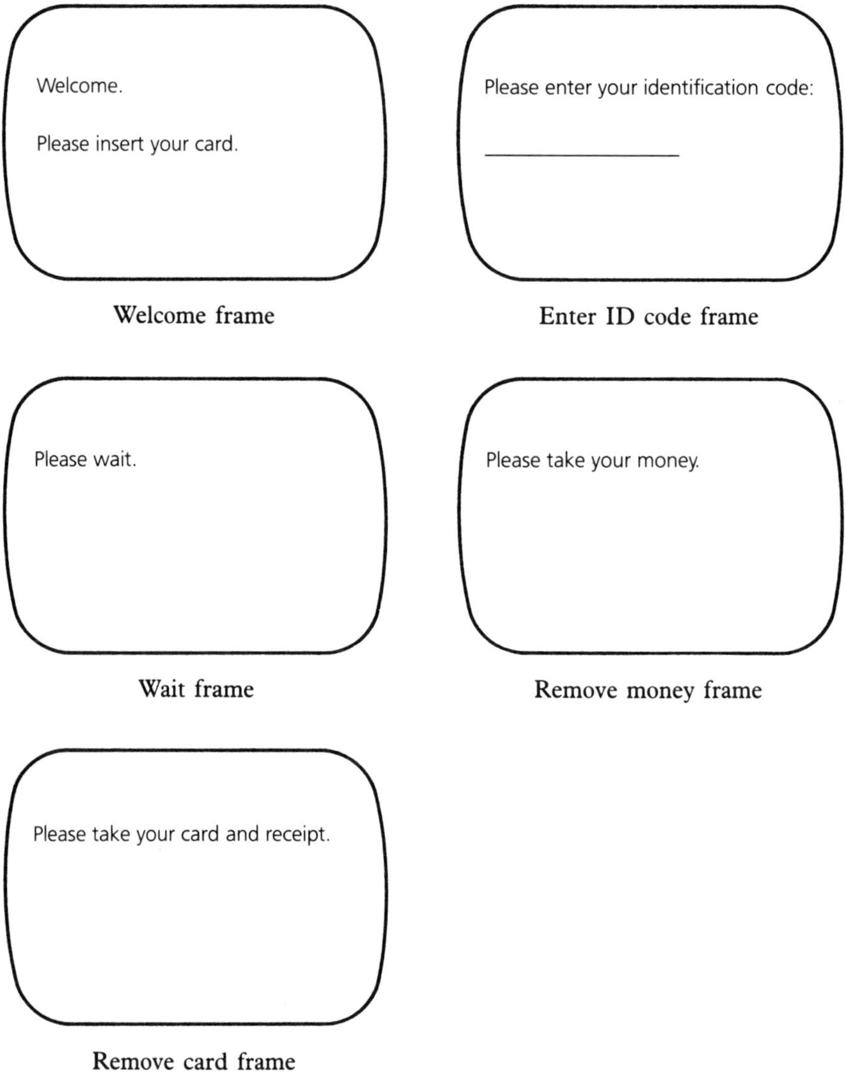

Figure 6-4. Revised screen frames for general instructions

To provide high-quality translations, we have hired a native speaker of Spanish to translate our English text.

In terms of the guidelines, voice output is appropriate for People's Bank ATMs because of the potential added value it offers: allowing people to use the terminals without having to read the instructions on the screen. Our original plan was to have the speech unit read what

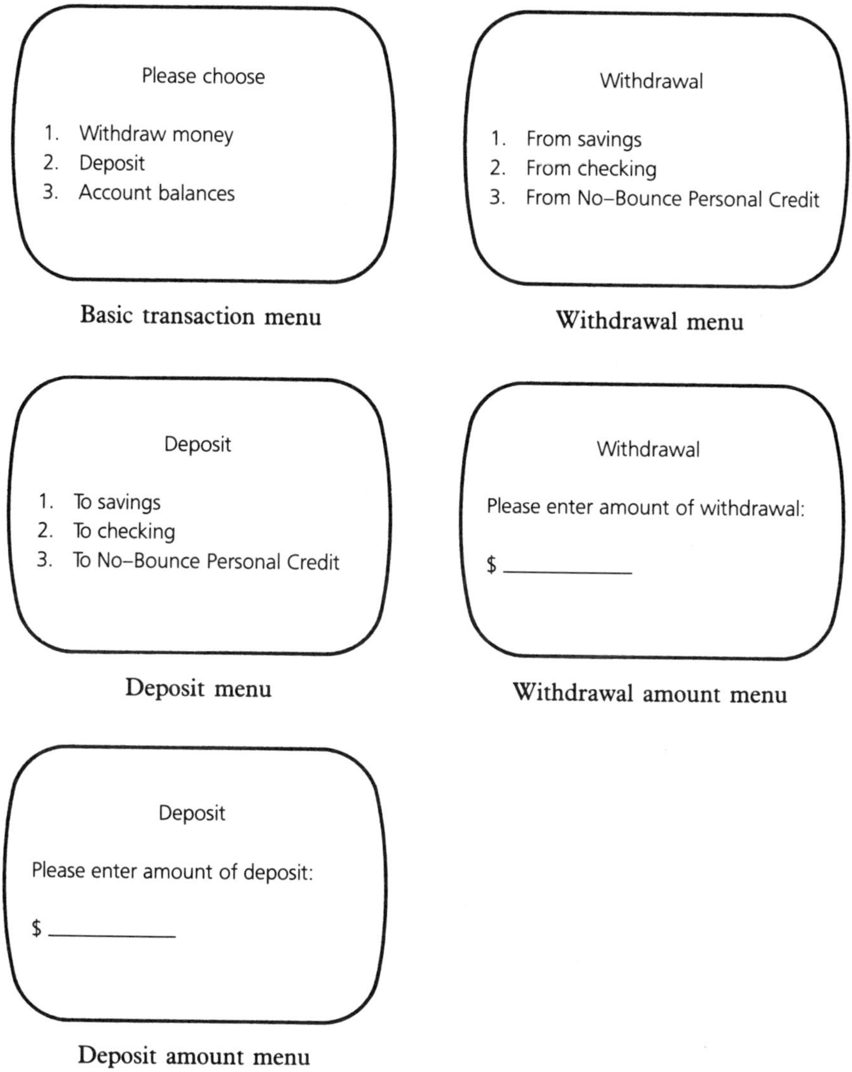

Figure 6-5. Revised screen frames for menus

appears on the screen. But when we try reading the menu frames out loud we discover that the words sound unnatural and don't really explain what to do. We decide to script the voice output independently, so as to express verbally the same idea as that presented on the screen. Figure 6-6 shows the parallel "lines" we have developed for screen and voice output.

SCREEN	VOICE
Please choose 1. Withdraw money 2. Deposit 3. Account balances	What do you want to do? Press 1 to withdraw money, 2 to make a deposit, or 3 to get your balances.
Withdrawal 1. From savings 2. From checking 3. From No–Bounce Personal Credit	Press 1 to withdraw from savings, 2 to withdraw from checking, or 3 to withdraw from No-Bounce Personal Credit.
Deposit 1. To savings 2. To checking 3. To No–Bounce Personal Credit	Press 1 to deposit to savings, 2 to deposit to checking, or 3 to deposit to No-Bounce Personal Credit.

Figure 6-6. Screens and associated voice messages

SCREEN	VOICE
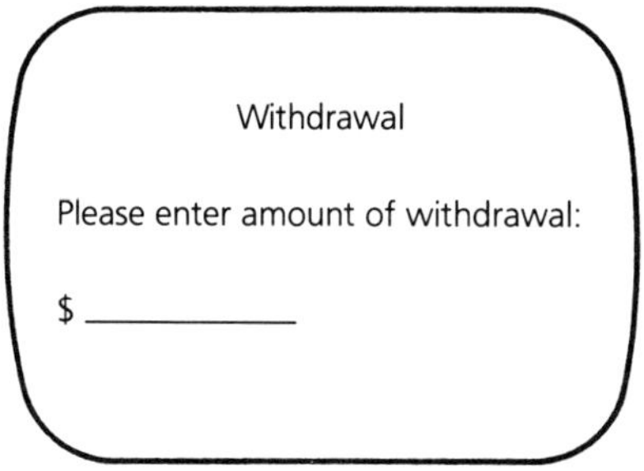	Please enter the amount you want to withdraw.
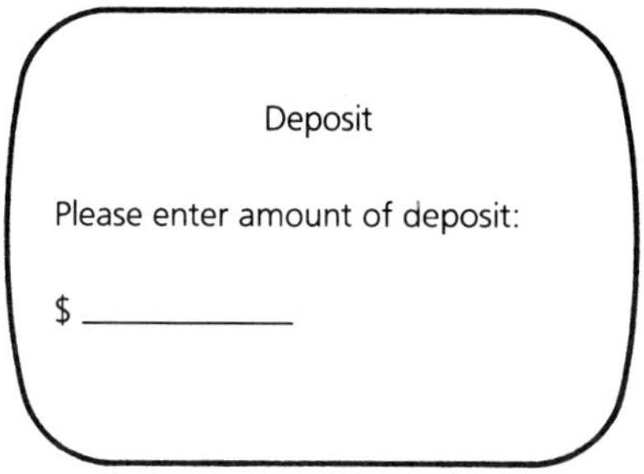	Please enter the amount you want to deposit.

Figure 6-6 continued

7 The Other Kind of Software

If you ask a schoolteacher or educational book publisher what "software" is, he or she will probably say that it's the books, movies, film strips, and other material available for teaching a particular subject. A complete computer system requires this kind of software, too: manuals, learning aids, help materials, and other documentation are essential to its productive use.

One result of a well human-engineered system is a reduction in the time and effort required of new users to learn about it. When the user must learn new vocabulary, new concepts, and new procedures, a number of aids, technical manuals, primers, reference manuals, reference cards, and on-line help facilities can make the process much more effective. In practice, many of these materials are of poor quality. This chapter explains why and how a good system design includes effective learning aids for the people who will use the system and how these aids can contribute to the design of a quality system. The guidelines presented here apply whether the people responsible for developing these aids are technical writers or system developers.

LEARNING

Understanding how people learn provides a framework for developing suitable aids. We know, for example, that most people have difficulty memorizing by rote. Information that is organized is much easier to learn and to remember than information with no apparent structure. We also know that people develop conceptual models for the whole environment within which they interact. They generate hypotheses about actions based on these models. Furthermore, people approach computers—as they do many other things—by establishing goals and then taking action [Card, Moran, and Newell 1980]. The action may achieve some of the goals, or it may force the creation of new goals.

Part of the problem for new system users is that there is an intervening step in the goal-action sequence. New users define goals but must then translate them to equivalent system goals before they can act. This step is a major problem for novice users.

Consider new users who are trying to understand cursor movement in a screen editor. If you ask them to point to a particular location on a paper page or on a terminal screen, they'll do so without hesitation. But ask them to move the cursor there, and what happens? There is no direct action corresponding to the goal. They must translate the "task" goal into "system" subgoals. What these subgoals are depends upon the type of cursor movement the system supports. If a data tablet or mouse controls cursor movement, the device preserves the notion of Euclidean distance, and the task is not too difficult. Video arcade games usually have such controls. But if directional arrow keys control cursor movement, the positioning goal must first be translated into city-block movements (down so many rows and over so many columns). And if cursor movement is by structural entities (character, word, sentence, paragraph), the original movement goal must be translated into these units. Not surprisingly, experiments show that cursor movement by mouse and similar devices is much faster than by grammatical entity key [Card, English, and Burr 1977].

Dealing successfully with a new system requires two kinds of learning. First, new users need to learn about the various procedures for accomplishing tasks, the details and step-by-step operations. Second, they need to learn how concepts and operations relate to each other. These two types of knowledge, procedural and contextual, require different learning approaches.

Designing learning aids is in many ways like designing the rest of the system. Users need to deal with a unified representation and with simple external behavior. For example, many design issues in screen layout apply directly to page layout in a manual. Evaluation is as critical to the design of learning aids as it is to the system design. Much energy goes into the learning aids; shouldn't we check to verify that they do in fact aid, not impede, the user?

Guideline 30. Treat learning aids as part of the system.

Each user approaches a system from a particular viewpoint, attempting to construct a single, simple, conceptual model of the computer. Since a major purpose of learning aids is to facilitate the development of this conceptual model, it is imperative that the basic system and the various learning aids be designed at the same time, in an integrated manner. Experience with the system, instruction, documentation, help, and error reports must all provide a consistent representation of the computer system.

INTEGRATING LEARNING AIDS

Another major reason for integrating instruction, documentation, help, and error messages with the design is that doing so will improve the rest of the design. Dealing early with these issues reduces the likelihood of discrepancies later. Because each component of the system relates to the whole in an important way, all parts will benefit from early attention.

Ideally, before building the computer, designers should understand the whole design so well that they could teach someone to use it. Teaching things is an especially good way to learn them. Trying to teach someone how to use an as-yet-unimplemented system, designers will learn what is simple and what is not, what issues are not dealt with in the design, and even something about how users will interact with the system.

User documentation should be done in parallel with design for much the same reason that instruction should be considered early: there is much to learn from documentation before the system is wholly designed, much less built. In many companies the technical writers who do documentation for computer systems are not treated as the equals of the designers, engineers, or programmers. This is unfortunate, since writers know much about systems that would be useful to incorporate into the design. After all, it's the writers who have spent years trying to bring order to system designs that fundamentally lack it. Writers, like instructors, must know the systems they describe in enormous detail. They usually know which concepts are hard to explain and which are easy.

Writers can have good ideas about design, and designers good ideas about documentation. In the development of the VAXstation 100 Software at Digital Equipment Corporation, the writers were part of the design team. The team scheduled its work so that the user's manual was being produced while the human interface was being designed. The human interface designers reviewed and helped rewrite the documentation, and the writers reviewed and helped rework the human interface design. The result of this arrangement was that concepts in the design that proved to be hard to explain or document could be reconsidered and changed, when that seemed appropriate, before the design was frozen. In conventional projects, a complex feature remains in the system and must be documented in all of its complexity. With integrated design, both parts of the system can become simpler.

Finally, many systems provide some kind of on-line assistance—documentation, explanations of error messages, programmed instruction. The value of these components of systems is scarcely ever evaluated formally, even though they can be extremely costly to produce. As with the error messages, documentation, and other learning aids, such facilities should be designed along with the rest of the system: if they are added later or developed separately they may not relate well to the whole. Many "help" systems are barely used because they are seldom integrated with the rest of the product.

An almost neglected issue is that of maintaining documentation, instruction, and on-line assistance when a system is changed. Including these in the whole design enables designers to provide design mechanisms for making updating easier and more efficient. In this respect too, integration of learning aids is a sound economic practice.

DOCUMENTATION: AN AID TO THE DESIGNER

The design of user documentation (such as primers, tutorials, reference manuals, and user's guides) should occupy an important place in the development process because documentation supports the user and is part of the human interface of the system. Developers have at their disposal a number of tools for specifying and evaluating a design—flow charts, program description languages, state diagrams, functional specifications, and other "languages" for describing the logic and structure of the system, how it works, and what it does. Almost all of these describe the system from the inside. To develop an effective user interface, designers need a way to characterize the system from the user's perspective, that is, from the outside. Documentation can perform this role.

Once a design has started to come into focus, long before any code is written, consider writing (or have someone else write) the user's guide, or tutorial. Using the documentation as a tool in *anticipation* of the actual system provides a tremendously effective design tool. As soon as the writer begins creating the user manual, feedback on the design also begins. If a writer finds it difficult to describe how to do something, the source of difficulty is probably the system, not the writer! Holes in the design, inconsistencies, and obscure constructs will become starkly visible. Iteratively adjusting the design appropriately and rewriting the manual results in a system more clearly thought out and more easily taught. And you get a good user manual in the bargain—all long before one line of code has been written.

Guideline 31. Write the user's guide first.

When the user's guide is written, just look at it. How much does it weigh? Is its size appropriate to the system? If writing the user's guide was a monumental undertaking, building the system may also require vast resources. (A simply described system, however, can also be hard to build.)

Give a copy of the user's guide to a representative user for review. He or she will be able to identify places that are confusing or ambiguous. This information will suggest areas for improvement in the design.

The following list describes the steps involved in early design feedback:

1. Write the user's manual from the design specifications.
2. Assess the issues and problems encountered in developing the document. Feed this information back into the system design.
3. Assess the coherence and clarity of the manual. Feed this information back into the system design.
4. Assess the ability of one or more "new users" to read and to understand the manual. Again complete the design feedback loop.
5. Continue updating the manual and repeating this process as the design progresses.

Writing the user's guide first instead of last has other advantages. It makes it easy to deal with incomplete or partial designs. Developing the user's guide before system implementation makes it possible to complete this part of the documentation at the same time as the system implementation. Written this way, the user's guide will never delay field test.

Another benefit is that describing the system from the outside will probably bring attention to many details that would otherwise go unspecified in the design until implementation time, with a resulting loss of unity. The documentation can help designers to focus on a finer level of detail and to integrate it into the design. The fewer the small clashes of detail with the overall design, the simpler the system will be to use, to describe, to build, and to maintain. Everyone wins.

METHODS OF DOCUMENTATION DESIGN

Designing documentation is like designing the rest of the system. It begins where system design begins: with an understanding of the user.

We need to begin the documentation design by reviewing the task analysis, use models, market requirements, and other information collected in anticipation of the system design. What are the overall goals of the effort, for whom is the system being built, and what are the constraints? A clear goal helps to focus the development of the documentation.

Once we understand for whom the documentation is being created, we can decide on an overall organization. For example, should there be a single document or several? The two basic categories of documentation are generally learning tools and reference tools. Some users will approach the system (whether or not by choice) by reading about it. Others will plunge right in and will refer to the documentation only when a question arises. Support for both learning styles is required. Will users always need two types of materials—those to learn from, and those for reference—or can a single document be created that satisfies both needs? Different purposes lead to differing requirements on the documents: user's guides require explanatory material; reference books require clear structure and indexes for easy access.

In either case, coherent structure is as essential to documentation as it is to the system itself. Users will be dealing with at least two conceptual models: one for the system and another for the documentation. We need to support them at both levels.

Guideline 32. Support clear conceptual models for documentation.

For users, understanding the documentation is a means of learning about the system. And since most users will view the computer itself as a tool, we need to be doubly sure that the documentation is as unobtrusive as possible.

Manuals that list commands alphabetically, one command per page, are difficult for new and skilled users alike. Users don't quite know where to look. Typically they have a task to perform and will be searching for a sequence of operations to support the task. They don't want to read everything about one command, but rather a little about the sequence of commands that will accomplish the task.

One way of organizing a tutorial manual or user's guide to facilitate learning is to use an "onion" model—that is, expose the system layer by layer. The first layer (discussed in the first chapter) would give a greatly simplified, uncluttered view of the system, including only basic, useful information on a set of commands. Forget the bells and whistles. A simplified description of the system provides an effective way to learn the basics. Subsequent chapters can take up additional capabilities and options. It is a lot easier for users to add to their conceptual models once they have a reasonable foundation.

Users often ask for more explanation, for a model of how things operate. They also often want less explanation: "I really don't care how it works. Just tell me how to do it!" They are looking for a step-by-step description. We can reconcile users' desire for both more explanation and less by providing both procedural information and explanatory information. The procedural information is a kind of verbal road-map that guides users from one place to another. It provides step-by-step information, but doesn't help much in novel situations or when the user has gone astray. The explanatory information is a type of survey map, showing the overall structure.

Knowledge of how people learn also provides guidelines for document content. To begin with, concreteness is essential. It is much easier for users to infer general rules from examples than it is for them to try to interpret a formal rule in a particular problem context. People are active processors of information, and there is much evidence that they generally prefer to deal with concrete specifications [Abelson 1976]. Let them exercise that preference and ability by allowing them to infer the general rules.

Nonetheless, formal descriptions can be useful for summarizing large numbers of commands and options. Summarizing is the key. Users may not be familiar with formal notations, which require years of experience to learn to decode. They may not be willing to invest time and effort in understanding the formalisms. Formal rules are useful for specifying and consolidating already learned information. For learning however, formal specifications should be avoided.

Consider the following formal description of a statement in some input language:

Print {literal | file-name }

It would be clearer, though just as powerful, to express it in this form:

```
Print "Abraham Lincoln"
Print myfile.dat
```

The corresponding example might look like this:

```
Print "My name is Joe."
Print File27.dat
```

Guideline 33. Examples, examples, examples.

It is impossible to overstate the importance of examples. Users need concrete examples of how things work. They need scenarios that show how to use features and options. Users need concrete procedures that they can readily apply, detailed examples that can serve as the basis for more general learning. Examples are little pieces of procedure that people can pick up and use. Documentation seldom provides enough.

The table of contents and index play important roles in documents of any significant size. The table of contents should contain a *very* modest amount of information about each chapter, enough to enable users to locate major areas of interest and understand the overall organization of the manual. A table of contents that lists every section heading in the text obscures the global structure of the manual. Three pages is the maximum size for a table of contents for any document, regardless of its size.

Guideline 34. An index is an information retrieval system.

Indexes, to be useful, must be much more than a sort-merge of important words in the document. The index is the information retrieval mechanism for the data base—the manual or book. It is the bridge between the information needs of the user and the content of the document.

TESTING THE DOCUMENTATION

Once the documentation has been developed, how do we know if it works? At the very least, we can check to see that nothing is left out, and that what is included is described accurately. But a better approach is to assess how effective the learning aids are. As a first step, we can give the documentation to representative users and ask them to read it and to comment freely on clarity, completeness, order, and the like, perhaps by writing notes and comments in the documentation itself. But the acid test is how well the documentation helps users learn about the new system. Representative users should be given the documentation and then asked to carry out a standardized set of tasks which could be accomplished on the basis of information in a section of the documentation. We may even want to compare how well users can do on the system with and without the documentation. In any event, we cannot simply assume that the documentation is good. If its purpose is to help users, we should verify that it achieves that purpose. Chapter 11 provides further information on testing and evaluation.

HELP! GUIDELINES

On-line help is particularly difficult to design into systems, especially large, general-purpose ones. Which information to provide under various circumstances depends intimately on the user's knowledge, situation, and abilities. Ineffective help is expensive for developers and users alike and is worse than no help at all. Users encounter help facilities at a sensitive time. They are admitting that they need assistance and are actively seeking it. To be frustrated at this point by an ineffective help facility will permanently discourage many users.

Guideline 35. Verify that help helps.

If help is to be provided, it should be uniformly available. The user must be able to get help without backing up, retyping, losing text, or changing context. In other words, the help provided must not disrupt the task or put a strain on the user's short-term memory. The more disruption that occurs in the process of seeking help and returning to the original task, the less likely it will be used.

Guideline 36. Don't let help interfere with the task.

New users may be unable to use a help facility even after they have heard about it, because they don't know what to do to get it. Active reminders such as prompts and references in error messages can be effective in making help accessible.

Help text should be in the language of the user. The system must always talk in terms of the application, never in terms of the technology. If something can't be said in terms that the user will understand, it shouldn't be said at all. Even something like "Data unavailable because of a communications failure," though not very specific, is better than "ERROR 21645–Data link CRC failure."

There are several types of help that designers can provide, corresponding to the following questions:

1. What does this command, error message, or the like mean?
2. What is the correct form of this command?
3. What command can I use to accomplish this task?
4. What went wrong?

A really good help facility at level 1 above (explaining the meanings of commands and messages) may be much better than providing some help at each of the levels.

As an example of these levels of help, consider a situation in which the system has failed to open a file. The usual sort of error message might be:

User: Search recipes for fish.

Computer: File not found: recipes.

In terms of the four levels of help information, the following responses might be given after a request for help.

1. What does it mean?

Computer: The information you requested about recipes is not available in your directory.

2. What is the correct form of this command?

Computer: Your command had the correct form:

Search recipes for fish.

3. What can I do to accomplish this task?

Computer: There is recipe information in the system <cuisine> directory. Try the command:

Search <cuisine>recipes for fish.

4. What went wrong?

Computer: You did not look in the right place for the information. No damage was done. Your current directory is <general>. Try <cuisine>.

These four possible approaches and system responses show how designers can relate help to the results from error processing. When a command processor has caught an error, a substantial amount of information is available to the system. If some of this context is saved, when the user requests help the system will have information upon which to base a response.

Guideline 37. Integrate help and error processing.

SPELLING CORRECTION AS HELP

Spelling correction is a useful form of help, one that can be both supportive and "friendly." There are two kinds of spelling correction: command and text. Command correction is relatively easy to implement and is not particularly demanding of system resources. It corrects mistyped command words in-line while making very few incorrect guesses. Since the number of words permitted in a particular context is usually very small, command correctors can usually be right. Nonetheless, it must be easy for the user to make the correction and go on if the wrong "correction" is made. Thus, command spelling correction must be fully integrated into the command processor. Table 7-1 presents a simple command spelling-correction method. To try to match a misspelled word to a word in a list of permitted ones, the system attempts a series of transformations to see whether they produce legal words. It constructs a list of all such possibilities. If only one word is found, the correction is made. If more than one word is on the list and the style of the human interface permits it, the system presents the list to the user to select from. Otherwise, no correction is offered.

Table 7-1. A spelling correction algorithm

Transformation	*Example*
All possible case changes (if significant)	prinT → print
All possible transpositions	pritn → print
All possible one-letter replacements	pront → print
All possible insertions of letters	prnt → print
Insertion of space (two words to check)	printit → print it
All possible deletions	prixnt → print

For example, consider the following list of command words:

help	done	quit
do	quiet	show

If the user typed "donr," the system would correct it to "done," the only match the rules generate. If "queit" were typed, the possibilities list would contain "quiet" (transposition) and "quit" (deletion). In this case, the system would not choose a correction.

It is desirable to ignore capitalization for all comparisons. See Peterson [1980] for a detailed discussion of spelling-correction methods.

Text spelling correction uses knowledge of natural language. The details of these methods differ from language to language. Since natural language presents an open set of possible words, the text corrector can only propose corrections and ask the user for resolution. Automatic correction can proceed in cases of common misspellings that are unambiguous. However, the user must always be able to override a correction in order to enter a word the system doesn't know. Text correction can be fast enough to keep up with user typing in real time, even on a time-shared machine. In a personal-machine environment, text spelling correction should be able to flag a questionable word before the user has typed more than a character or two beyond it.

LEARNING AT PEOPLE'S BANK

How will people learn to use the People's Bank money machines? Because there will be no user's guide or other independent documentation, the machines must be self-documenting. The design attempts to accomplish this by presenting as-you-go instructions. In addition, we have specified that an instructor will lead new users through their first transaction on the machines to ensure that they understand the process. This instruction will cover the following concepts and tasks:

- What the machine will and will not do
- How to choose an identification code
- How to insert the identification card
- How to use the handset for spoken instructions
- How to enter the identification code
- How to make menu selections
- How to make withdrawals
- How to make deposits
- How to get account balances
- What to do in case of mistakes or other trouble

8 Human Interface Styles

"HELLO-GOODBYE."

There are three basic interactive styles of control in human interfaces: command, menu, and direct manipulation. Most operating systems on time-shared and personal computers use command interfaces, which require the user to create an utterance stating what he or she wants the computer to do. Thus the user is responsible for knowing what to say. Just as a foreigner can learn enough English to instruct a waiter ("Please, a hamburger"; "Bring french fries"), the user of a command interface may underutilize the language. But the structure of the conversation is the same, as both the command processor and the waiter are able to understand stylized utterances. What makes both English and command languages special is that just the right thing can be created to say what's wanted. "I'll have a hamburger on an onion roll, medium rare, with a slice of onion, ketchup, and a double order of fries."

Like restaurant menus, which avoid long discussions with customers about what the cook will and will not do, what materials are available, and what they might cost, the menu style on a computer presents

Cartoon courtesy of Sidney Harris, Great Neck, New York.

the user with selection among a number of choices. Unlike commands, the choice of utterances is from a fixed set. Menus may come in trees, so that making a selection in one menu elicits another, for a subsidiary choice. With menus, users never have to remember what the choices are, because they are all presented. The menu may not tell users how to get what they want, but it does tell them what they can get from here. Users have only to recognize the items and to understand their meaning.

Finally, direct manipulation interfaces represent objects that users act upon directly [Shneiderman 1982]. Like a restaurant with a buffet, users take the items they want. They put their own slice of onion on their hamburger. Screen editors that display a document and allow modification by pointing and typing are of the direct manipulation type. Other examples are the document-based interfaces of the Apple Lisa, Apple Macintosh, and the Xerox Star.

People provide two kinds of input to computers: control and data. Control information tells the computer what to do; data, what to do it to. The distinction is often blurred, and each of the three control styles can also be used to enter data, as shown in Figure 8-1. There are also many cases in which commands and data are indistinguishable. Prompted yes-no questions are one such case. Nonetheless, it is usually possible to attribute an overall style to data entry as well as to control.

Few human interfaces consist of a single basic style. A command processor may provide help in the form of a menu as a reminder. A menu system may ask for typed data at some point. Similarly, a screen editor may use either commands or menus to specify what action is to be taken. So the style of a particular interface is the particular mixture of command, menu, and direct-manipulation styles incorporated into it.

Any I/O device used for controlling an interaction can be made to support different styles. Figure 8-2 shows examples of function keys used in each of the three basic styles. Labeling keys with all of the available choices creates a menu on the keyboard rather than on the screen. Putting command words on the keys produces an interesting command-and-menu hybrid in which the words are selected menu style, but the sequences of them create commands. When function keys are used in a direct manipulation interface, the keys select the actions to be performed at the location indicated by a pointing device.

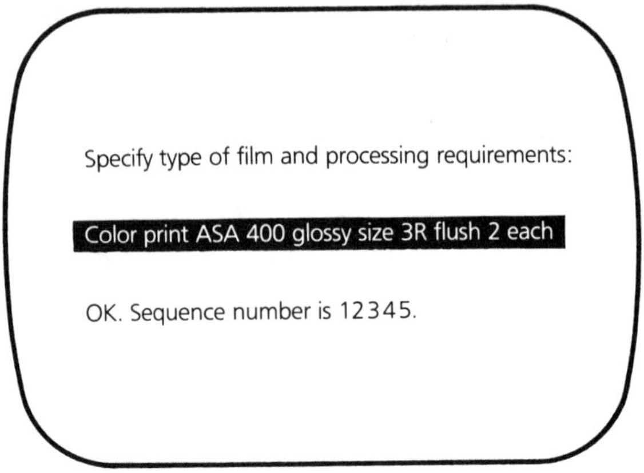

Screen A

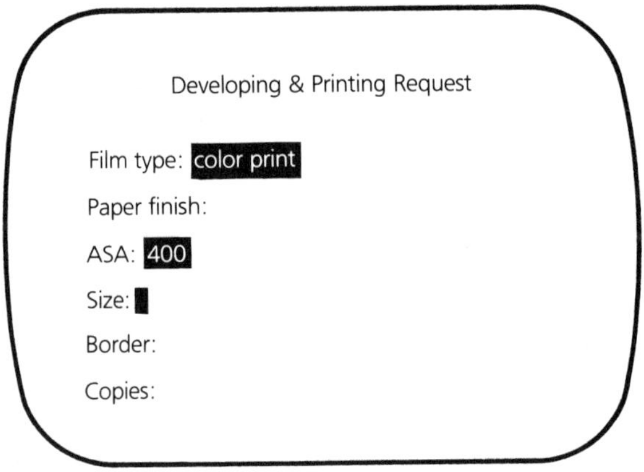

Screen B

Figure 8-1. The three interactive styles applied to data input. In command style (Screen A), the user types a complete sequence of command words in response to a prompt from the computer. In direct manipulation (Screen B), the user selects a field, moves the pointer to it, then types the desired data.

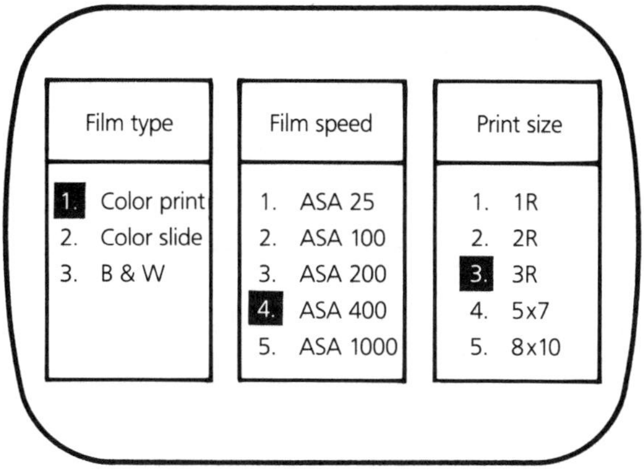

Screen C

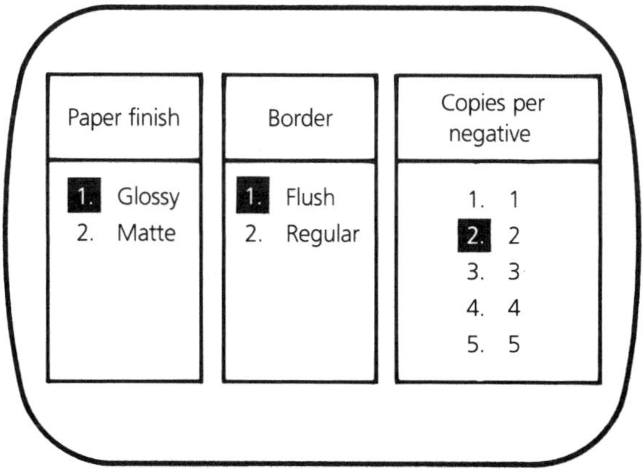

Screen D

Figure 8-1 continued. In menu style (Screens C and D), menus appear in sequence and the user presses a number key to select from each one.

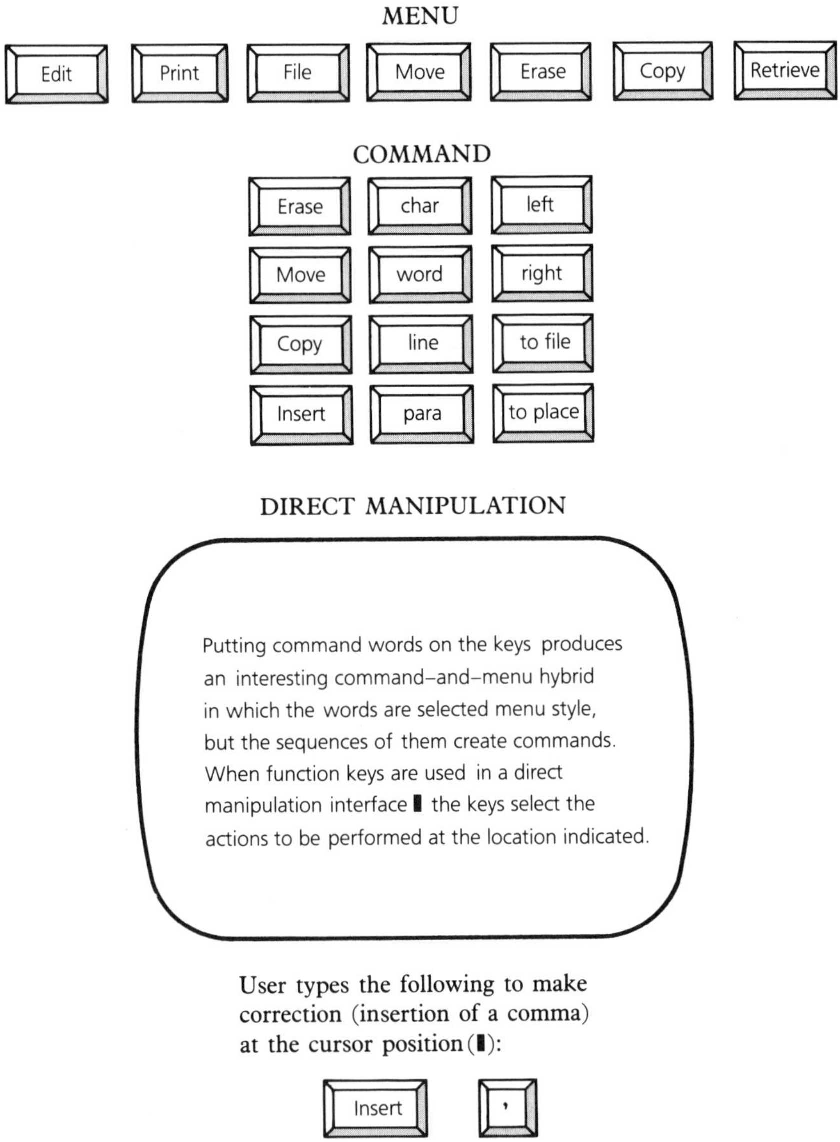

Figure 8-2. Use of function keys in each interface style

We frequently hear that systems should be built to allow switching between styles, such as between menu and command modes. Menus are supposed to be good for novices because they require little learning, but too slow for proficient users. Commands are fast and flexible, it is maintained, and their extra utility is worth the extra learning time to sophisticated users.

An interface with two distinct control modes presents a number of problems: it makes the interface more complicated for the user, it takes more effort to implement, and it is likely that neither mode will be optimized as well as it might have been if the effort had not been split between the two. Frequently the modes have separate lives, with features that can be used in one mode but are unavailable in the other. Such a design reduces ease of use. A menu-plus-command system may leave the menu mode too incomplete and may make the command mode too complicated and difficult to use [Hersh 1982b].

Guideline 38. Avoid multiple style modes.

A conceptual objection to mixed style modes is that they confuse the interactive style with the external myth. A well-designed interface of any style will have the efficiency of motion necessary to avoid wasting the user's time. Two stylistic modes that have the same external myth behind them will differ in their ease of use only in terms of their quality in each mode. Only complexity is added with the extra mode. If the user's conceptual model is not shared between the modes, then the user really has two separate but overlapping systems, much more complicated than either would be alone. We believe that it's far better to put design and development efforts into a single well-executed interface.

COMMAND-BASED DESIGNS

Many computer professionals are comfortable with the command style of controlling computers, but other users may have problems. They may fail to grasp the syntax that is required or the fact that it's a formal language with rigid limits. Even once they are familiar with a system, people may have difficulty remembering command words, punctuation, and the sequences needed for an operation.

Beyond the traditional command-style interfaces, there are natural-language parsers (see Figure 8-3). Natural language parsers are within the subject matter of artificial intelligence (AI). They require a knowledge of the subject domain and a suitable, complex grammar. Although a few excellent ones have been built [see, for example, Woods, Kaplan, and Nash-Webber 1972 and Harris 1977], they are extremely difficult to construct. The dangers of using natural language parsers, from a human interface perspective, are that users may come to expect

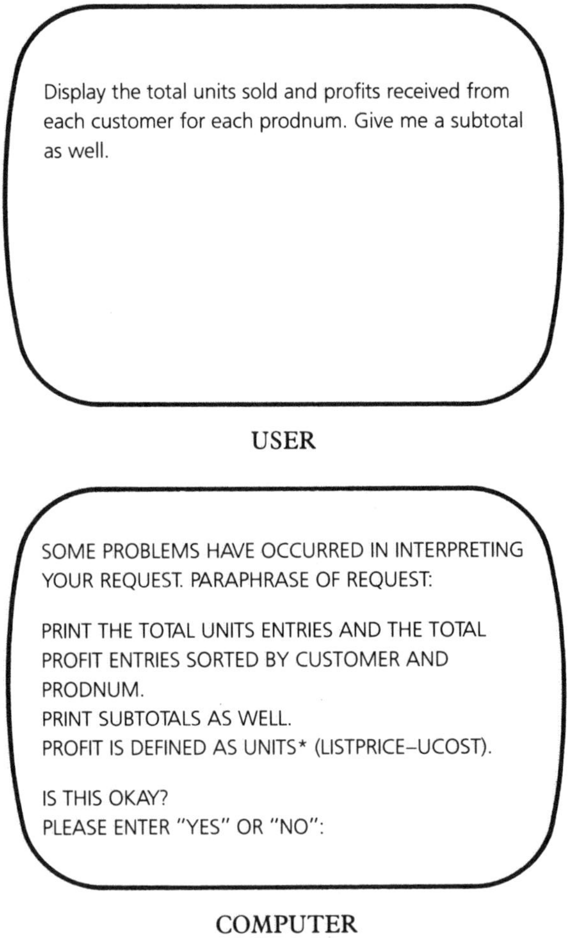

Figure 8-3. A natural language parser (RAMIS II database management system, *Datamation* 1983)

too much from them, and that without enough AI technology, the processors will do too little. The results are frustration and less control of the system.

For many applications, a natural language interface is too sophisticated. Most people using systems that do not require the user to express much will find it easier to type in a number or to answer "yes" or "no" than to type in a full sentence. On the other hand, in a system that requires a rich form of expression to provide sophisticated control, a simple command scanner interface may be too unwieldy to work effectively. Nevertheless, designers need to have strong indications that natural-language or other artificial-intelligence approaches are essential to a system before incorporating them as human interfaces. Aside from the fact that they do not automatically provide a panacea for all human factors considerations, these methods can be extremely expensive.

With any command interface the user will learn what language the machine does and does not understand. The input processor will be easy to use to the extent that the user can make good predictions about what it will understand, and to the extent that the processor tolerates small variations in how its commands are expressed.

There are command scanners of varying complexity and sophistication. The right choice for an application depends on what the scanner is called on to do. A very simple scheme recognizes only single letters for each word in a command. Such a design is very limited, and can accommodate only a few command types. Later additions to the system or translations into other languages may be awkward or impossible. If the letter *S* is already used for *Show*, and you want to add a *Set* command, you're stuck. Rather than using the best word, you must resort to using a synonym. The principal virtue of one-letter command processors is that they are easy to implement.

One improvement to a simple command scanner is to show the user the full command. In general, it is desirable to echo all commands readably, even if what the user has typed is terse. The single-letter-command processor is a special case of command scanners that allow abbreviations. Abbreviations are useful because they minimize the amount of typing required of the user. With such a scanner, instead of

Set line width to 72

the user can type

```
slwt 72
```

Though economical in terms of keystrokes, the result is cryptic. A good compromise is to allow the user to type the abbreviation but to have the computer echo the full command so that it is readable.

More elaborate command scanners allow users to type in sequences of words. As we mentioned in Chapter 6, these may rely too much on punctuation as a means of carrying meaning. Consider this example:

```
PRINT TEST2/SPACING=2;TEST3.DAT/SPACING=1/FORMS="Mailing labels"
```

There is so much punctuation-dependent syntax here that the command is unreadable. The period is used as part of the file syntax, the slash introduces a switch, the equal sign acts as a separator within the switch, quotation marks protect a string name, and the semicolon separates groups of files. This conventional monitor command language, which requires the user to know when to use which separator, is extremely unfriendly.

A common example of a friendlier command line still includes a slash:

```
PRINT TEST2/DOUBLESPACED
```

Here the slash serves to identify DOUBLESPACED as a modifier. An equivalent statement that relies more on natural language constructs might be:

```
PRINT TEST2 WITH DOUBLE SPACING
```

This command involves more typing but is a lot easier for users to learn and to remember.

Guideline 39. Don't rely on punctuation to carry meaning.

A more sophisticated kind of command scanner provides a more interactive procedure for the assembly of the command line. It allows the user to "negotiate" the command with the computer, until an acceptable instruction is attained. Then the user confirms this command, usually by pressing RETURN. These more sophisticated processors provide help, command completion, and spelling correction, all in-line with the command.

Often users forget what options or variations are permitted in commands. Having typed half a line of a command, they find it frustrating to have to cancel the line in order to find out what can be typed next, only to have to retype it. A command processor should let users find out what can be done at any given point without losing what they have already typed in. One method, used in the TENEX operating system, allows the user to type in a question mark [Myer and Plummer 1973]. The computer responds with a list of choices, retypes the line up to that point, and allows the user to continue from there. In other words, a sort of in-line menu is provided. Another possibility is to show a menu of choices elsewhere on the screen. What matters is that the prompting not interfere with the typing of the command, and that it be visible while the user continues the line.

As noted above, users don't always want to type whole command words, especially if they are long. Nonetheless, the computer can always display the full command, which is usually much more legible. Some command processors provide a way to expand an initial sequence of letters into the full command once enough have been typed to constitute a unique specification. This function provides a surprisingly comfortable style of interaction. By echoing the remainder of each word, the command scanner indicates that the sequence has been understood and provides a maximally readable typescript. The Bolt Beranek and Newman Hermes system is a good example [see Rude, Melone, and Mooers 1979]. Figure 8-4 shows how a scanner completes to the "point of ambiguity." That is, when more than one command word is possible to complete from the letters typed by the user, the scanner completes as much as is possible, up to the spot where more information is necessary.

Commands designed to resemble natural language in their syntax require small connective words, such as "the" and "to." A command processor that habitually ignores such words may end up ignoring words that mean something important to the user. One solution to this problem is for the computer to provide "guide words" for the user as the command is entered. This scheme is shown in Figure 8-4.

Figure 8-4 also shows how a command might be created interac-

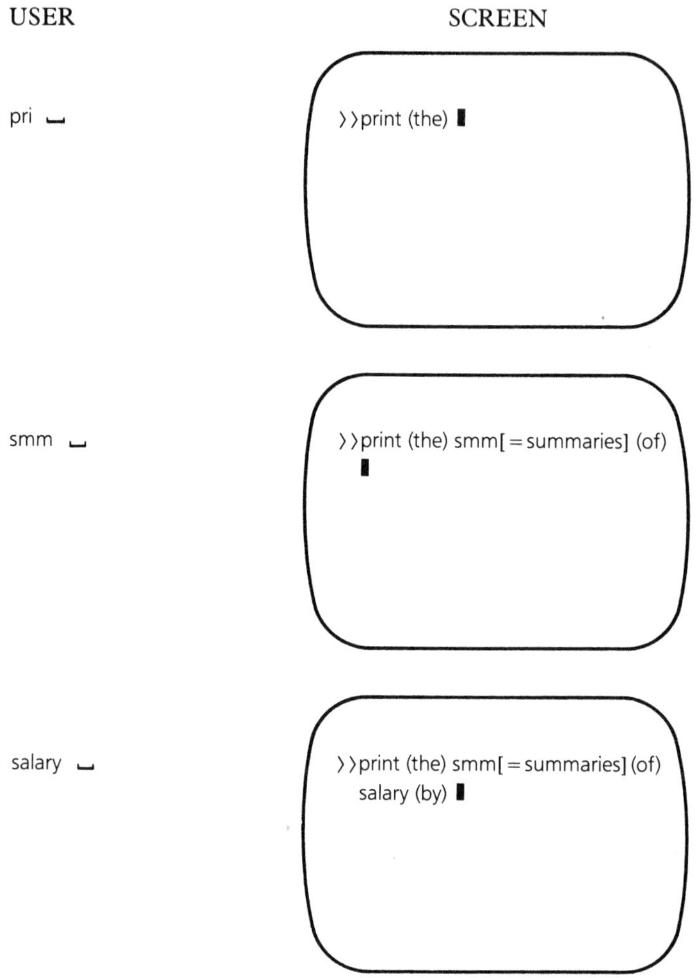

Figure 8-4. Command scanner incorporation, completion, guide words, and help

tively on a sophisticated command scanner constructed in accordance with the ideas discussed above. The diagram shows how the user and the computer work cooperatively to create the command that the user wants. There is a high degree of interaction. The user first types "pri," which is the beginning of the "print" command. The computer dutifully echoes. "␣" indicates that the user typed the space bar on the typewriter. This is the computer's cue to try to complete part of a command, and it responds with the rest of the word "print" plus a

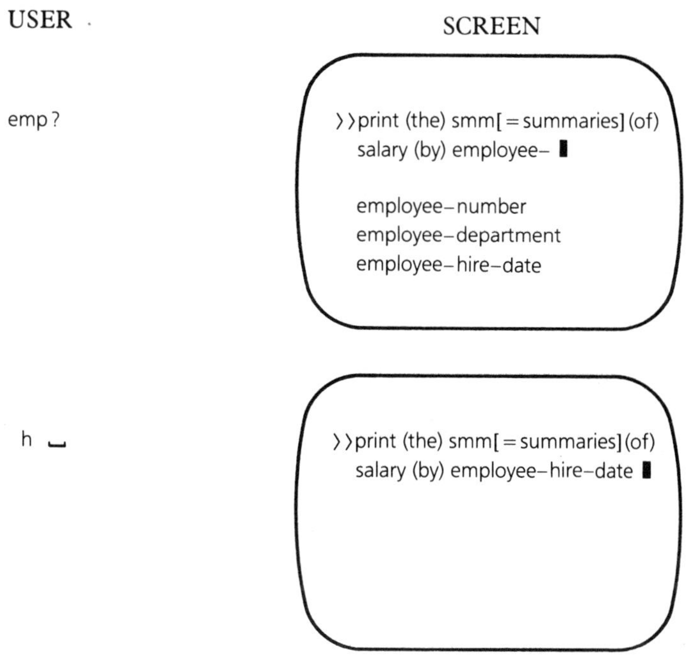

Figure 8-4 continued

guide word that cues the user about the next piece of the command. The user mistypes the first part of the next word, and the computer corrects it, showing the correction but moving right along. If the correction had been wrong, the user could have deleted characters back and retyped. That is, what's on the screen behaves just as if the user had typed it. The user continues, specifying "salary," and then reaching a point where he needs some information on the available options, types "?" A list of options appears. The list does not disturb the command line, and the user continues. When the command is complete, the user presses RETURN to confirm that this is what he wants done.

MENU-BASED DESIGNS

The menu style of control is especially popular for systems intended for the noncomputer oriented. Menus have the virtue of making explicit what choices or operations are available. A menu interface serves as its own memory aid. Because the basic user action is selecting, menu interfaces may require little typing and are appropriate for systems without full text keyboards. Since commands are not typed, there is no question of misspelling. Similarly, syntax errors may be avoided.

On the negative side, menus limit user expression to a finite number of choices, unless some alternative is provided for more general input. Long menus are undesirable for human-factors and practical reasons. As a result, when there are many possibilities to select from, some sort of hierarchy of menus is necessary. Navigating through a poorly structured or overly complex hierarchy will cause difficulties. Users can get lost or they may become impatient with making multiple selections in order to get to where they want to be. The organization of menu structures must match the task and the external myth, or even simple things will be confusing. Menus work best when there is little or no delay in getting the next one.

Guideline 40. Keep menus short.

Five or six items is a practical maximum for frequently used menus. Such menus are easily searched and remembered. As a result, their structure is less important to finding entries. Frequently used menus can be in an order based on convenience and frequency of use. Longer lists, undesirable in general, are harder to search. Structure can be quite helpful in finding items. Switching between one kind of ordering and another can itself be a source of confusion, so some simple rationale that the user can internalize is required. For example, the names of files, a potentially long list, might always be alphabetical, but the names of commands (a short list!) could be ordered by expected frequency (see Figure 8-5). Ordering should not change from session to session, user to user, or among related functions, because consistency is also important.

Guideline 41. Label menus.

Menus should have some kind of label, such as a header, so that they are easily identified. Structured menus also need position (state) information that shows how the user got there, such as a list of the previous

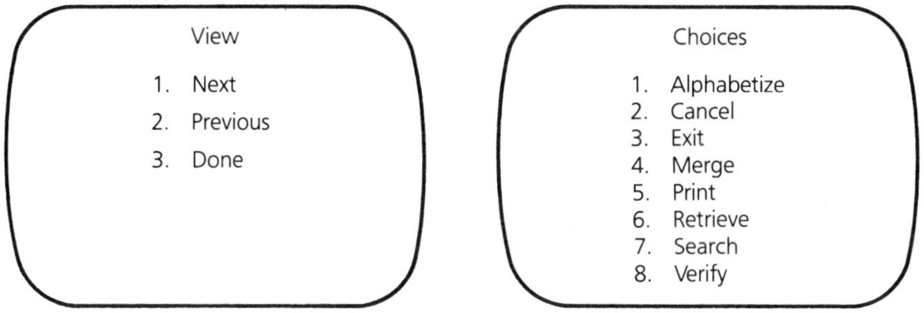

Figure 8-5. Menu ordering by structure and by frequency of use

selections. People cannot keep track of their state in menu structures of any considerable complexity. Three levels of depth is a practical maximum. Figure 8-6 shows two ways that state can be reflected on a screen.

The language of menu items significantly affects the quality of a menu interface. Menus may consist of descriptions of actions, formal language such as one would find in commands to do similar functions, or even pictures (icons) indicating the results of each selection. The language criteria discussed in Chapter 7 apply to textual menu items, and Chapter 11 gives procedures for evaluating icons.

The use model and the natural order of operations in the task should be the basis for menu structure. Because submenus represent a kind of mode in themselves, it is desirable to have relatively few of them. At any given position in the structure, users should be able to do what they want, given where they are in the task. Since menus represent modes, they should follow the external myth and be appropriately labeled.

DIRECT-MANIPULATION-BASED DESIGNS

Direct-manipulation interfaces represent objects—such as documents and forms—on the screen and allow the user to manipulate them directly by pointing, typing directly into them, and performing other operations *in situ* [Shneiderman 1982]. The user may select specific actions via function keys, menus, or keyboard commands. As a result, direct-manipulation interfaces invariably also have some menu or command character. Screen editors usually have interfaces of this type.

The advantage of direct manipulation is that it helps create concrete,

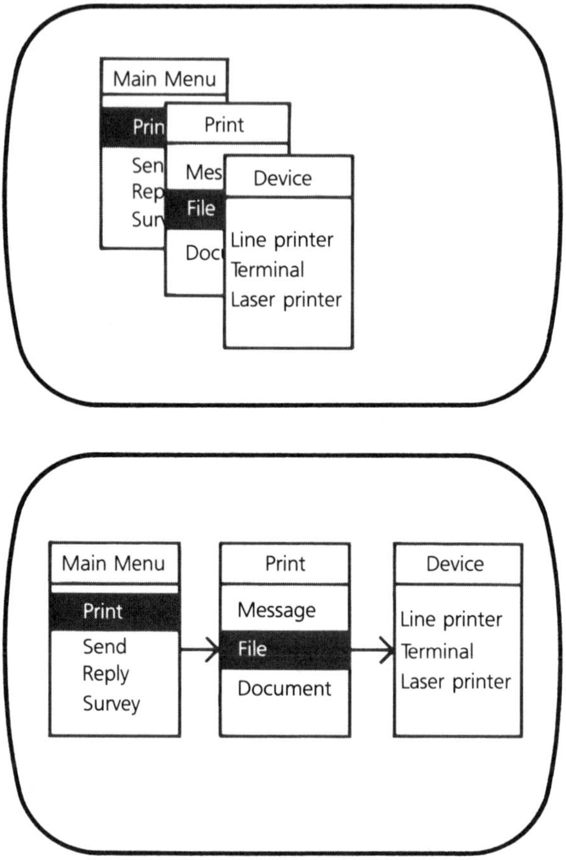

Figure 8-6. Examples displaying menu state

literal conceptual models. Users do not need to imagine what is happening to the item they are manipulating—they can see it. Also, greater simplicity is possible than with other styles when it comes to indicating where an action is to occur, because pointing replaces other types of specification. Pointing is easier than saying. The virtues of direct manipulation are exploited best with a graphical input device (such as a data tablet, joy stick, mouse, touch screen, or track ball) instead of with commands or function keys for cursor movement. Pointing devices are discussed in Chapter 10.

Direct-manipulation interfaces can make substantial computational demands on the systems that support them. More information is presented at one time than with menu or command systems. This data must be made visible on the screen and kept up to date. Direct-manipulation interfaces also require more frequent service from the computer. Real-time response is required for many actions, because the user is involved in feedback loops when pointing, typing, or otherwise acting on an object. What may not be computationally simple will frequently appear to be simple on the screen, and thus will require better response to look good. Reformatting or rejustifying text is a clear case in point: users expect such operations to happen in an instant. The next chapter provides response guidelines that apply to direct-manipulation interfaces. Finally, representing full documents on a screen may require displays of greater capabilities—larger, and with higher resolution and performance—than would be needed if another style of user interface were employed.

Guideline 44. Use a pointing device.

Guideline 45. Respond to direct manipulations in real time.

Guideline 46. Match objects in the interface to the external myth.

The objects upon which the direct-manipulation interface works must make sense in terms of the external myths. Direct manipulation should not be applied to conceptually dissimilar things. Therefore, if the external myth supports the representation of documents on the screen and if the user must edit a previously typed command, the command must be made part of a document. Applying direct document actions to something else—say, to a buffer—would be inconsistent.

The three basic styles—command, menu, and direct manipulation—combine freely. They mix the way colors mix: what constitutes a good mixture depends on the job. The important task is to build an interface with one coherent style, because styles do interact with external myth. Like external myths, they create expectations for users. Thus the style of other interfaces the user employs may affect the choice of a human interface style. One style of human interface is not automatically superior to another. Quality is independent of style and can be built into an interface, whatever stylistic choices are made.

FORMS AND STYLE

In business environments, most information is stored and communicated in a highly organized format, although it may not always be apparent that the data are embedded in a structure. Data are organized in forms such as purchase orders, invoices, time cards, bills of lading, travel vouchers, employment applications, and pay stubs. People use forms to withdraw money from banks and to reconcile the differences when the statement and check register do not agree.

Two salient features of forms are that they are highly structured and relatively static. Forms are perceptually organized, that is, structured visually. Associated data elements on a form are associated physically. On pay stub forms, for example, the voluntary deductions are grouped together, as are the taxes. Cumulative information such as year-to-date income is clearly separated from current information.

The highly organized nature of forms allows a viewer to scan a form quickly for pertinent information while ignoring the irrelevant. The structure exists as the grouping of associated fields, with segmentation of groupings by spaces, lines, or borders. Without these separations, the form structure would be much less apparent. This fact is evident to anyone who has used lineless forms on a CRT display.

Much of the utility of the form's structure comes from its relatively static nature. If every time someone used a form the information were arranged differently, utility would be greatly diminished. This is one reason that the IRS is reluctant to modify the 1040 tax form each year and, when it does, to alert taxpayers to the modifications. People expect forms to remain relatively constant.

Forms also embody the accepted information-handling procedures of an organization. The fields to be filled in tell a new user which information is required and which is optional. The signature block reflects organizational policy by indicating who must approve or certify facts and transactions represented by the form. Without forms, policy and procedure manuals would be referenced more frequently and errors of omission and commission in conveying information would increase dramatically. Thus forms help tell the user what information is needed for carrying out a procedure within the organization. They promote consistency in the behavior of organizations.

A particular combination of styles yields a screen representation of paper forms. Forms interfaces have been in use for years, but they have tended to be computer driven, controlling where the user enters data. More recently, forms with direct-manipulation interfaces have appeared. This combination provides a clear external myth, one related directly to the familiar paper forms people use every day. With direct manipulation, the labels in forms provide light-handed prompting, while leaving the user in charge and able to do things in his or her own order.

SEQUENTIAL AND CONCURRENT OPERATIONS

Concurrency is a concept that has found great use in computer hardware and in system software, but it has been underutilized in human interfaces. In designing systems, the simultaneous performance of a number of related parts of the task increases speed. Pipelining, array processing, interrupts, and look-ahead carry are all examples familiar to hardware designers. In software, timesharing, real-time operating systems, and multiprocessing all allow a number of independent services to be provided concurrently, even though there is a single machine doing all the jobs. This capability can make activities economical that may not warrant the price of separate, dedicated machines. In this sense, economics drives both hardware and software parallelism.

Parallelism in human interfaces allows *users* to be more efficient. People do not necessarily do what they do in a logical, sequential way. Their behavior depends critically on personal styles, on the task, and on the situation.

Guideline 47. Let the user choose the order of tasks.

It may not always be possible to structure a computerized task in the same way as its manual equivalent, but doing so may be advantageous. The resulting interface can be natural and comfortable in a way that a technically expedient interface rarely is. Task analysis should reveal whether the activity is inherently parallel or serial (or some mixture). To accommodate individual stylistic differences for a given task, an interface should provide flexibility. Usually, the designer cannot know what order a user will prefer for tasks of any substantial complexity. It is necessary in these cases to leave it to the user to choose.

If the application and use model warrants, it is desirable to let users have several things going at one time. It's a common feature of everyday life that people are interrupted, are prevented from finishing tasks, and do several things at once. It's frustrating to lose one's place in these tasks or to be forced to start a partly completed task over again.

Not only are people capable of concurrent activities: many prefer them. Computer systems can facilitate concurrency by keeping track of the tasks and their states. Thus, the computer is not necessarily actively working on several things simultaneously, but is allowing the user to be in the middle of many things at once.

Drawing, for example, is a highly concurrent task in the sense that the draftsman is normally free to draw any of several sections of the picture in any order. There may be parts that are usually done together—some local structure to the task—but it's usually sensible to break with even this structure from time to time. Imagine drawing a plan for a house. A computer that forces you to complete the outside walls before doing any of the inside ones—and doesn't allow outside wall changes once any inside walls are specified—would be limiting and frustrating to use. Rather, the parallelism occurs at a conceptual level. The draftsman can work on the kitchen for a while, then on the porch, then on energy loss, then on the kitchen again. In this case the challenge would be to design a system that knows something about architecture but that leaves the user free to work on whatever he or she wants.

Banking transactions on the other hand are generally serial. With a live teller, it is certainly possible to suspend processing of a transaction, say a withdrawal, until another issue is resolved, say a deposit, and then to complete the first transaction. This kind of thing happens, but it is not the norm. An electronic teller is designed to deal with the normal rather than the exceptional transaction and would not be expected to handle such a situation. Nonetheless, forcing customers to do things in a particular order may be unnatural if the order is not inherent in the transaction. If you have both a deposit and a withdrawal to make, the machine should not force you to make one or the other first. Not everyone approaches the task in the same way.

In a database system it is usually easy to ask a question that will take the computer a long time to answer. Although throughput may actually degrade when several queries are processed in parallel, users' productivity and perceptions of the system may improve as a result of this type of transaction. Concurrency allows users to be doing something even though the computer is busy.

Most current message systems lead the user through a sequence of questions to send a message. The system asks the same questions the user would have to answer on a memo form: the names of those to receive the memo, the subject of the memo, and the body of the message. For some people and situations, this sequence is not natural. A manager drafting a memo about the status of a project might write out the body and then decide to send a copy to someone not thought of at first, say the department business manager. Or, the manager might decide that the topic is not accurate and want to change it. Making such changes concurrently on a piece of paper is easy. In midsentence the user can change a subject line, add or delete a recipient, or correct a spelling error in a previous sentence. A high-quality human interface would provide the same kind of flexibility.

INTERFACE STYLE FOR PEOPLE'S BANK

Every automatic teller machine we know of is largely based on menus, whether shown on a screen or realized in an array of buttons. For the finite tasks involved, with their very limited sets of choices, menus seem to provide the greatest ease of use. Some teller machines also provide a moderate amount of command character in the choice of

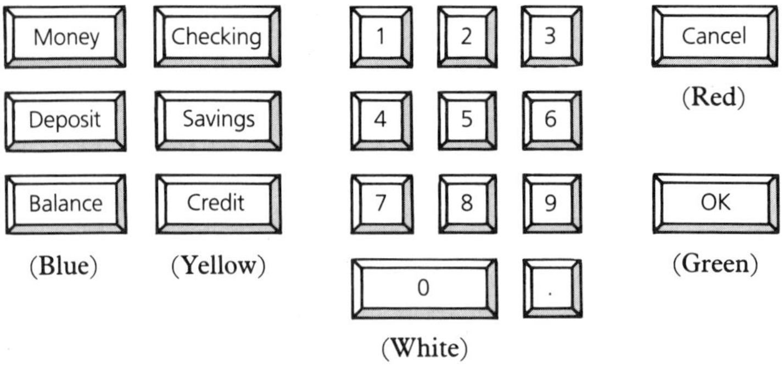

Figure 8-7. Command-oriented key layout

buttons. For our purposes, the array shown in Figure 8-7 is one possible approach.

One machine in current use does just this, with prompting such as "Select transaction type—use blue keys," leading the user through the creation of a command. For our multilingual requirement, however, each button would have to have two legends, and there is the possibility that syntax might not match easily between the two languages. The keys would end up cluttered. If touch-screen technology were available, we could put the buttons on the screen and provide the correct labels in the user's language. Unfortunately, the ATM vendor does not provide touch-screens.

Another possibility is a direct-manipulation style, which would represent documents on the screen for each transaction type. When the transaction was complete, the customer would have a printed copy (receipt) just like the screen image. Thus the machine interaction would more closely parallel the live-teller transaction with which customers are already familiar. Again, we choose not to pursue this possibility, but note that it is available should testing reveal that users do not understand the machine transactions.

The menus we have designed for People's Bank generally meet the menu guidelines detailed in this chapter. The titles carry some state information, but not all of it. The "amount" frame should indicate which account a deposit or withdrawal affects. We must use six different frames to cover all cases, not just the two we had. Figure 8-8 shows these new frames. There are at most three levels of menus, the worst case being when a deposit or withdrawal is selected and the user must choose the account and then enter the amount. The menu tree structure is shown in Figure 8-9. Menus are punctuated correctly and are printed in upper- and lowercase letters for legibility. None of the menus is very long.

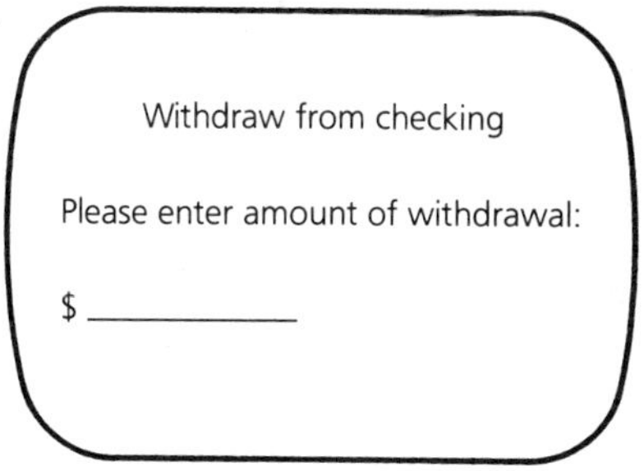

Withdraw amount from checking frame

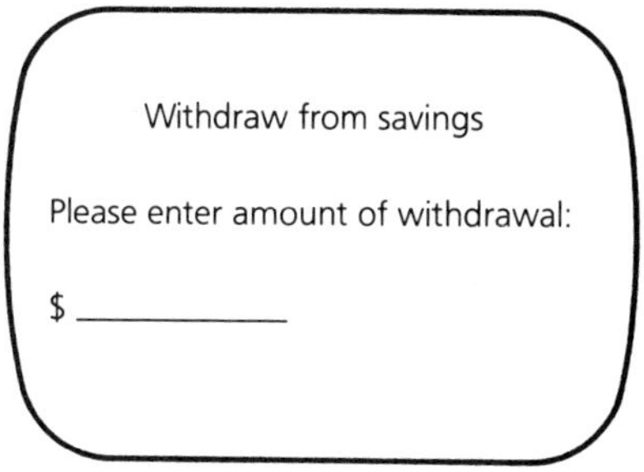

Withdraw amount from savings frame

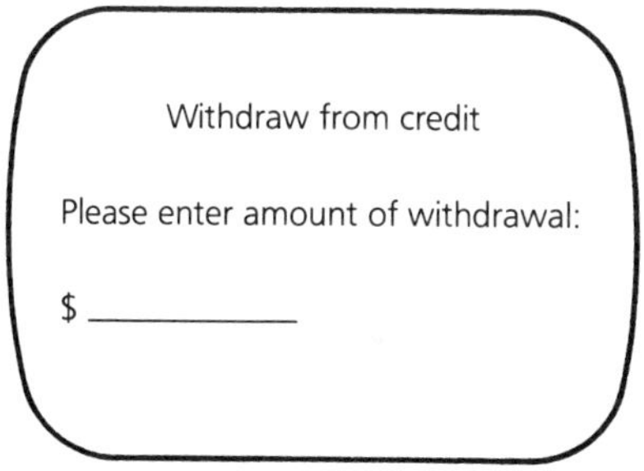

Withdraw amount from credit frame

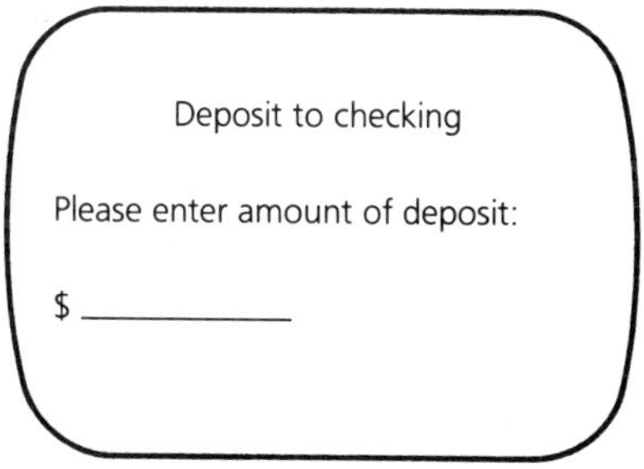

Deposit amount to checking frame

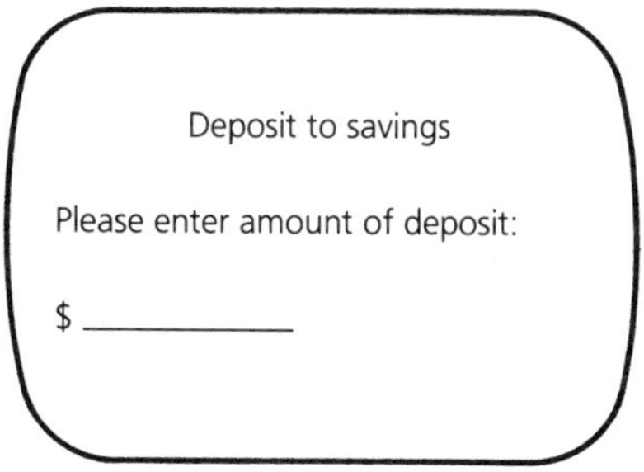

Deposit amount to savings frame

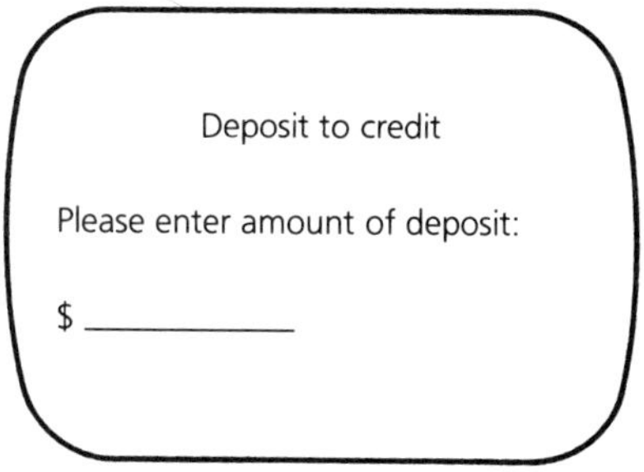

Deposit amount to credit frame

Figure 8-8. Menu frames including state information

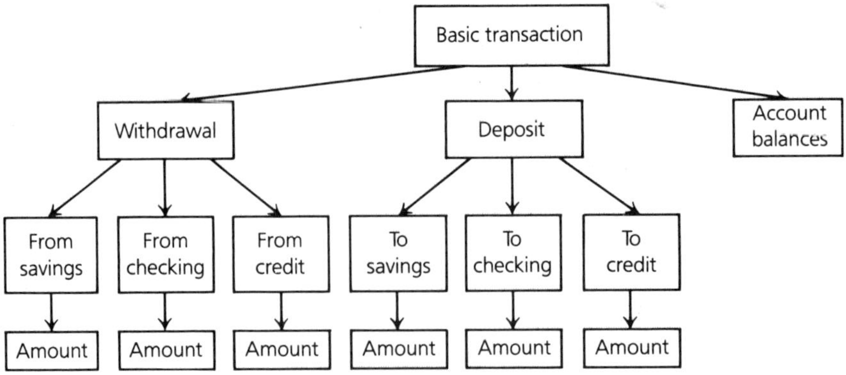

Figure 8-9. Menu tree structure

9 Responding to Users

The user needs to know what is happening on the computer's side of the interaction. This information returned to the user is called feedback, and includes both responses during normal operations and responses when there is a problem. If feedback is not current, correct, clearly expressed, or visible, the user may think or do the wrong things.

FEEDBACK ON NORMAL OPERATIONS

The goal of feedback is to provide high-quality, timely responses to keep the user well informed and comfortable. In extreme cases bad feedback can even cause system failure. In one system we know of, users did not know when the system was working, because of poor response. Data entry required that users hit the "send" key when a record was ready for processing. Pressing this key transmitted all the data on the terminal screen, but for many seconds there was no acknowledgment of the receipt of the data. To deal with the lack of response, users got into the habit of hitting the "send" key six or eight times just to make sure that it had worked. Performance degraded because of frequent reprocessing of data and elimination of duplicate entries. The moral: a system should keep users informed even when things are fine. Otherwise it's like being ignored in a conversation; people don't like it.

Guideline 48. Acknowledge user actions—quickly.

There must always be a response to the user. If processing will take any appreciable time, immediate acknowledgment is necessary. People are quick to attribute meaning to events. If acknowledgment does not always come, or if it comes at varying times, users will incorporate this information into their conceptual model of the system.

A blank screen is a likely indication that the terminal or computer is not working. Even if users come to expect the blank screen as part of normal operation, when the system does break they may become confused. When a system becomes heavily loaded or would otherwise be unresponsive, two defenses are possible: make the acknowledgment the first thing done after input or run the acknowledgment part of the code at higher priority. Some operating environments make prompt acknowledgment much easier than others. For long computations, the terminal could simply show "Working" or a similar message. Providing the percentage of task completed, partial results, or counts of items found is useful in some environments.

Inadequate response can cause functional confusion for users. Consider a screen-oriented editor that uses a "mouse" as a pointing device. If the procedure is to press the button to get a menu and if the menu appears positioned with a first menu item at the indicated position, the user may learn to press the button twice in succession for that particular case. If the user is faster than the computer, the second press could be lost or could cause the wrong action. Situations like this can be annoying and can lead to materially lower throughput because the user is afraid of doing the operation too fast for the machine.

Although the system should always assume that the user has performed an action deliberately, in a few cases no response to an action can mean that the action is meaningless and has no effect. If, for example, you have to design a system around a keyboard with keys that are not used, the system can consistently ignore them. The user soon learns that the keys do not do anything.

Guideline 49. Provide an easy way out.

A system could allow a panicked or impatient user to respond as would a participant in a conversation. Conversers have ways of changing the subject or of otherwise extricating themselves from an unsatisfactory interaction. A cooperative system would allow the user to interrupt a task to do something else, in effect saying, "Excuse me for a moment. . . OK, I'm back. Where were we?" In situations in which the user stops some task, good feedback dictates that the system acknowledge the interruption and make it clear to the user how to resume the task or how to proceed in some other way.

Guideline 50. No surprises.

The more complex a system is, the more surprises it generates. One example is a compiler that eliminates multiple spaces and tabs in comments. If the user has gone to the trouble to make a table or other spatially structured comments, these omissions will result in the loss of some useful information and in annoyance to the user. Other cases involve side effects of commands, as when a user explicitly sets a mode or value, but some other action invisibly changes or overrides it. For example, some terminals allow users to select white characters on a dark background or the other way around. This setting can also be changed under program control. Programs that change the setting for whatever reason countermand the user's intentions, especially if they do not return the terminal to its original state after doing whatever they do. There are even programs that set terminals to the white-on-black state when they have finished running, so as to return the terminal to its "original condition." This works only for users who have set their terminals for white-on-black. What we call the *Principle of Least Astonishment* dictates that the computer tell users when it is not following their instructions to the letter, as when it makes a necessary spelling correction. It's hard to avoid surprises, but the basic tool for doing so is awareness of the user's conceptual model.

Guideline 51. Confirm information content, not literal input.

When confirming a command, the system shouldn't merely repeat what the user typed. It should try to state what it has understood. A paraphrase, based on the content extracted from the command, allows users to decide whether the computer has understood their intended meaning.

A sample dialogue from an instructional program called SOPHIE [Brown, Burton, and Bell 1974] illustrates these points. This system has a sophisticated natural language interface and permits students to do electronic troubleshooting of a simulated instrument:

User: WHAT IS THE OUTPUT VOLAEG?

Computer: =VOLTAGE
THE OUTPUT VOLTAGE IS 30.03 VOLTS.

User: IS THAT CORRECT?

Computer: IN A WORKING CIRCUIT THE OUTPUT VOLTAGE IS 30.07 VOLTS.
THAT VALUE IS CORRECT.

User: CHANGE THE LOAD RESISTANCE TO 30 OHMS

Computer: THE LOAD IS 30.0.

User: NOW WHAT IS THE OP VOLTAGE

Computer: THE OUTPUT VOLTAGE IS 1.82 VOLTS.

User: WHAT SHOULD IT BE?

Computer: IN A WORKING CIRCUIT THE OUTPUT VOLTAGE IS 29.88 VOLTS.

User: WHAT IS THE VBE OF THE CURRENT LIMINTG TRANSISTRO

Computer: =TRANSISTOR
=LIMITING
THE BASE EMITTER VOLTAGE OF Q6 IS 36.23 MILLIVOLTS.

As you can see, SOPHIE makes spelling corrections and informs the user of each one. Then it gives answers containing a paraphrase of the input question, so that the user knows what the machine has understood. A short answer like "29.88 volts" could convey the impression that the machine understood, even in cases when it did not.

Guideline 52. Don't distract.

Actions and reactions made by the computer should all be meaningful and should not draw the user's attention away from what is important and central. We know of one graphics editor that slides the whole graphics image down on the screen every time a command is to be typed. The justification is to make room on the screen for the command. As a result the whole visual field is disturbed, when a spot for the command could have been reserved (or temporarily used and restored).

ERROR HANDLING

A critical component of any system is the way it responds to mistakes, errors, incompatibilities, hardware contingencies, and other things that are wrong. Making errors of one sort or another is simply a feature of being human. Many of our everyday activities are guided by the detection of errors. We use this information to correct our behavior and thus to achieve our goals. For example:

- We dial a wrong number, discover the fact, and try again.
- We hammer nails to hold something together, test it, and hammer more if the result isn't adequate.
- We look at the copies coming from the copy machine, find them too light or dark for our taste, adjust the dark/light control, and try again.
- We write things, read them, and make changes, repeating the process until we are satisfied with the result.

So, making errors is the norm. While we generally focus on the result rather than on the errors we made along the way, the errors are a necessary part of the path to the goal. Norman [1982] calls these unintentional errors "slips," while deviations and errors of intent he terms "mistakes." Thus, if you decide to take your umbrella with you and forget it, that's a slip. If you decide not to take it because you think it won't rain but it does, you've made a mistake.

Computer systems can be extremely sensitive to human errors. Because people normally make many slips, the consequences of these slips should be very minor, giving users feedback so they can do better on the next try. In contrast, the system may or may not detect mistakes at all, since what makes an error a mistake is the deviation from the user's intention; in general the system can't know that a command is a mistake. Mistakes with computers may require the user to undo or repeat work.

Because people make slips routinely, they are used to noting the deviation from the desired result and making corrections. But the deviation must be seen in proximity to the error, while the information is still "hot." Although we suggest not forcing users to deal with problems on the spot, most problems are best fixed at the time they occur. In systems that must process input long after a slip occurs, good error checking not only avoids unnecessary use of computing resources in the form of incomplete runs and the like; it also avoids interruptions to the user while he or she is doing something else. Good and timely feedback supports the perception that the computer is helping rather than obstructing progress.

Guideline 53. Report errors simply and in context.

Some time ago, one of us compiled his first program in an unfamiliar computer language called BLISS. The one-page program generated three pages of diagnostic messages, 35 in all, and the compiler summarized them as follows:

```
Information:     13
Warnings:        18
Errors:           4
```

For a person with little computer experience, such a deluge of diagnostic information would be demoralizing. Systems need not present the user with all the problems in one command, program, or data set.

While it is important to provide a maximum of useful information, redundant reports and those that are consequents of errors already reported serve no useful purpose and may well give offense.

Error messages should also avoid "garbage" information, which adds to the volume of the message, but not to its utility. Dumps, tracebacks, error logs, and the like should be saved for experts to analyze. In turn, the user won't ignore succinct, interesting, informative messages.

Guideline 54. Be polite.

Consider this message:

```
Fatal flaw at line 25.
```

It is insulting and overdramatic. It is supposed to mean that the program was unable to figure out what the user wanted, because the input did not obey a syntax rule. But the user, in this case a programmer, probably meant the program to do something. The computer could acknowledge this and even accept some of the blame, instead of abusing the user. A good principle for avoiding accidental rudeness is to assume that the user always meant something by his or her input. Computer programs should be humble. If the computer can't make sense of it, then the fault is the system's, not the user's.

Guideline 55. Don't blame the user.

The best system never assesses blame at all, but if it must, then the computer should take the blame. A neutral description of what happened lays the blame on no one. For example, "Too many inputs" could be expressed as "Two inputs expected, but three were found."

Guideline 56. Avoid error codes.

An error message should help the user determine what to do. Error codes do not serve this function well. Because there is no longer a premium on storage space for messages, error codes now have little value and are simply garbage that users must wade through to get to the English part of a message. Codes are sometimes used to index errors in documentation. This function is better performed with simple key words or another unobtrusive scheme.

The other set of concerns for reporting errors involves their content and meaning. An inaccurate error message is counterproductive. One portable computer that talks BASIC gives a *syntax* error message when the value of a loop limit exceeds 999, an undocumented implementation limit. This is a semantic error rather than a syntactic one. It's the wrong message.

Guideline 57. Don't mislead.

Consider this dialogue:

User: Rename apple.txt pear .txt

Computer: %Maximum parameter count exceeded

The intent of the command is to change the name of a file from "apple.txt" to "pear.txt", but the user mistakenly typed a space in the second name. From the program's point of view, the problem is that there are too many inputs for the particular command because the space acted as a delimiter. The error message, however, reads as if some greater transgression has occurred. It implies that some overall limit has been exceeded, rather than that it has found one too many items as input to the command.

Next consider the message given when a particular personal computer is booted without a system diskette in place:

ROM DISK LOADER FAILURE

From the programmer's point of view, the message makes perfect sense. The loader in read-only memory failed to load a program. But users may be left with the impression that a hardware failure has occurred, especially if they know that a ROM is a piece of hardware.

A few systems give vague responses indicating that "something is wrong here." One program we've used for word processing processes a special binary file to produce another file that is in turn used by a document formatter. Its only message is "CONFUSED," which is not much help in finding out what went wrong.

Guideline 58. Fix problems.

Here is another error report:

```
            GOTO (10,20,30) N
                            ↑
?COMMA MISSING IN COLUMN 22
```

This error message is an old favorite from the early days of FORTRAN compilers. The program discovered exactly what was wrong and was clearly in a position to fix it but did not.

A programming system called INTERLISP [Teitelman 1974] has an impressive error correction facility called DWIM, standing for "Do What I Mean." It can correct spelling errors, typing errors, and many other mistakes during input without causing users to lose context or even necessarily requiring them to take any explicit action. Under normal circumstances, these capabilities make DWIM very friendly. A friend of ours, however, was working late one night and was making liberal use of DWIM to change his lowercase procedure names to the required uppercase. Thus he was saved the awkwardness of typing many shifted characters on his keyboard. For each such "error," DWIM made the correction, politely noting the change. After several hours of such fixing, it printed the following message:

```
You seem to be having trouble with this.
```

DWIM had been counting! Although we don't object to an occasional light response by a computer, our friend was not amused by the message. The moral: don't expect a program to make inferences about a person's state of mind. You will either be wrong or insulting, a no-win situation.

Guideline 59. Don't personify the computer.

The other extreme is to be too chatty and make the computer out to have a personality:

User: Print aardvark

Computer: I don't understand the word "aardvark".
Please rephrase your question and ask me again.

Attributing human characteristics to the computer is presumptuous. Few systems have the requisite intelligence, and computers do not as yet have feelings, bodies, or other human attributes. Chatty first-person messages may elicit English input that won't work at all or may lead users to believe that a person is communicating with them via the machine.

Guideline 60. Distinguish between success and failure.

Consider this computer response:

%DEBUG-I-EXITSTATUS is %SYSTEM-S-NORMAL, normal successful completion

Because it has the form of an error message, this message does not give the impression that everything is fine, even though that is what it says. Such a response is like putting a red sign declaring "In Order" on a public telephone. It should be easy for users to notice that something has gone awry. A visual distraction, beep, or other polite attention-getter is particularly helpful during routine, frequently performed operations that nearly always work. Failing to get users' attention may allow them to compound the problem by taking an inappropriate action.

Guideline 61. State errors in terms of the external myth.

One of the greatest difficulties with error messages is that they tend to state the problem in terms of events within the computer rather than in terms of the application. Consider the difference between:

Unable to open file DSK3:[SYSTEM.FONTS]TIMES-ROMAN.FONT

and

The Times Roman typeface is not available.

Designers should always ask: "What does this event mean to the user?" Then they can make sure that the system tells the user what caused the problem and hopefully what to do to correct it.

It is exceptionally difficult to deal with system, hardware, and internal errors, because the user has little or no context in which to understand them and because many such messages are not directly related to the conversation. After all, they are not part of the external myth. The conditions may not even relate to something the user did.

If the error is not part of the user dialogue, the system should interrupt politely, and only if the message is important. Recoverable system errors that don't relate to user actions should be reported only to systems people, via a system log, message file, dump, or other means. If the user's context is not lost because of the error, the system should attempt to recover before alerting the user to the problem. For example, the fact that a block on a tape had to be read a few times before it came in correctly is immaterial.

Guideline 62. Make it easy to correct mistakes.

It must be easy to make corrections. Having to retype a long command to fix a typing error wastes time and resources. Experience with word-processing systems has shown that people type much faster if they know they can easily fix the mistakes they make.

One excellent idea for a command interface is to allow users to edit the previously issued command just as they do for text, as in the following dialogue:

User: Print repoetdata on letter printer

Computer: Can't find file REPOETDATA

User: Use report for repoet

Computer: OK, trying REPORTDATA.
File REPORTDATA printed on letter printer.

Guideline 63. Combine error and help processing.

There should be close ties between a system's help and error facilities, because it is when something has gone wrong that the user may need some assistance. The help facility can use the context of an error to direct the user to the right sort of information. Since error messages are usually associated with user slips, getting right to the point with a little well-aimed help can keep the slip from escalating into a major hassle with the system.

Error handling can also be designed to provide additional semantic information about the genesis of an error. Explained in external terms, a traceback can provide users with meaningful information, made available as part of the help facility when an error has occurred. Consider this scenario:

Computer: Error—Unable to create a new spreadsheet.

User: Why?

Computer: Unable to create a new spreadsheet
... because unable to open a new backing file,
... because unable to preallocate sufficient memory,
... because not enough disk memory is available.

Although this explanation might not mean anything to a nontechnical user, it does describe the problem in simple terms. A user could easily jot the information down or read it over the phone to someone who could help, without getting bogged down in numbers or codes.

DESIGNING OUT ERRORS

The set of possible errors in a system should be a constraint on design, not a consequence of it. Designers can control errors by enumerating all the slips that can possibly occur and specifying an associated response by the computer. Although mistakes are harder to control, because the system may not sense them directly, analysis of the user's task and situation will also allow discovery of many of the possible errors of intent. By structuring the system well, designers can influence even these errors.

Guideline 64. Design the error behavior of the system.

Consider a capability in a business information system that allows users to draw graphs and charts from sets of data that already exist. Suppose four possibilities are available: pie chart, bar chart, line graph, or point graph, as shown in Figure 9-1. For each type of drawing, users can specify further information about scales, labeling, and so on.

Although the problem may immediately suggest a structure for the set of commands, it is valuable to defer the decision a bit and consider a number of alternatives. For each, what are the mistakes a user could make? What difficulties in the program might have to be reported to the user?

Consider a command interface. We assume that the data set is already specified or known from context. The interface might have commands like these:

```
Pie chart
Bar chart
Point graph
Line graph
Set x scale linear
Set y legend "Sales (Dollars)"
Draw
```

With this interface, these are some of the possible errors:

- Unknown command
- Too many arguments
- Too few arguments

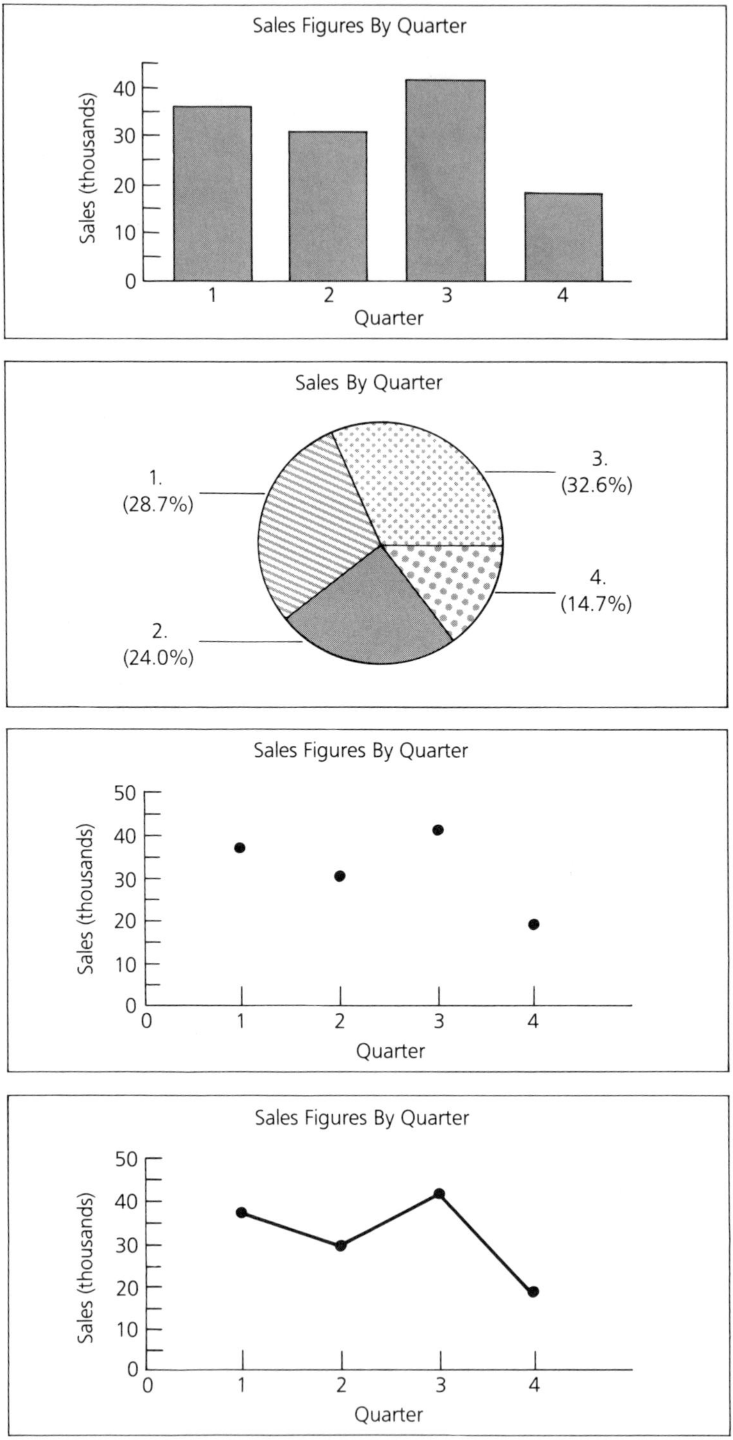

Figure 9-1. Examples of business graphics

- Unknown scale type
- Scale not applicable to pie chart
- Chart or graph form not specified
- Scale type not specified
- Legend text too long

Some of these errors could be eliminated by "defaults," that is, settings to be used unless overridden. Unless specified otherwise, the result would be, say, a graph with linear scales and connected data points. Specifying defaults helps some but can still lead to surprises for users.

A second possible design would have the computer prompt the user for the information it needs. A typical dialogue with prompted parameter specification would be:

User: Draw
Computer: Plot type? (Chart, graph):
User: graph
Computer: Connected points?
User: yes
Computer: X scale (log or linear):
User: linear
Computer: X legend:
User: Year
Computer: Y scale (log or linear):
User: linear
Computer: Y legend:
User: Sales (Dollars)
Computer: Your graph is being drawn.

In this structure there are no commands, and thus no syntax errors; the "not applicable" and "not specified" kind of errors disappear. Its disadvantage is that it forces a sequence on the user. As a result, slips have greater consequences here than they would in the command design.

Another possibility is a menu, direct-manipulation design. Only appropriate menus are presented, with later choices determined by earlier ones. The first menu presents a choice of overall type:

Chart type

☐ Pie
☐ Bar
☐ Graph

Once a bar chart is selected, for example, the system presents a menu with the appropriate choices for that type of drawing.

Errors possible in this design are nearly the same as in the previous one. The user might still fail to specify a needed piece of information, but providing tentative selections in the "bar" and "graph" menus would overcome any omissions.

A final design is a variation of the basic menu design. The various menus are presented simultaneously as part of a single form, although using a form is not essential to the idea. The innovation here is that selections remain visible and accessible once choices have been made. The user is free to go back to earlier menus to change selections. The form itself is a dynamic one: subsequent fields change depending on selections made earlier, that is, nearer the top of the form. Once the user selects a bar chart, the rest of the form changes to be appropriate for describing a bar chart.

This last design can be carefully constructed so as to avoid *all* error messages related to specifying the graph or chart to be produced. Users can still fail to get the graph or chart that they want, but there are no inputs that cause the computer to respond with an error message. The effect of instructing the computer is always seen in the resulting picture. In other words, slips and mistakes are entirely in the problem domain. Seeing an undesired result is certainly in the category of error feedback but there are *no* explicit error messages. This effect is achieved by:

- Presenting only relevant choices
- Marking default choices provisionally, so that no deliberate selection activity is involved
- Allowing regression: if an earlier choice is changed, the subsequent menus change accordingly.

By considering various designs for error behavior, designers become aware of the options available for optimizing error handling. It may not be possible in a particular situation to eliminate all errors as in the last example. But it is always possible to make the situation better than it would have been if no error design occurred.

RESPONSE TIME

When a computer needs a noticeable amount of time to accomplish a task, immediate acknowledgment of input tells users that they've successfully done their part. But there is still the question of how long it is reasonable for other things to take.

Guideline 65. Allow people to work in real time.

Tasks involving hand-eye coordination require feedback in real time. In effect, any delay in a sensory-motor feedback loop interferes with smooth, coordinated actions. Responding in real time means that the computer keeps up with the person. The criterion is not whether there is a noticeable delay, but rather whether the delay degrades human performance. Tasks involving sensory-motor feedback can be very demanding on computers. Echoing is a familiar case, often handled with special hardware or high-priority service routines. Tracking the puck on a digitizer tablet is another case in which real-time response is needed.

Some feedback is required for every user action. After two to four seconds, people start to wonder if what they have done has worked, or they begin to think about other things. The two-to-four-second rule follows from observations of conversations. When one party in a dialogue stops talking, the other will usually commence. If there is an unanticipated silence in the conversation, the interchange quickly becomes very awkward.

The long-distance telephone network, for example, provides subtle feedback while a request is being processed. Although there is no specific meaning advertised for the small clicks, pops, beeps, and other noises callers hear between dialing a call and being connected, these sounds have a structure that callers can discover, and they provide some useful information about the progress of the call. For example, the background noise level changes when the audio channel to the remote exchange is established. This feedback is satisfying because it usually means that the wait is almost over.

Guideline 66. Announce long delays.

When the response time is much longer than two to four seconds, for instance with a complex retrieval operation, the system should inform users of a rule change for the conversation. Options include a graphic indicator such as a timer clock, hourglass, or bar chart showing actual progress, or at a minimum a statement that it will take some time to finish what was requested. A user not adequately informed that the system is processing will start to think that something is wrong. A little feedback can go a long way toward improving the perception of good response without actually improving performance.

Irregular response times make a system seem unpredictable and can cause frustration. Generally, it is more important for response time variability to be low than for the average response time to be low [R. B. Miller 1968]. As the mean response for a particular operation increases, variance becomes more noticeable, and thus, important. Variation in response time usually conflicts with user expectations and confuses the user's model of how the system works.

Guideline 67. Make delays make sense.

Delays ideally should be proportional to perceived processing effort. For instance, it may be acceptable to wait a few seconds for a purchase order to be retrieved by content. If the user's model is that of conventional paper documents, such a wait would be consistent with (and a vast improvement over) the situation in a conventional office. Waiting the same few seconds for a machine to multiply three items by a purchase price of $20 and to show the total would not be acceptable because the perceived effort to do the task is very small, and because computers are supposed to be good at arithmetic.

The central idea in the design of response time is: response is good, adequate, or bad only in terms of the user's perception.

Response is good, adequate, or bad only in terms of the user's perception.

Actions can be categorized into the ranges of response time on the basis of their conceptual (as opposed to computational) difficulty. Users find it easier to accept long responses when the task appears to require a lot of work. Unfortunately, the perception of effort does not necessarily correspond to the actual amount of computation. For example, sliding an image across the screen in response to a light pen may require a great deal of computing, but the motion must seem smooth and quick because the act is conceptually simple. It is just a physical motion of an object represented on the screen.

Appropriate response time can be one of the hardest human interface requirements to achieve. Because technology and available resources are frequently cost sensitive, designers need good information on how users react so that they can argue for the resources to make the system fast in the right places and can save money in areas that don't demand high performance.

Computation delays should not force users to be idle. In practice, however, it can be hard to determine the productivity impact of having to wait. Sometimes users make good use of waiting time to plan their next task, or to talk to a client, and the impact of waiting is minor. The challenge for designers is to know what it is worth to speed up a system. Often the decision requires a tradeoff between resources and costs versus productivity. One approach is to ensure that the user can always do something useful while waiting for something else.

Consider the setting of response time goals for a document-preparation and information retrieval system. Table 9-1 shows a possible range of responses for the operations performed by the system.

Table 9-1. Response times possible for an information retrieval system

- "Zero" (no visible delay)
  - Cursor movement
  - Echoing
- Short (up to about 1 second)
  - Procedural informational requests (help, status)
  - Acquiring menus
  - Scrolling, page flipping
  - Detection of syntactic "type" error
  - Detection and automatic correction of a misspelled word
  - Display a document, file, report, etc.
  - Retrieve a document, file, report, etc., by name or location
  - Detection of semantic command error
  - Retrieve a single document by content (keyed field)
  - First feedback from a data base search
  - Store a document
- Long (maybe several seconds)
  - Retrieve a single document by content (not keyed field)
  - Make paper copy of a single-page document
  - Retrieve a document from on-line remote data base.
  - Test for system fault (go/no-go)
- Very long (more than 60 seconds)
  - Archive retrieval
  - External data base inquiry
  - Make paper copies of long documents

RESPONSE ISSUES FOR PEOPLE'S BANK

For the People's Bank system, we need to address feedback, response times, and error handling. We already dealt with feedback issues for our ATM design when we designed the menus. Feedback is provided by the sequence of menus, which include the appropriate state information.

Response time is an issue for the automatic teller machines. From the user's viewpoint, the machine is providing a service only to him or her; it's not time sharing. Response should thus not vary noticeably with loading on the central system or network. We therefore specify that account and authorization data be prefetched when the user inserts the card and is entering the password, rather than in response to a particular transaction request. This should smooth out the response time over the interaction. We further specify that the transition from one frame to the next take less than one second. This will avoid delaying users or causing them to wonder whether anything is wrong.

The following are the error conditions for a particular existing ATM system:

- Machine out of service.
- Faulty card—please contact the bank.
- Incorrect password—please enter identification code again.
- Identification code incorrect three times—please contact bank.
- Machine out of cash (other transactions permitted).
- Cash withdrawal must be a multiple of $10.
- Unable to obtain balances.
- Unable to perform transfer transaction.
- No receipts available (proceed if no receipt is required).
- Transaction canceled at your request.
- Transaction canceled (time up). Do you want another transaction?
- Card withdrawal limit exceeded.
- Machine failure. Transaction not completed.

These amount to a great many things that can go wrong. We have decided to modify the design of People's Bank ATMs to reduce both the number of messages and their rather technical content. This strategy will involve a tradeoff that the management of People's Bank finds hard to accept: when anything is wrong with the machine, we'll have to take it out of service, even if some transactions would still be possible. The result is a requirement for more machines or more frequent servicing at each location, but we believe this is an acceptable price for minimizing complexity for users.

The list of errors for People's Bank machines is much shorter:

1. Sorry, machine out of service.
2. Your card appears to be faulty—please contact the bank.
3. Withdrawals must be multiples of $10.
4. Identification code not understood.
5. Machine withdrawals for this account are limited to $350 per day.

The "machine out of service," message covers all mechanical failures, including lack of cash, lack of receipts, and communications failures. If a fault occurs during a transaction, the customer's card is returned and this message is shown on the screen.

Similarly, rather than have a separate message when the identification code is given incorrectly too many times, we'll respond with "Your card may be faulty—please contact the bank." This message is in line with the principle that the customer is always right. We treat the problem as ours and not the user's.

We've gone to some lengths to take the blame in messages four and five above. We started with:

4. Incorrect identification code—please try again.
5. Money limit exceeded.

These still suggest that the user is wrong somehow. For the first, we considered Shneiderman's suggestion [1982] for timesharing system passwords: "The password you typed does not match the one stored." This seemed far too complex for the purpose, but it has the right flavor. Finally, we settled on the wording shown.

If a transaction is canceled, the machine simply returns the customer's card and goes back to the "ready" state. Similarly, after any error, the card is returned. When the card is removed, the machine returns to the "ready" state.

We can now eliminate the "Delay" frame. Since data is prefetched and all other processing is local, no noticeable delays are possible within a transaction. If prefetching fails, we will return the card and put the machine out of service until network access resumes.

10 Presentation and Representation

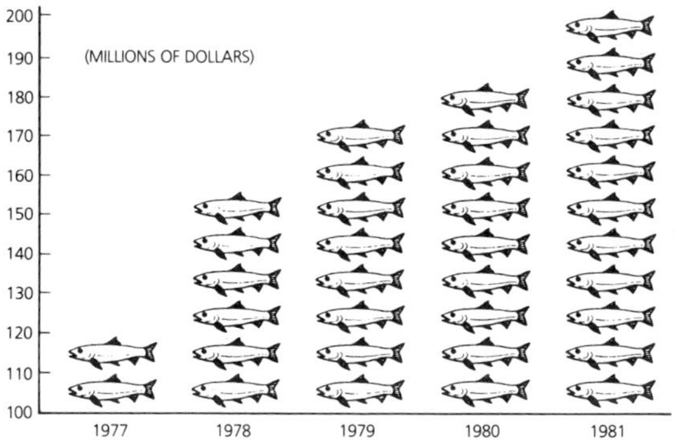

Designers must make choices about how the system will present information to users. These decisions involve both hardware and software issues: what displays, keyboards, and arrangement of keys and legends to use; what information to display; what other input devices to use and how software should treat them.

The relation between hardware and software varies from project to project. Ideally, both are designed together to meet the goals of a project. The computer industry frequently separates hardware and software efforts, the various components of a system being designed and built by separate groups under separate management at different times. A new software product may be conceived for an existing hardware product, or vice versa. Accordingly, it is frequently impossible to do a complete system design.

PRESENTATION OF DATA

Information can be presented to users directly with a display of some sort or transcribed into some other medium such as paper or film. The

Chart showing increasing commercial value of the Massachusetts fish catch courtesy of the Office of Senator Paul Tsongas, Washington, D.C.

design of documents, forms, and other media may require specialized knowledge, though many ideas and principles are common to all. In this chapter we are concerned principally with the active display of information on a CRT or similar dynamic device.

Guideline 68. Respect the rules of good presentation on paper.

A host of issues relate to effective presentation. Some of these are described below.

Uppercase text is harder to read than normal upper- and lower-case text. Try reading this material:

[DE COLMAR'S ARITHMOMETER] IS CONSTRUCTED CHIEFLY OF A BRASS PLATE *AA* FURNISHED WITH EIGHT SLOTS AS SHOWN; DIRECTLY UNDER THESE SLOTS ARE MOUNTED EIGHT DRUMS, EACH HAVING NINE ELONGATED COG-TEETH OF SUCCESSIVELY DECREASING LENGTH; OVER EACH DRUM, AND BETWEEN IT AND THE SLOT, IS MOUNTED A SQUARE SHAFT ON WHICH SLIDES A PINION WHEEL, SO AS TO CATCH ANY NUMBER OF TEETH ON THE DRUM [Hannyngton 1871, p. 244].

Our bet is that you got our point in the first couple of lines and skipped down to here. Because people have to read uppercase text more slowly, it should be used sparingly, for emphasis, only if no other distinctions are available.

Text should be large enough to read easily; that is, the visual angle—the angle subtended by a letter—must be large enough that the reader experiences no eye strain. The angle depends on both the size of the text and the viewing distance, as Figure 10-1 shows.

The DIN (*Deutsche Industrie Normen*) standard specifies characters a minimum of 2.6 mm high. The standard is based on a nominal viewing distance of 500 mm and a range of 450 to 600 mm. Character height should be adjusted accordingly if the viewing distances are not within this range. Characters are measured, for purposes of the standard, from the top to the bottom of a capital letter, as shown in Figure 10-2. At normal eye-to-screen distances, 2.6 mm is still a bit small. We recommend 3.0 to 3.25 mm as the minimum height for ordinary text and normal reading distance. The crucial factor is the clarity of text under the conditions of use. With high-resolution screens (3 pixels per mm or

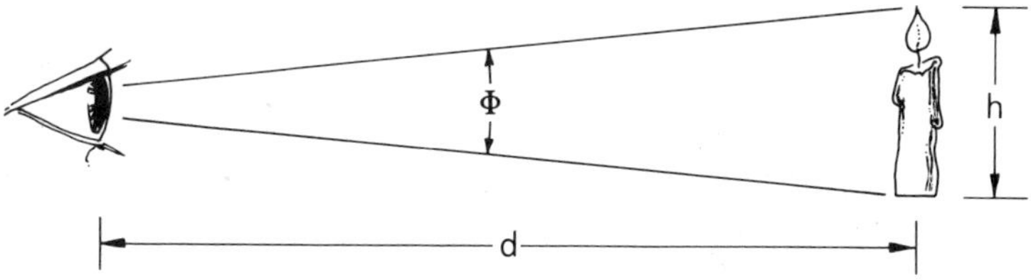

$$\Phi = 2\tan^{-1}\left[\frac{h}{2d}\right]$$

where:

Φ = Visual Angle
h = Height of object
d = Distance to screen

Figure 10-1. How visual angle depends on size and distance

better), the DIN standard height may prove adequate at normal terminal viewing distances. In any event, if little information need be presented, we recommend the user of somewhat larger text.

The quality of the text font is also an issue, especially as characters get bigger. As shown in Figure 10-3, larger characters created by replicating dots (pixels) can be *less* legible than their smaller counterparts, and thus have little advantage unless a font appropriate to the size is used.

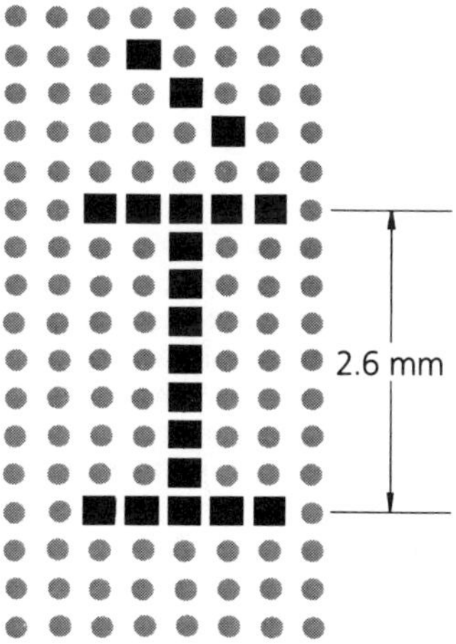

Figure 10-2. DIN standard character height measurement

Figure 10-3. Replicated pixels versus proper fonts

Hyphenation is a normal part of printing and, used sparingly, causes readers little trouble. However, it takes more effort to read a hyphenated word than the same word not hyphenated. Many text- and word-processing systems attempt to hyphenate automatically. Hyphenation can be overdone, as Figure 10-4 illustrates.

We suggest a cautious approach to hyphenation. Proper nouns, such as people's names, should never be hyphenated. Other words should be hyphenated only at morphemic boundaries, that is, at places that leave the units of meaning in the word intact. For example, *restrict-ive*

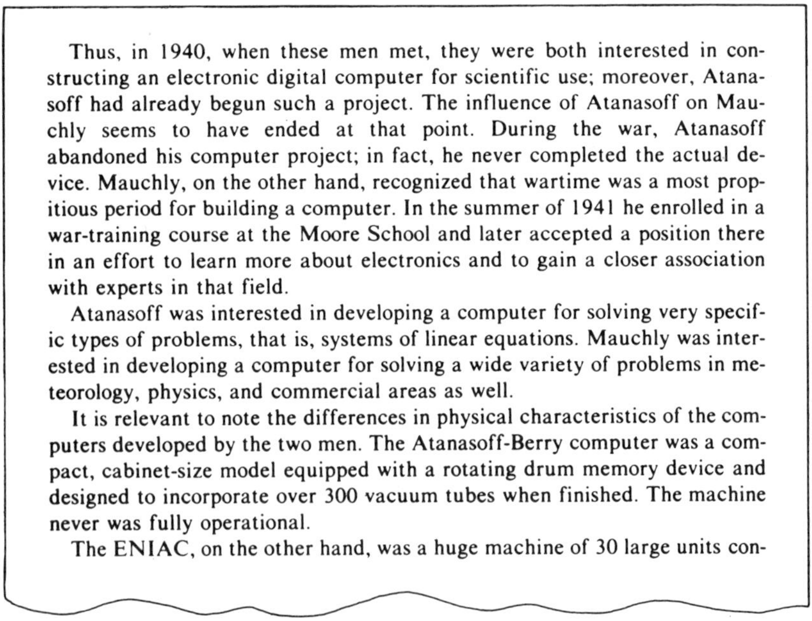

Thus, in 1940, when these men met, they were both interested in con-
structing an electronic digital computer for scientific use; moreover, Atana-
soff had already begun such a project. The influence of Atanasoff on Mau-
chly seems to have ended at that point. During the war, Atanasoff abandoned his computer project; in fact, he never completed the actual de-
vice. Mauchly, on the other hand, recognized that wartime was a most prop-
itious period for building a computer. In the summer of 1941 he enrolled in a war-training course at the Moore School and later accepted a position there in an effort to learn more about electronics and to gain a closer association with experts in that field.

Atanasoff was interested in developing a computer for solving very specif-
ic types of problems, that is, systems of linear equations. Mauchly was inter-
ested in developing a computer for solving a wide variety of problems in me-
teorology, physics, and commercial areas as well.

It is relevant to note the differences in physical characteristics of the com-
puters developed by the two men. The Atanasoff-Berry computer was a com-
pact, cabinet-size model equipped with a rotating drum memory device and designed to incorporate over 300 vacuum tubes when finished. The machine never was fully operational.

The ENIAC, on the other hand, was a huge machine of 30 large units con-

Figure 10-4. Badly hyphenated computer-set type

is better than *re-strictive* because the latter division suggests that the prefix *re-* ("to do again") is part of the structure of the word. Similarly, the word "European" is listed in the dictionary as "Eu·ro·pe·an," suggesting that it can be correctly hyphenated as "Eu-ropean," "Euro-pean," or "Europe-an." The first and last of these divisions is likely to cause the reader to stumble momentarily because either the first or second part suggests the wrong thing. Our rule for hyphenation is far more restrictive than the possibilities shown in dictionaries based on syllables.

In English, justification of text at the left margin is the norm, but justification at both margins does not necessarily increase readability unless spaces are equalized between words, as the examples in Figure 10-5 show.

Text with Uneven or Ragged Right Margin

I never cease to get a kick out of the end of each day when, frazzled and
exhausted, I hit my UDK3! My terminal comes to life. Words driven by a
list processing routine flash across the screen as the machine assembles all
the day's messages (the hours of work, calls, problems, requests handled)
in order of priority, merging them into a format I designed years ago. Then
finally I hear the sound of the printer snapping to attention and purring
away, with a lot more vigor than *I* feel at the moment.

Text with Justified Right Margin and Unequal Spacing

I never cease to get a kick out of the end of each day when, frazzled
and exhausted, I hit my UDK3! My terminal comes to life. Words driven
by a list processing routine flash across the screen as the machine
assembles all the day's messages (the hours of work, calls, problems,
requests handled) in order of priority, merging them into a format
I designed years ago. Then finally I hear the sound of the printer
snapping to attention and purring away, with a lot more vigor than
I feel at the moment.

Text with Justified Right Margin and Equal Spacing

I never cease to get a kick out of the end of each day when, frazzled and
exhausted, I hit my UDK3! My terminal comes to life. Words driven by a list
processing routine flash across the screen as the machine assembles all the
day's messages (the hours of work, calls, problems, requests handled) in
order of priority, merging them into a format I designed years ago. Then
finally I hear the sound of the printer snapping to attention and purring
away, with a lot more vigor than *I* feel at the moment.

Figure 10.5. Justification affects readability

Guideline 69. Present lists vertically.

It's much easier to find an item in a short list. When possible, limit lists to fewer than about seven items. Horizontal lists are harder to read than vertical ones. If several columns of items are necessary, arrange the items vertically in each column, in whatever order is natural. Figure 10-6 shows the right and wrong arrangements of an alphabetical list. Try finding the item "GTE" in each list.

Right (alphabetized vertically)

ATT	GMC	ITT
DEC	GTE	MCI
FBI	IBM	RCA
FCC	ICC	SRI

Wrong (alphabetized horizontally)

ATT	DEC	FBI
FCC	GMC	GTE
IBM	ICC	ITT
MCI	RCA	SRI

Figure 10-6. Horizontal versus vertical ordering in lists

Guideline 70. Identify output data.

Some data are self-identifying, and some are not. July 2, 1982, will be understood to be a date, but 7/2/82 is less clear from its form. Context always helps. The context and the identification should work together, so users have less to remember.

Guideline 71. Number from 1; measure from 0.

People count items, events, choices, or other discrete objects, beginning with 1, not 0. Scales of measure, however, start at 0, rather than 1.

A period, parenthesis, or other suitable punctuation is effective for separating labels from list items, as shown in Figure 10-7.

Right	*Wrong*
A. apple	A apple
B. oat	B oat
C. hair	C hair
D. ear	D ear
E. land	E land

Figure 10-7. Right and wrong punctuation for labels

Use a typeface that enables a reader to distinguish readily between zero and the letter *O*, and between the number one and the letters *I*, *L*, and *l*.

Guideline 72. Use formatting and ordering to clarify structure.

Related groups of data are easier to read when they are in columns. Right-justifying integers and aligning decimal numbers to the decimal point also help, as Figure 10-8 shows. Indentation and sectioning help to clarify structure by allowing "chunking" of data into a smaller number of groups, particularly in long lists. A structured list of no more than about 5 or 6 groups of items is far better than 50 undistinguished items (see Figure 10-9). Liberal use of white space also helps make the structure clearer. Structuring lists provides a model for users to predict

Location		*Intensity*
X	Y	
10	15	2.06
20	10	12.61
100	5	.70
0	100	.006

Figure 10-8. Proper alignment of numbers

Structured list		*Unstructured list*	
Most active stocks		Closing prices	
PatrickPtr	UP 9.1	CLaEl	31 3/4
Peobody	UP 8.2	CeMPw	13 1/8
ChockFON	UP 6.7	CnSoya	14 5/8
Mattel Inc	UP 5.6	CVtPS	14 3/4
ThompMed	UP 5.3	CentrDt	14
		CntryTl	8 1/4
LIL Co	OFF 18.2	Cenvill	23 1/2
Medtronic	OFF 16.0	Crt-teed	17
EvanPD 1.4pf	OFF 13.4	CessAir	21 1/8
Evan Pd	OFF 11.5	Chmpin	22 3/8
Shoetown n	OFF 9.7	Chml pf1.20	23 1/8

Figure 10-9. Benefit of structure in lists

where to find something they are looking for, though not all users can make good use of this information [Levy 1982].

The arrangement of items requires some judgment, but the guidelines are similar to those for ordering menus (Chapter 8). Short lists can be arranged by frequency of use, interest, or some other content criterion. If an unstructured long list (more than six or seven items) is necessary, it can be organized alphabetically or in some other appropriate way. It is important to verify that users perceive the structure imposed on the data. A logical presentation is illogical to those who don't know the rule.

Structure is partly determined by the intended use of the data. Presenting large amounts of data in more than one way may help. Cross-references or indexes also help users find what they want. In on-line applications, it may be more appropriate to provide selective access to large sets of data rather than attempting to display it all.

Guideline 73. Use graphs and charts.

People generally have difficulty interpreting and comparing sets of numbers. This fact accounts for the great popularity of business graphics systems, which represent numbers into concrete, spatial representations. Figure 10-10 shows a typical use of computer graphics for

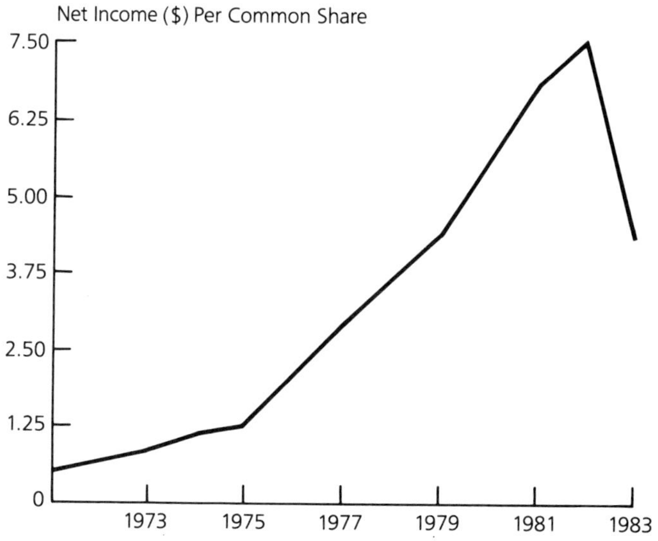

Figure 10-10. Typical business graphics

business applications. When the exact numbers themselves are also important, they may be included; otherwise, the graph or chart can speak for itself, with numbers read off the axes when desired.

Many systems present "frames," a sequence of related screen images. Each frame specifies an activity or stage in the user-computer interaction. Forms-based systems frequently use such sequences. Design goals for these frames include coherence across the whole interface, establishing clear and correct expectations and avoiding confusion.

Guideline 74. Avoid clutter.

Presenting too much information can be detrimental. The user needs enough information to know what's happening, but not so much that it detracts from what is important. Avoiding clutter is a matter of good taste. We have to seek ways of presenting data, often much data, simply and usefully.

Commonalities in frames can be used to develop reasonable expectations about where information will be. Putting the same or similar things in the same place adds a spatial component to the user's conceptual model. There are many techniques for achieving this consistency. One is to divide the screen into regions or windows that have different functions. With a frame-oriented interface, the arrangement of each frame supports its recognition.

Whatever may be displayed on a screen, it is necessary to distinguish among types of information. When it is desirable to call the user's attention to something on a screen, the item is made brighter, made to blink, or otherwise distinguished from the normal presentation. These distinctions are called *visual attributes*.

Visual attributes are not confined to computer screens. For example, in a forms application, a difference in typeface helps to distinguish the labels of fields from the text contained in them. This is just an adaptation of conventional practice in paper forms, as can be seen in Figure 10-11.

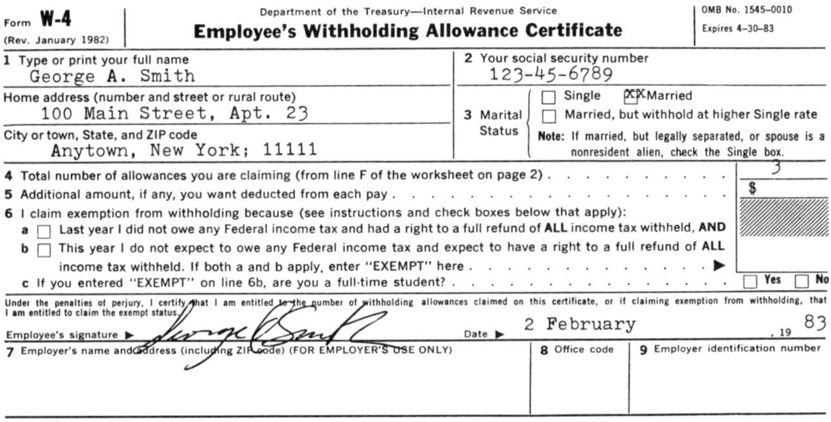
Form **W-4** (Rev. January 1982)
Department of the Treasury—Internal Revenue Service
Employee's Withholding Allowance Certificate
OMB No. 1545-0010
Expires 4-30-83

1 Type or print your full name
George A. Smith
2 Your social security number
123-45-6789
Home address (number and street or rural route)
100 Main Street, Apt. 23
3 Marital Status
☐ Single ☒ Married
☐ Married, but withhold at higher Single rate
City or town, State, and ZIP code
Anytown, New York; 11111
Note: If married, but legally separated, or spouse is a nonresident alien, check the Single box.

4 Total number of allowances you are claiming (from line F of the worksheet on page 2) 3
5 Additional amount, if any, you want deducted from each pay . . . . $
6 I claim exemption from withholding because (see instructions and check boxes below that apply):
a ☐ Last year I did not owe any Federal income tax and had a right to a full refund of **ALL** income tax withheld, **AND**
b ☐ This year I do not expect to owe any Federal income tax and expect to have a right to a full refund of **ALL** income tax withheld. If both a and b apply, enter "EXEMPT" here . . . . ▶
c If you entered "EXEMPT" on line 6b, are you a full-time student? . . . . ☐ Yes ☐ No

Under the penalties of perjury, I certify that I am entitled to the number of withholding allowances claimed on this certificate, or if claiming exemption from withholding, that I am entitled to claim the exempt status.
Employee's signature ▶ George A. Smith Date ▶ 2 February, 19 83

7 Employer's name and address (including ZIP code) (FOR EMPLOYER'S USE ONLY)
8 Office code
9 Employer identification number

Figure 10-11. Visual attributes in the paper world

A screen editor may need to use several kinds of visual attributes, to distinguish different kinds of text on the screen. These types of text may include:

- Text being edited
- Text selected for a special operation, such as erasure

- Markers that show the limits of text
- The cursor (typing position)
- Information not part of the text, showing modes, names of files, and status
- Properties of the text itself, such as roman, italic, and boldface

If many distinctions in the text are necessary, it may be difficult for the designer to find enough additional attributes. Text-only terminals provide a small set of attributes, such as reverse video, underlining, brightness, and blinking. Bit-map displays offer a greater range of choices, including variable fonts and more detailed layout, thus facilitating human interface design.

A variety of dimensions are available for creating attributes. Because people pay attention to changes in time or space and habituate to steady states, any mechanism that enhances contrast will help users distinguish among kinds of data. Too much contrast, however, disrupts performance of the task. Figures 10-12 through 10-22 present several kinds of visual attributes that can be useful in creating distinctions. These include:

- Blinking
- Borders
- Brightness
- Color
- Font
- Indicator
- Layout
- Shading
- Shape
- Size
- Text

Visual attributes should be chosen so that they interact well, because it may be necessary to apply more than one attribute to a given object. The field next to be entered in a form may need both a "field name"

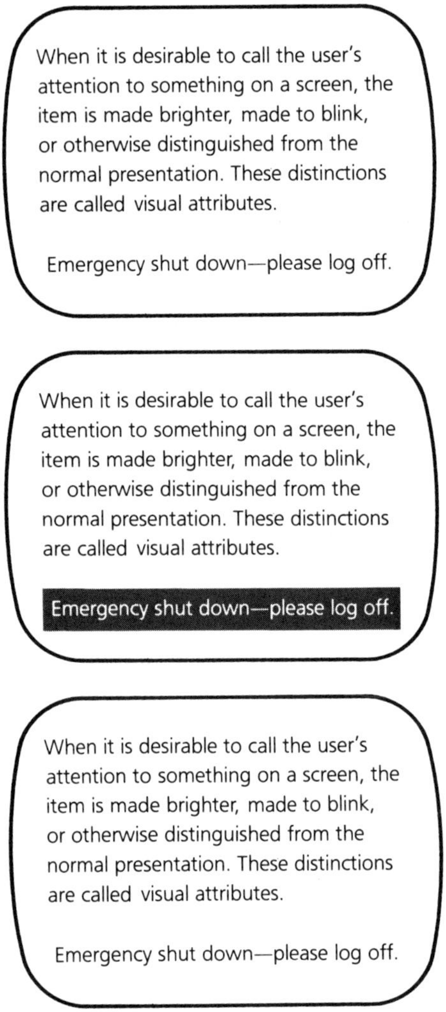

Figure 10-12. Blinking as an attribute: Blinking is a strong attention-getter, very difficult to ignore. It should be reserved for emergencies and other critical situations.

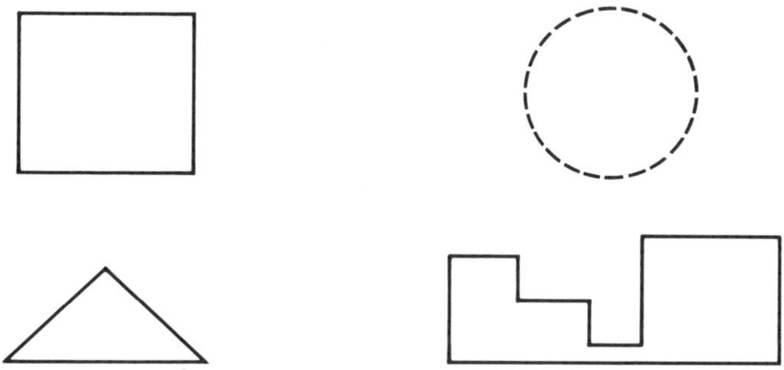

Figure 10-13. Borders as an attribute: Many distinctions are made possible by outlines such as dotted lines, broad shaded regions, and the like around an object. However, care must be taken that borders are not confused with the objects they enclose.

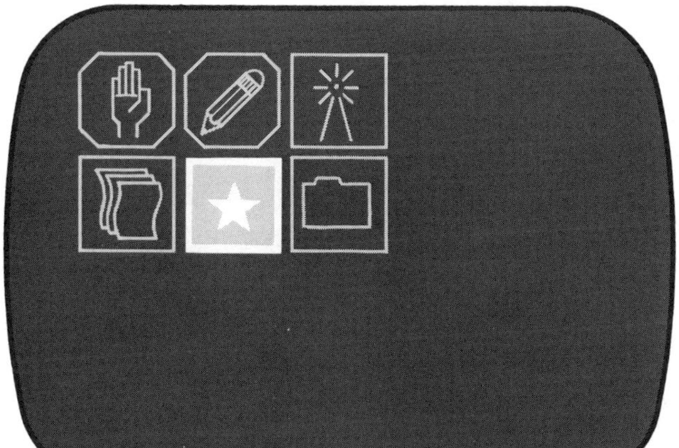

Figure 10-14. Brightness as an attribute: People can distinguish only a few levels of brightness, but clear distinctions can be achieved when contrasts are established with only one or two other levels. Extremes must be avoided: very dim items may be unreadable or invisible; very bright ones, unpleasant.

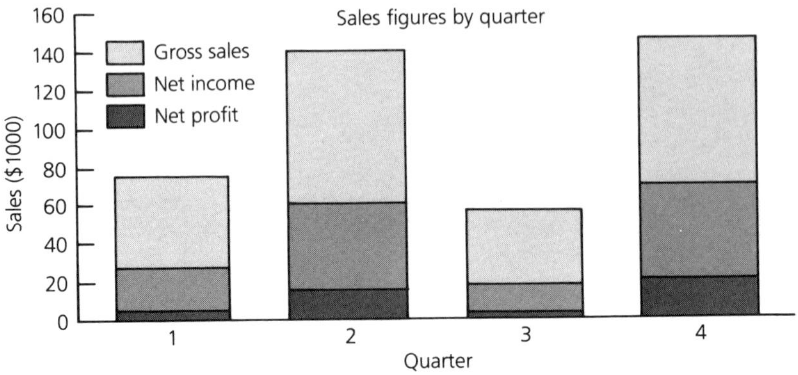

Figure 10-15. Color as an attribute: Colors offer many possible distinctions, but garish ones can be distracting or even disturbing. For the few people who are color-blind, it is necessary to provide redundant information.

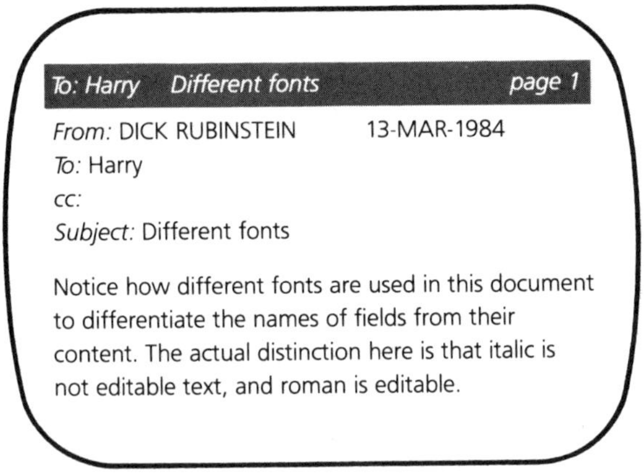

Figure 10-16. Font as an attribute: Variations such as italics and bold type fonts allow systematic distinctions among strings of text.

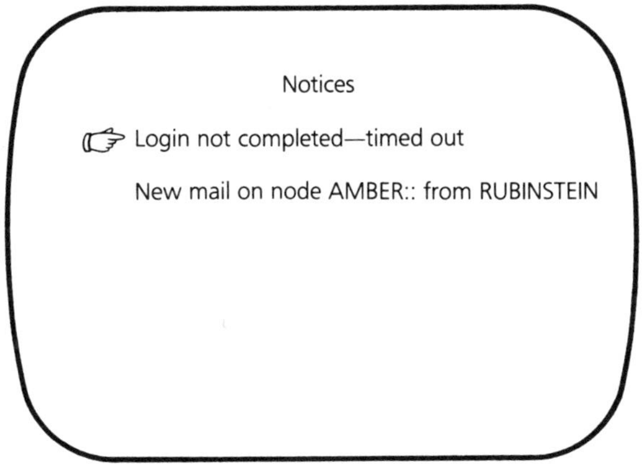

Figure 10-17. Indicator as an attribute: An easy way to call attention to something is to add some kind of pointer, such as an arrow, next to it. Underlining of text is another example.

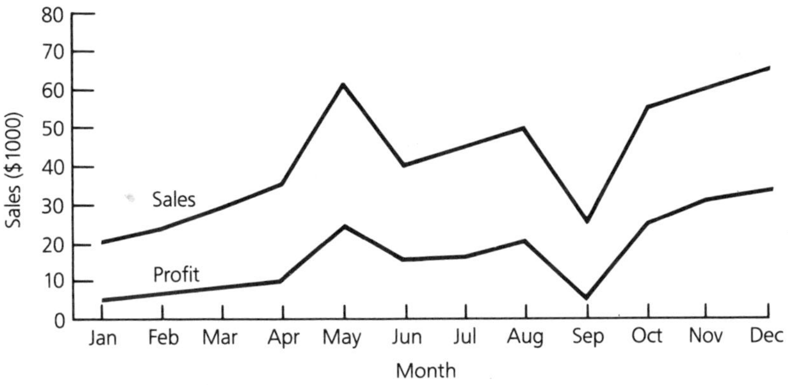

Figure 10-18. Text as an attribute: We frequently use textual labels without thinking of them as visual attributes. Symbols can be used to mark data points, to distinguish screen regions, and so on.

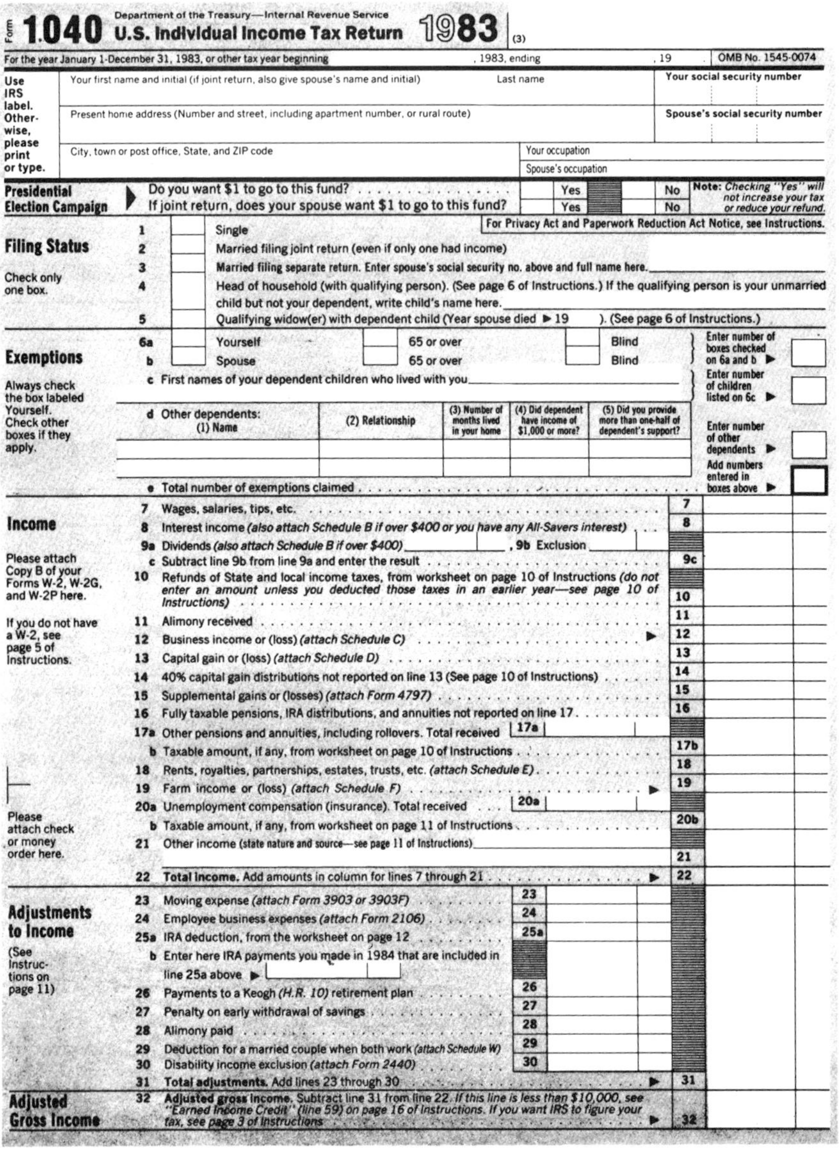

Form 1040 Department of the Treasury—Internal Revenue Service
U.S. Individual Income Tax Return 1983 (3)

For the year January 1-December 31, 1983, or other tax year beginning , 1983, ending , 19 | OMB No. 1545-0074

Use IRS label. Otherwise, please print or type.
Your first name and initial (if joint return, also give spouse's name and initial) | Last name | Your social security number
Present home address (Number and street, including apartment number, or rural route) | Spouse's social security number
City, town or post office, State, and ZIP code | Your occupation | Spouse's occupation

Presidential Election Campaign ▶ Do you want $1 to go to this fund? Yes No
If joint return, does your spouse want $1 to go to this fund? Yes No
Note: *Checking "Yes" will not increase your tax or reduce your refund.*

For Privacy Act and Paperwork Reduction Act Notice, see Instructions.

Filing Status
Check only one box.
1 Single
2 Married filing joint return (even if only one had income)
3 Married filing separate return. Enter spouse's social security no. above and full name here.
4 Head of household (with qualifying person). (See page 6 of Instructions.) If the qualifying person is your unmarried child but not your dependent, write child's name here.
5 Qualifying widow(er) with dependent child (Year spouse died ▶ 19). (See page 6 of Instructions.)

Exemptions
Always check the box labeled Yourself. Check other boxes if they apply.
6a Yourself | 65 or over | Blind
b Spouse | 65 or over | Blind
Enter number of boxes checked on 6a and b ▶
c First names of your dependent children who lived with you
Enter number of children listed on 6c ▶
d Other dependents: (1) Name | (2) Relationship | (3) Number of months lived in your home | (4) Did dependent have income of $1,000 or more? | (5) Did you provide more than one-half of dependent's support?
Enter number of other dependents ▶
e Total number of exemptions claimed
Add numbers entered in boxes above ▶

Income
Please attach Copy B of your Forms W-2, W-2G, and W-2P here.
If you do not have a W-2, see page 5 of Instructions.
7 Wages, salaries, tips, etc. 7
8 Interest income *(also attach Schedule B if over $400 or you have any All-Savers interest)* 8
9a Dividends *(also attach Schedule B if over $400)* , 9b Exclusion
c Subtract line 9b from line 9a and enter the result 9c
10 Refunds of State and local income taxes, from worksheet on page 10 of Instructions *(do not enter an amount unless you deducted those taxes in an earlier year—see page 10 of Instructions)* 10
11 Alimony received 11
12 Business income or (loss) *(attach Schedule C)* ▶ 12
13 Capital gain or (loss) *(attach Schedule D)* 13
14 40% capital gain distributions not reported on line 13 (See page 10 of Instructions) 14
15 Supplemental gains or (losses) *(attach Form 4797)* 15
16 Fully taxable pensions, IRA distributions, and annuities not reported on line 17. 16
17a Other pensions and annuities, including rollovers. Total received 17a
b Taxable amount, if any, from worksheet on page 10 of Instructions 17b
18 Rents, royalties, partnerships, estates, trusts, etc. *(attach Schedule E)* 18
19 Farm income or (loss) *(attach Schedule F)* ▶ 19
20a Unemployment compensation (insurance). Total received 20a
b Taxable amount, if any, from worksheet on page 11 of Instructions 20b
Please attach check or money order here.
21 Other income (state nature and source—see page 11 of Instructions) 21
22 **Total income.** Add amounts in column for lines 7 through 21 ▶ 22

Adjustments to Income
(See Instructions on page 11)
23 Moving expense *(attach Form 3903 or 3903F)* 23
24 Employee business expenses *(attach Form 2106)* 24
25a IRA deduction, from the worksheet on page 12 25a
b Enter here IRA payments you made in 1984 that are included in line 25a above ▶
26 Payments to a Keogh *(H.R. 10)* retirement plan 26
27 Penalty on early withdrawal of savings 27
28 Alimony paid 28
29 Deduction for a married couple when both work *(attach Schedule W)* 29
30 Disability income exclusion *(attach Form 2440)* 30
31 **Total adjustments.** Add lines 23 through 30 ▶ 31

Adjusted Gross Income
32 **Adjusted gross income.** Subtract line 31 from line 22. *If this line is less than $10,000, see "Earned Income Credit" (line 59) on page 16 of Instructions. If you want IRS to figure your tax, see page 3 of Instructions* ▶ 32

Figure 10-19. Layout as an attribute: Larger objects, such as forms, may be visually distinguished by their overall configuration. Combinations are virtually unlimited. Layout is a powerful attribute because it makes use of people's extensive pattern-recognition abilities.

Figure 10-20. Shading as an attribute: Shading patterns (hatched lines, textures, and gray levels) provide a number of distinct attributes. Text cannot be shaded effectively unless gray scale or high resolution is available.

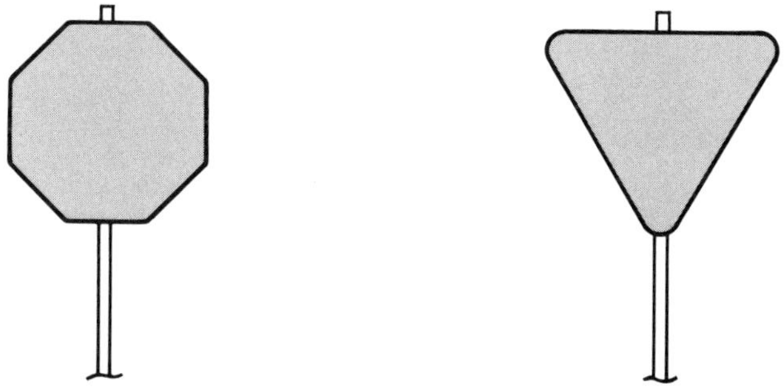

Figure 10-21. Shape as an attribute: Shape is an effective distinguishing feature, underutilized in displays but common elsewhere.

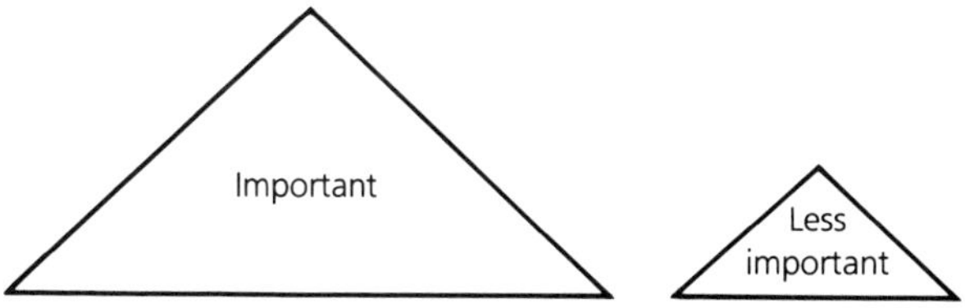

Figure 10-22. Size as an attribute: Size often correlates with importance. Changes in size can be an attention-getting attribute, similar to blink.

Guideline 75. Visual attributes must compose correctly.

attribute (say, italics) and "attention" (perhaps a blinking cursor). Attributes should be distinguishable from each other when more than one is present. Figure 10-23 shows both good and poor combinations of attributes.

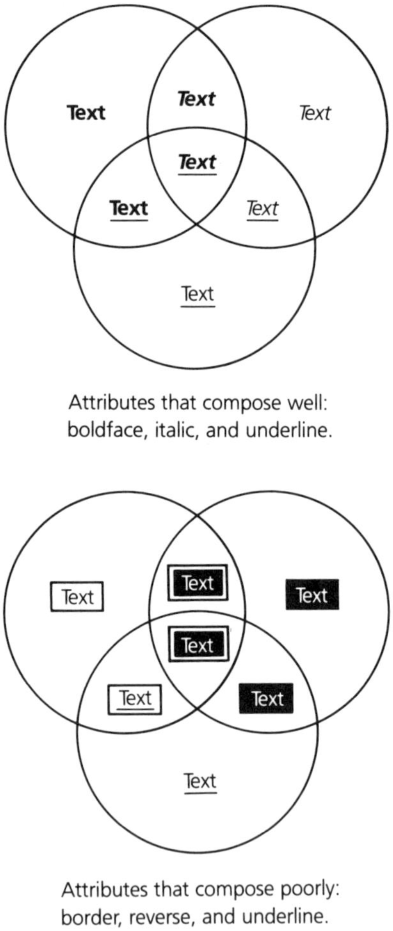

Figure 10-23. Good and poor interactions of attributes

Guideline 76. Don't overwhelm the user with visual attributes.

Some simple attributes are just too powerful. Reverse video, blinking, and bright colors are the worst offenders. They can be annoying, especially if the user, having noted them, wants to ignore them. They may also interfere with the legibility and accessibility of other information on the screen. (See Figure 10-24.) People are good at discerning relatively small differences, so a light-handed approach will achieve useful distinctions between items. Similarly, people can be overwhelmed by many distinct attributes. Care should be taken to avoid busy-looking displays.

Guideline 77. Make semantics of attributes clear and consistent.

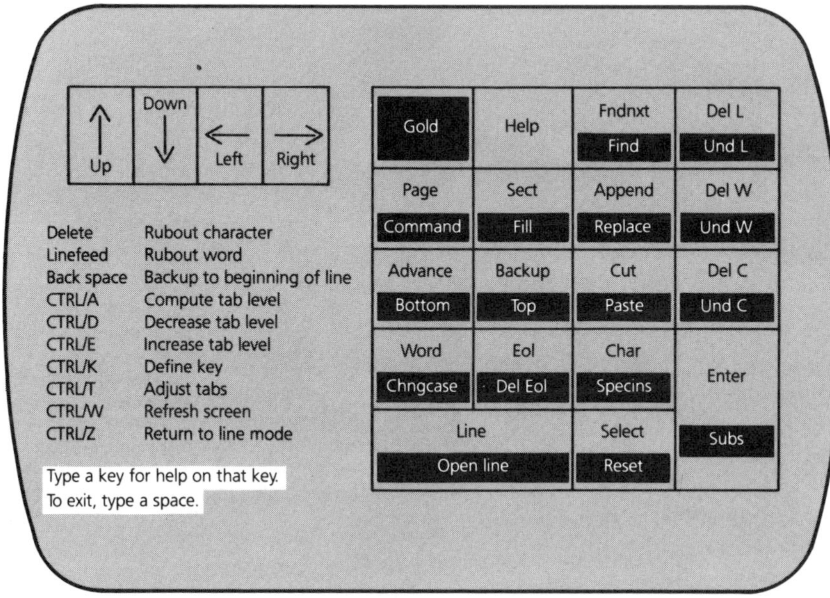

Figure 10-24. An example of overwhelming attributes

Each attribute should have a clear and consistent meaning. Two distinct attributes should not be used for the same purpose, nor one used in two different ways, because visual attributes become part of the user's conceptual model. In a text editor, for example, an explicit way of showing the limits of the text would be to represent the file as a document. Then the physical borders would delineate the beginning and end as well as the right and left sides (not of the text, but of the paper document as it would look printed). This is a spatial distinction; what's inside the border is the document, and what's outside isn't. Thus, it is easier for the user to make text outside these limits represent other information, such as the name of the document and its status. These attributes are closely intertwined with the user's model of what is represented on the screen.

Another issue in data representation is codings. Unlike attributes, codings represent quantities rather than properties. Figure 10-25 shows the results of one study on different ways to represent data [Engel and Granda 1975].

Code	*Maximum number of items**	*Evaluation*	*Comment*
Color	11	Good	Little space required. Location time short.
Numerals and letters	Unlimited for combinations of symbols	Good	Little space required if contrast and resolution is good. Location time longer than for color.
Geometric shapes	15	Good	Little space required if resolution is good.
Size	5	Fair	Considerable space required. Location time longer than for color or shapes.
Length of line	4	Fair	Will clutter display with many signals.
Brightness	4	Poor	Poor contrast effects will reduce visibility of weaker signals.
Flash rate	4	Poor	Interacts poorly with other codes.

*To give overall accuracies of 95 percent or better.

Figure 10-25. Methods of data representation

Most of the dimensions used for attributes can be used for coding data quantities. These methods apply when distinctions must be made reliably without necessarily comparing one item directly with another. Finer distinctions may usually be made if comparisons are possible. Thus bar charts allow a number of fine comparisons, but the length of isolated lines is of limited use for categorizing quantities.

Some choices of coding strategies are hard to relate to the quantities represented. It is essential to choose relationships that are easily worked into conceptual models. For continuous data the representation may be continuous, or ranges of values may be lumped together to create a small set of distinct values. Figure 10-26 shows continuous quantities related directly to a spatial conceptual model.

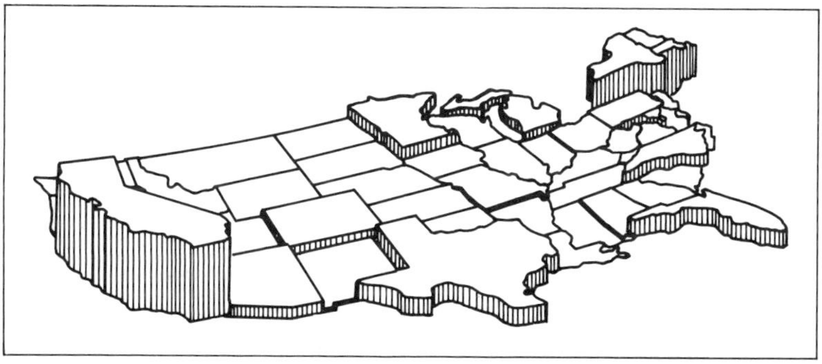

Figure 10-26. Hybrid of a bar chart and map

To understand how codings work, consider the design of a sea-battle game in which the following quantities must be represented on a screen:

- Four classes of ship
- Six nationalities of ship
- Percentage of cargo capacity in use
- Percentage of fuel left
- Condition of ship (good, damaged, burning, sinking)

A natural coding for class of ship might be size and shape. The nationality of each ship might be coded by color, by a flag, or by a text legend. Brightness or length would be inappropriate. Coding cargo capacity would be more difficult because it is a continuous variable. A number would allow fine distinctions, but would require more user attention than is desirable. Length would afford a rough reading. In this case, however, the height of the water line on the ship would be ideal, because it is directly related to the physical situation. Fuel remaining is another continuous variable. Perhaps a gauge (thermometer style) would work. Finally, condition could be coded with angle, modifications to shape, flashing, or even animated smoke.

DATA INPUT

Whereas the goal for output of information is consistency and predictability, the goal for input is flexibility of expression for the user. Different problems brought to the system should allow for different representations of data.

Numerical data frequently have associated units of measure, such as feet, milliliters, tons, volts, or acres. A system that allows users to specify these units when inputting data eliminates the repetitive task of converting measurements before entering them in the computer. It also eliminates the likelihood of errors due to human slips. The fewer times users handle data, the smaller will be the number of faults introduced. Typically, people introduce a 1 percent error rate when transcribing numbers [Rosenthal 1978].

Guideline 78. Allow flexibility in formatting input data.

The input of data should not depend critically on tabulation or other formatting. Old FORTRAN packages such as early versions of SPSS for example, in a holdover from punch-card input, required users to enter data in particular columns of the input records. Another error-prone strategy is to require users to identify a data item by relying on its order in a typed record. If information is carried by the format of data, systems should provide a structured way to enter it, so that the format is captured along with the data, without forcing the user to express the format unassisted.

Guideline 79. Provide prompting or cuing for input.

There are many ways to cue users about what information is required. The best allow users to express the information in their own order. This flexibility is a virtue of forms-based systems, which allow free movement from one field to another. Field labels provide cues about which items go where. Command-oriented input styles use prompts to label the input.

Guideline 80. Allow shorthand and abbreviations in input.

Entering information requires a substantial amount of effort, so anything the system can do to make the user's task easier will be welcome. To save the user from having to enter the same units of measure, or commands repeatedly, the system should accept abbreviated forms of input but produce nonabbreviated output.

Guideline 81. Make frequent inputs easy to express.

Commonly performed actions should be easy and quick. In information theory, this concept is called *frequency encoding*. If you are sending a message, the things you send most often should be encoded with the shortest symbol. That's why the symbols for *e* and *t* in Morse code are just "dit" and "dah," whereas the code for *q* is "dah dah di dah." People can communicate instructions to a machine more efficiently if frequently performed sequences have short, sensible means of expression.

Similarly, the expression of common actions should be easy and quick. One study of function usage for a word processor discovered that 90 percent of the commands were of just five types [Whiteside et al 1982]. This finding suggests that users optimize their activity by relying on a few commands do most of the work. On this word processor, functions are accessed via typed commands and function keys. Putting the most important commands on the function keys would go a long way toward optimizing the information density for commands to the system.

REPRESENTATION

An important part of an external myth is how data and control information are represented. The human interface design must specify the representation of data and control information to be received from or given to the user.

Representation of output should be compatible with the input representation. We call this principle *input/output equivalence*. A unified treatment for input and output contributes directly to a simple, consistent internal model. People do learn by imitation [see Bandura and Walters 1963]. They make inferences from what the computer says, so if the form of output does not obey input rules, users may be misdirected [Mooers 1983].

Choosing an appropriate representation is serious business, because users may already represent ideas and concepts in a particular way. Programs should understand the user's choice of representation. Figure 10-27 shows two different representations coexisting within one system.

Accommodating the user's representation of data can be technically difficult. Consider a system for printed circuit layout. If the user knows certain rules, such as "two adjacent wires must be no closer than x inches," the program must use this representation to check and adjust both input and output for consistency with that rule. Nonetheless, constraint rules provide a convenient form for the user to express the information. Some AI technology exists for dealing directly with such rules [Sutherland 1980, Davis 1982]. Constraints are a good way to represent rules that users present.

Concrete representations are better than equivalent abstract ones, though they are also more difficult to achieve. Screen editors, for example, can represent a document as if it were paper copy, accurately showing size, position, and typeface. If formatting instructions also appear specifying how it will look after a formatting operation, the

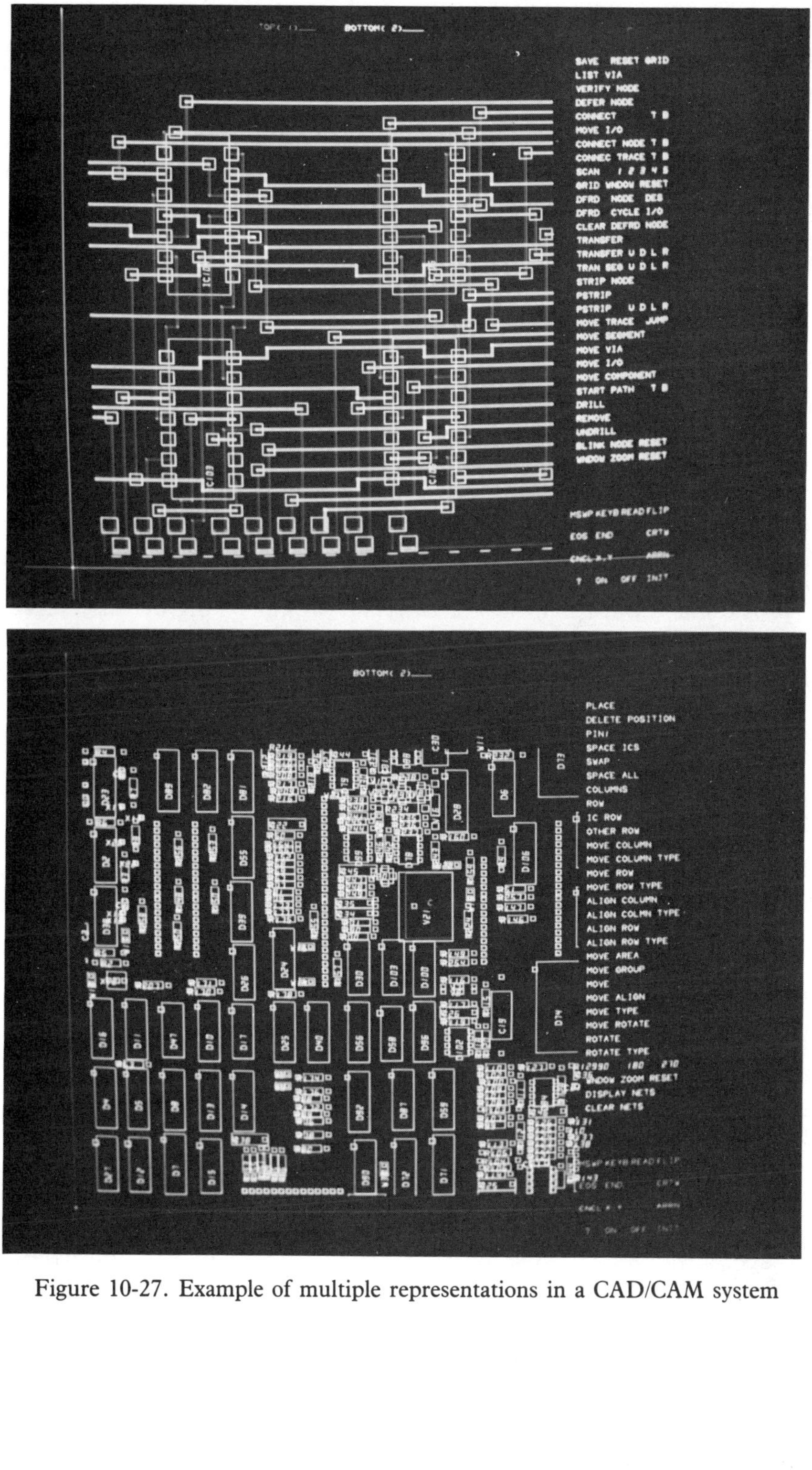

Figure 10-27. Example of multiple representations in a CAD/CAM system

representation becomes more abstract. The further the screen image is from a literal picture of the paper copy, the more abstract the representation, and the further removed from the user's conceptual model of the document. Changes made on the screen may be reflected immediately in the appearance of the screen version of the document, or a recomputing step may be necessary to bring the screen up to date. Again, the further removed the process is from the updating of paper copy, the more abstract the representation.

INPUT/OUTPUT DEVICES FOR HUMAN INTERFACES

There is a diversity of hardware for building high-quality human interfaces. The services provided by a computer are delivered via terminals, displays, sensors, printers, plotters, and other data transducers. The devices of greatest interest in human interface design provide specialized or high-quality control (input) and display (output).

Positional input (pointing) devices can promote a highly interactive interface not easily matched in other media (see Figure 10-28). Graphics operations using pointing devices include:

- Pointing—indicating a particular place or object on a screen
- Selecting—choosing from a list of items, frequently in a menu
- Drawing—operating much like users do with pencil and paper, to produce line drawings, sketches, or even "paintings."

Some graphic input operations resemble pointing:

- Digitizing—tracking a sequence of pointing positions, such as on paper maps, and interpreting the results
- Control of input variables—using the pointing device to adjust the setting of a graphic knob, gauge, switch, or other input device in a simulation
- Positioning—moving objects around on the screen.

All the pointing and digitizing devices described below are in commercial production. They vary widely in characteristics, virtues, level of specialization, and the problems they pose in human interfaces.

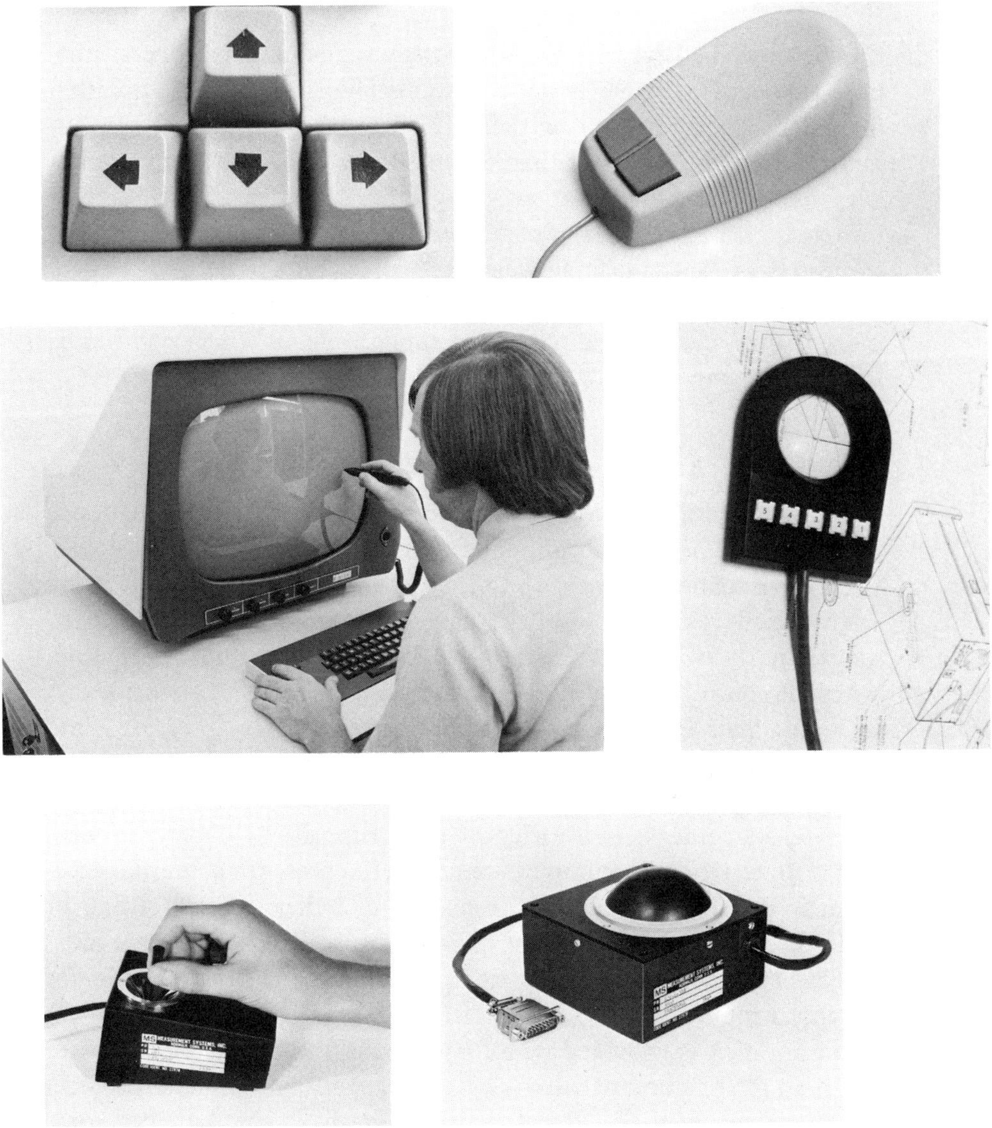

Figure 10-28. Pointing devices. *Top row,* cursor keys and mouse; *center row,* light pen and graphic tablet; *bottom row,* joy stick and track ball.

Cursor Keys

Cursor keys, the keys with arrows on them found on most general-purpose keyboards, require many operations to achieve a single pointing operation. Their presence on the keyboard makes them more convenient to use with text input than other devices. However, they are not very useful for pointing at anything other than text, because their movement is tied to units of characters and lines. All motions must be expressed as "city-block movements" along horizontal and vertical paths, rather than at an angle. People find direct motion at an angle more natural most of the time. For applications in which pointing is frequent or important, we recommend other devices.

Joysticks

Computer joysticks, like their archetypes in aircraft technology, are levers that can be moved right or left, forward or back. Despite providing a clear spatial relationship to the variable being controlled, many commercially available joysticks have low accuracy, low resolution, and are fairly awkward to manipulate. Incorporating a nonlinear scale, with fine control provided near center and coarse control farther away, increases their effectiveness. Joysticks are sometimes integrated into keyboards and terminals. As separate devices, they consume a modest amount of desk space.

Joysticks come in two varieties, proportional and binary. Proportional units send the computer a number representing the displacement from center in each axis. Binary units indicate which of four or eight directions from center the stick is displaced. The latter are inexpensive and are used in many video games, but are nearly useless for graphical input.

If a joystick is provided with force-feedback control, the computer can read the position of the stick in two dimensions and apply a reaction force to the stick. This allows more realistic simulation of some physical situations, such as an airplane control stick.

Mice

A mouse is a small graphic input device held with the hand and rolled around a flat surface, frequently the surface of the desk or a piece of paper laid on it. A flexible wire connects the mouse to the terminal or computer. Mice do not roll away, and therefore do not get lost when placed on a desk. Most people have the spatial memory necessary to put their hands back on the mouse without looking at it. A mouse has one or more function buttons, used to trigger specific actions, and it works well in close quarters, because the user can lift it and reposition it for comfort, without moving the screen pointer. Effective use for drawing and fine control requires some experience. Graphic tablets are generally preferred for these functions. Holding a button down while moving the mouse can cause arm fatigue and should be avoided. For a comparison of mice with other pointing devices, see Card, English, and Burr [1977].

Track Balls

A track ball is a bit like a mouse turned upside down. It consists of a sphere mounted in a housing. The user can rotate the sphere in any direction by just pushing it. Like a joystick, a track ball occupies a modest, fixed area. Some are small enough to be integrated with keyboards. Because the military has long used track balls as control devices, there are some high-quality ones available. Track balls have the advantages of high resolution, ease of location by touch alone, and unlimited motions (incremental, relative output).

Touch Panels

The most natural way for people to point is with a finger. Touch panels sense where a human finger is pointing. Two kinds of touch panels are available: those placed on a horizontal surface, tablet style, and those attached directly over the screen. A screen-mounted unit allows the user to point directly at what is displayed but can cause arm fatigue. Small touch pads can be incorporated directly into some keyboards, providing easy access and less fatigue during use.

Touch panels have limited resolution, as much because fingers are blunt instruments as for technological reasons. A human interface that uses a touch panel must take this limitation into account. Some touch panels get around the size-of-finger problem by calculating the centroid of the contact area to give finer positioning. Use of a stylus with a touch panel achieves higher resolution, but the stylus must be put down before the user can type. Finally, some account of parallax must be made, because otherwise the user and machine may disagree about what's being pointed at.

Light Pens

Rather than emitting light, as the name suggests, a light pen contains a photocell that senses light from the screen. Because light pens can sense only positions on the screen that are lit, a tracking cursor or a solid background is necessary for drawing or pointing at a location where no object exists. Another option is to light the entire screen. One color display uses a blue background to ensure that the system can sense the pen anywhere on the screen. Screens with black text on a white background can be provided with the same capability.

A light pen consumes essentially no desk space, but the user must put the pen down to type and pick it up again to interact with the screen. Light pens are best at menu selection. In vector-drawing displays, they provide an easy linkage between the logical structure that is creating the picture and the spots on the screen that are lit. As with touch panels, arm fatigue is a potential problem.

Graphic Tablets

Graphic tablets, also called digitizers, data tablets, or data pads, consist of an active surface and a cursor (puck) or stylus attached via a cable. The user positions the cursor or stylus anywhere on the surface; the computer can sense where it is. The size of the working surface can range from a few inches square to drafting table size. Some tablets can even sense the stylus location in three-dimensional space.

The stylus or cursor provided with the graphics tablet is the most important design variable for human interfaces. Buttons provided on cursors allow the user to indicate a position or to initiate one of several functions. A cross-hair viewer, sometimes containing a small magnifier, permits accurate positioning of the cursor in relation to a drawing or other graphic data placed on the tablet. If the application is primarily digitizing, a cross-hair cursor may be the best choice, especially if precision is essential. Careful choice of the number and function of buttons will mean the difference between a simple interface and one that is confusing or complicated.

A pen or stylus can be used for both drawing and pointing. Instead of a button, pens have a switch activated by pressure on the tip. Some tablets can sense when the instrument is near them. If a stylus is used it is essential to consider differences between pointing and drawing uses. Pointing and digitizing tasks usually use the pen "down" switch to mean "record a data point," much as a cross-hair cursor button is used. For drawing, however, the force required to close the "down" switch must be very low. This sensitivity allows the operation of the "down" switch to correspond to the user's perception of having the pen in contact with paper. If the user is pressing hard enough to write with the pen, then the sensor should report that the pen is down.

Graphics tablets present at least two potential distractions: any reference material that might be pointed to is away from the screen, and if a pen is used, it must be found and picked up for each use. Furthermore, tablets used at a desk or work station occupy a sizable portion of the work surface.

Keyboards

Only rarely are the layout and labeling of the keyboard designed along with the software and the rest of the system. Yet the physical part of the human interface deserves the same consideration as the other parts, so that physical structure and behavior remain integrated. The design of the keyboard layout and labeling should be part of the same process as the design of the external myth, use model, and functional capabilities.

Guideline 82. Design keyboards as a part of systems.

Guideline 83. Simplify keyboard layouts.

Guideline 84. Group keys according to function.

Figure 10-29. Separate text and control

Grouping keys is an opportunity to create a clear relationship between keys and functions in the human interface. Keys should be grouped logically according to function. Mixing function types within groups works against the formation of a simple conceptual model and may induce confusion between keys with dissimilar uses.

A corollary of logical grouping is to avoid putting function keys in the alphanumeric part of keyboards. Similarly, keys for special symbols should not be mixed into function key groups. Non-computer-oriented users bring expectations about typewriters to a keyboard. Typewriters generally do not intermingle printing functions and control; on a typewriter, return and tab are printing operations, not control operations. Separating text from control results in a clearer conceptual model of the keys' functions, as shown in Figure 10-29.

Guideline 85. Separate text and control on keyboards.

Guideline 86. Avoid multiplexing keys.

The Hewlett-Packard HP-35 calculator was the first to have keys smaller than fingers. The idea spread through the industry. The HP-35 was simple, elegant, and easy to use. By fitting 35 keys on the surface of a hand-held unit, the device could provide many functions requiring only a single keystroke. Most scientific and programmable calculators made since then have multipurpose keys that change meaning depending on what key is hit first. Now designers are running out of places to put the alternate functions associated with each key. Calculators are harder to use as a result.

A shift key is fine for printable symbols within the alphanumeric part of a keyboard, but not for changing the meaning of function keys. "Gold" keys or "auxiliary function" keys that change the meaning of function keys are similarly confusing. Multiplexed keys represent subtle state changes in the human interface. They force the user to associate multiple, situation-dependent meanings in the conceptual model with a single key. The result is a complex, error prone system. Multiplexing also makes it difficult to label keys with the functions they perform for each state, increasing the burden on memory.

Labeling keys involves making consistent distinctions between functions. Many functions can be designated by either nouns or verbs, describing the result or the process, respectively. If special keys are used for processes, we recommend using verb forms for all functions, noun forms for all objects. This strategy poses no difficulty for clear-cut instances of verb forms (such as *create*, *delete*, *draw*, *erase*, *get*, and *withdraw*) or noun forms (such as *menu* or *PERT*). But many words used to designated computer operations can be either verbs or nouns, as the following list shows:

Address	File	Picture	Store
Blank	Help	Print	Trace
Call	Link	Program	Transfer
Default	Load	Record	Trap
Display	Mask	Run	
Dump	Paragraph	Stack	

Such a word used as a label on a function key (say, to *file* or *help*) will acquire a verbal meaning in the conceptual model. Legends should be based on the external myth and verified with the methods described in Chapter 11. Testing labels on users will reveal any potential misinterpretations.

Abbreviated legends can also be ambiguous. It's better to spell out words and to use smaller type, or even to use icons or pictures, than to use ambiguous abbreviations.

The internal codes generated by keyboards should be invisible to users. If escape sequences are used, the software should interpret them rather than echo the constituent characters, which will have no meaning to users. Such mysterious characters represent a chink in the armor of the consistent external myth designers should try to create.

Subject to the constraints above, it is desirable to locate keys so as to minimize hand motion. When and how the hands move to hit keys will affect the speed with which operations can be performed and the degree of fatigue involved in using the keyboard. Keying realistic sequences on a mocked-up keyboard can give designers a good idea of user needs.

Displays

The trend in displays is toward bit-map devices, which display one or more bits of information for each position (pixel) on a screen. Bit-map displays are displacing both calligraphic displays (also called random-access or line-drawing displays), and the simpler, text-only displays. Bit-map technology provides generally good support for human factors, but it also has some drawbacks.

Bit-map displays can display text of many sizes and typefaces. They can intermix text and graphics and display half-tones, real gray-scale images, and even color. High-resolution models permit display of a great deal of information on a single screen. For all these reasons, bit-map displays offer greater flexibility and thus provide possibilities for better human design than their more limited predecessors.

On the other hand, some functions such as scrolling that were accomplished by special-purpose hardware in other displays must now be done in other ways, and performance may suffer as a result. Scrolling a bit-map region requires moving each pixel. Suppose the user wants to scroll an area containing 500,000 points—a real possibility on a high-resolution display—and that it takes one microsecond to read or write each point. Moving a pixel requires both a read and a write, so the result is one million memory accesses, for a total time of one second. This is a long time to wait for the display to make room for one line of text.

Several alternatives can keep performance high: special hardware to speed up scrolling and region manipulations, or different styles of interface that do not depend critically on scrolling. Forms-based and direct-manipulation interfaces avoid scrolling problems.

PRESENTATION AND REPRESENTATION FOR PEOPLE'S BANK

Figure 10-30 shows the layout and legends for the ATM keyboard for People's Bank. It's a very simple keyboard, because the design does not require many functions. Note that the vendor normally supplies English legends of "OK" and "CANCEL" for confirmation (when entering amount) and terminating the transaction. Instead, we will use the keycap icons shown in the figure, because we want to avoid multilingual legends on keys.

Because users of the People's Bank ATMs will not enter commands, there is no danger that they might copy the wrong things off the screen, but we still want to create some visual distinction between the menu choices and other text appearing on the screen. It must be easy for users to learn that the items listed correspond to numbered buttons on the keyboard.

The icons shown in Figure 10-31, used instead of item numbers in screen menus, would create a concrete visual link between the screen items and the buttons that are to be pressed. We recommended this approach to the hardware people, but they said that the terminal display will not reproduce such pictures. This is a constraint we must live with, because the system must be built with available hardware. If we

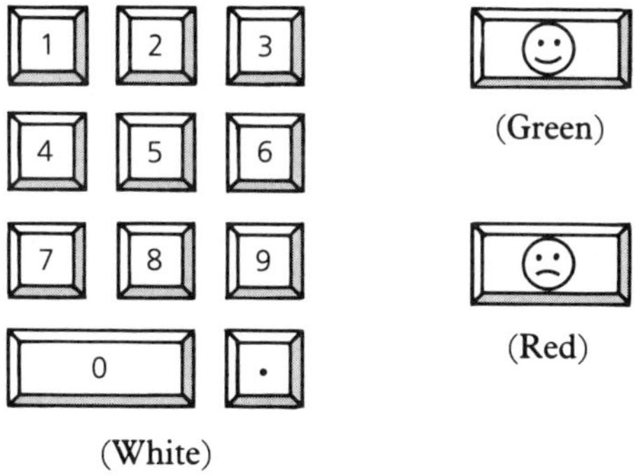

Figure 10-30. ATM keyboard layout and legends

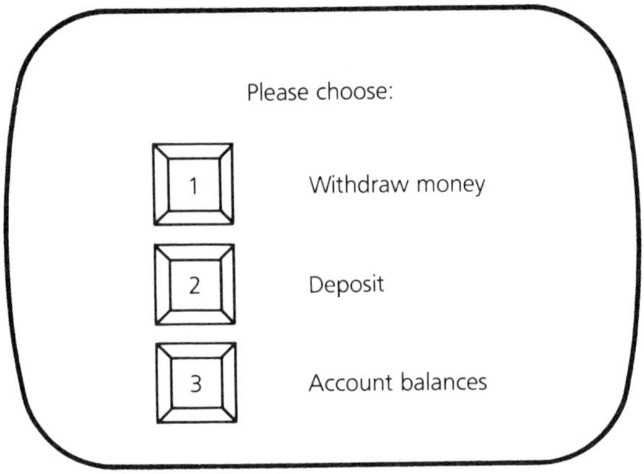

Figure 10-31. Proposed button icons

could have used a bit-map display, we would have employed icons for item markers.

Because the standard ATM won't support icons, we decided to use the lines separating the menu header from the choices as visual distinctions. The hardware will do reverse video; we will make the header reverse video and leave the items in normal text well separated by blank space, as shown in Figure 10-32.

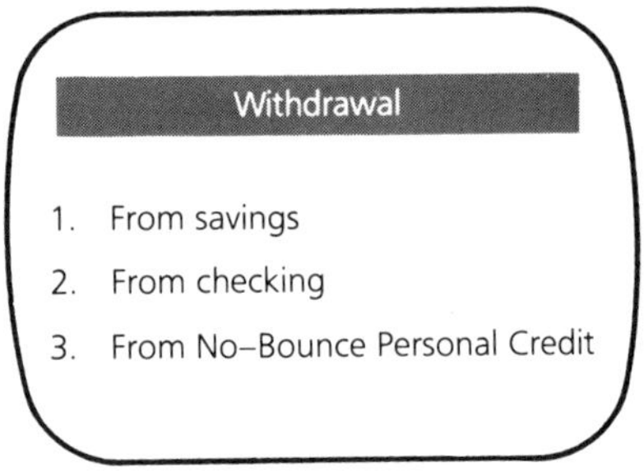

Withdrawal menu

Figure 10-32. Sample ATM menu with attributes

11 Testing Systems

User testing is one of many things designers can do to make sure that systems work effectively for their intended users. In the 1960s, one manufacturer set up a test facility to investigate how computers could be used in teaching children. Even though the idea of teaching machines had been around for some years, it was a novel project. It was using prototype evaluation, a human factors technique, to uncover problems with a computer system design. The way the children were to interact with the computer was also novel: to answer questions, they used a light pen to point at things on the screen. One thing the evaluators learned from this study was that the children stuck the light pens in their ears, and the ear wax blocked the photocells so that the light pens couldn't detect light coming from the display screen. The systems could not be kept working! The designers of the system had never foreseen this problem.

Virtually every engineering design is evaluated in some manner before it is released. Before production, for example, automobile manufacturers routinely evaluate various aspects of the design such as

Drawing by Jan van Wessum; courtesy of Jan van Wessum, Amsterdam, The Netherlands.

safety, performance, and cost of manufacturing. Failure to conduct such tests would expose them to a wide range of possible problems in the marketplace and in the courts.

Hardware, system software, and human interfaces may all have problems that evaluation can find and measure, but although errors in hardware and system software persist until corrected, errors in user interface design merely force users to accommodate to the system. Users compensate for problems by devising special ways to interact and to live with the system. In doing so they develop peculiar habits and complex conceptual models.

Given that a user's state of knowledge is constantly changing, trying to evaluate the quality of the user interface can sometimes be like trying to measure with a rubber ruler. This does not mean, however, that evaluation shouldn't be done. Most software developers are not in a position to carry out formal experiments to assess user system performance or error rates. But it is possible for a developer to do an informal assessment with a minimum of effort.

Overall, our philosophy of evaluation is simply: You build it, you test it.

You build it, you test it.

DESIGNING AN EVALUATION

For research in human factors, formal experiments are usually necessary, but for practical system assessment, a much more informal evaluation may suffice. Our goal as designers is not to discover basic scientific truths, but rather to have an objective look at our own systems in the light of day.

As with the other components in the development process, evaluation requires planning before doing. It is necessary to choose in advance the right kind of evaluation for any particular product. There are three relevant criteria for an adequate evaluation:

1. Appropriateness to the product or system
2. Reliability—obtaining similar results on repeated evaluations
3. Validity—measuring what is supposed to be measured.

Appropriateness

The first step is to select an evaluation approach that is appropriate for the product or system being developed. What is the system to accomplish and what will be done with the test results? Must the system meet initially established criteria, such as the ten-minute rule? If so, an absolute evaluation is appropriate, comparing real performance with the specification. Because there are fixed standards, results are relatively easy to interpret. If the ten-minute rule is to be the criterion, for example, either a majority of users can learn to accomplish the task in that time, or they cannot.

Guideline 87. Articulate the evaluation goals.

Another way to evaluate a system is to compare it to the corresponding manual operation it replaces. Many computer-based functions have their origins in manual operations. Success of many systems depends on bettering the previous way in which things were done, so the old methods provide a basis for comparison in evaluation.

Some time ago, the Foreign Technology Division of the U.S. Air Force built an immense retrieval system containing abstracts of the world's scientific and technological literature. Search analysts would submit their questions and the system would respond by printing the number of documents retrieved. They could then print out the retrieved abstracts and enter a more specific query. After a little time using this system, many analysts developed a more efficient strategy: without looking at any of the retrieved abstracts, they would revise and resubmit queries until only 50 to 100 documents were retrieved. At that point they would have the entire retrieved set printed out and would read the abstracts to find the desired ones. Thus the analysts discovered that it was easier just to read hard copies of the final set of documents than to try to obtain a still smaller set of relevant documents by submitting additional computerized queries. If this strategy had been discovered during an evaluation of the design of the system, designers might have been able to consider integrating both computer-based and manual operations into the use model of the final system.

Building the best possible product is not always what is wanted. Sometimes it is enough to show through comparative evaluation that your system is better than the competition's. In a competitive marketing environment, doing much better than the competition may not be worth more than doing a little better. It might be sufficient to be able to show that secretaries can produce two more letters per hour on word processor A than on word processor B, or that new users can learn to use system X in one hour, whereas it takes a full day of classroom instruction to learn system Z.

The most powerful evaluation techniques employ actual users. Testing can occur at many points in the overall development process. Measuring user performance early in the design of a system can provide useful data for detailed design decisions. For example, a designer may want to assess two alternate methods of error recovery or to choose among several possible command names. Measuring users' performance on each of the alternative design proposals before the design is finalized may make it possible to get the design right the first time.

As the system begins to take shape, behavioral analysis of the details of task performance becomes important for assessing the specific expectations, confusions, and errors experienced by users. These issues may be more important than how fast functions can be performed. Detailed information about how users perform their tasks exposes potential problems and suggests possible solutions early in the development process. Later, as the system approaches its final form, global performance measures are useful for determining competitive positions and for providing concrete feedback to those responsible for developing learning aids.

Assessing both learning behavior and behavior after mastery can be important goals of an evaluation. In a learning situation the evaluation should measure how easy it is to learn to use the system. A system may be efficient to use once it is mastered but be difficult for novices to understand. If a system will be used by a constant flow of new users, then fast learning becomes a much more important goal than if a fixed set of people will use it on a regular basis. Air traffic control towers and control rooms in nuclear power plants are two places where performance of systems outranks learning time. But even when steadystate performance is not critical, performance after learning is usually an important consideration. Even though users tend to adapt their behavior to the idiosyncrasies of a system, the system may be unnecessarily inefficient for knowledgeable users, as when a designer produces an "idiot-proof" system in an attempt to make one that is easy to learn. General, menu-driven systems tend to have this problem. Experienced users will often see potential shortcuts that are unobtainable because of a rigid menu structure.

A final consideration in designing an evaluation is whether formal or informal evaluation is more appropriate. There are no easy rules for this choice. If the system is a commercial product or if economic or safety consequences are relevant, a formal evaluation is in order. On the other hand, if the evaluation is for the designer's own use or if the effort is a midnight project, an informal evaluation is appropriate. It is worth noting, however, that midnight projects often become commercial products.

Reliability and Validity

Once we've determined the goals and appropriateness of a particular evaluation approach, we need to ensure that the evaluation will be useable. First of all, the evaluation must be reliable—that is, someone else should be able to do the same evaluation under similar conditions and obtain essentially the same results. Reliability comes from maintaining controlled conditions in the evaluation. We also need a fair, or *valid* assessment, one that truly addresses the stated objectives. Validity is making sure that what you say you are measuring is what you are actually measuring.

Components of an Evaluation

Any evaluation is composed of four parts:

1. A system prototype or simulation to be evaluated
2. One or more users
3. One or more standardized tasks to be performed
4. Some way of observing or measuring what's happening (or not happening).

The system under evaluation should be stable and well defined, closely resembling the final design. If the user interface changes during the evaluation, the results won't be reliable.

Selecting Users

Selection of test users or subjects involves several considerations. First, they must be participants who will act in good faith during the evaluation—they must be disinterested in the results. Second, enough subjects must participate to balance out differences from one person to the next. No two people are identical. Using a single subject may provide substantial insights, but the likelihood that someone else selected at random will produce the same results is probably low. Depending on its complexity, an informal evaluation requires at least four subjects to produce fairly reliable results. If there is wide variation in the results, however, it may be desirable to increase the number of subjects to obtain consistency in the outcome or to identify the aspects on which there is variation.

Guideline 88. Select subjects who are unfamiliar with the system.

A designer or implementer who has been involved with a system for months or even years has a deep understanding of the system and its underlying software structure. His or her conceptual model is both comprehensive and accurate. Designers are not good subjects because they know too much about the system under test. Obtaining reactions akin to those of actual users involves testing the user interface with someone who has never used the system before, who doesn't know the idiosyncrasies of the interaction or how the software is organized. This subject must build his or her conceptual model based on the external myth presented, providing a useful test of the system.

Although we've consistently taken the position that the user is always right, during evaluation it is especially important to ensure that the users are representative of those who will actually use the particular system. Thus, if the subject has difficulty trying to perform a particular function, we must know whether it is reasonable to expect the target users to understand the task the system is performing. If the system is an electronic mail system destined to replace paper interoffice mail and the user is an experienced office worker, then the answer is yes. The user probably understands at a conceptual level such functions as sending, receiving, and forwarding. But if the system performs a finite-element analysis (for a structural engineering design), the same office worker will have difficulty no matter how well the user interface is designed.

Guideline 89. Select subjects who are representative of the target user population.

People pursue different careers partly on the basis of their abilities and interests. As a group, people who go into insurance or secretarial work differ in abilities, interests, and work styles from those who go into computer science, programming, or design. The target profession's vocabulary, perspective, and way of defining procedures may be radically different from the way the designer has envisioned them. Subjects who share the designer's perspectives rather than the target users' can create an insurmountable bias. For example, if the system is to be used by both accountants and astrophysicists, then representatives from both groups should be included in the evaluation.

Users who are unfamiliar with computers deserve special consideration. Many people are afraid of computers and have misconceptions about them. The attitude of first-time-users may affect their interactions strongly. Accessibility for these users should be examined separately from a general evaluation of the system.

Selecting Tasks

Having determined who the subjects will be, we need to choose the proper tasks for them to carry out. Not any task will do. The tasks must represent those in the use model for the test to be valid. Further, the tasks should make the evaluation relevant for subjects, since they provide a context in which subjects will interact with the system. For example, with an information retrieval system, the tasks might be to answer a set of questions of interest to subjects by obtaining pieces of information via the system.

Guideline 90. Use representative tasks.

Guideline 91. Standardize the tasks.

Part of designing the task is designing the evaluation procedure. The entire evaluation process should be standardized. All subjects should be given the same information in the same way. If system users are to read the documentation or otherwise prepare themselves before performing tasks, then subjects must do so before proceeding with the test. If the tasks are timed, each subject must be timed in the same way. If subjects are trained one day and tested on another, the delay must be constant for all. Individual variability will result in differences between runs, but the evaluation design should minimize any other variations.

Selecting the Measurements

Having the system, subjects, and task in hand, we need a standardized method of observing and measuring behavior. Some performance and attitude measurements that are appropriate (and usually necessary) for human factors evaluations include:

- Human performance measures
  - —Reaction time
  - —Error rate
  - —Behavioral analysis
- Attitude measures
  - —User perception
  - —Self reports

Human performance measures typically refer to reaction times or error rates. Reaction time, or the time needed to complete a particular task, is taken to be an indicator of task difficulty. Error rates refer to either the number or severity of errors. Physiological measures such as pupil dilation, pulse rate, and electromyographic (electrically sensed muscle) responses are also used as measures of human performance but are generally inappropriate for informal evaluations. Finally, behavioral analysis is observing the behavior of users and relating what they do to aspects of the design.

Attitude measures, which involve users' perceptions of reality (in this case, the computer), are necessarily subjective and do not always correlate with performance measures: tasks perceived as easy may actually be performed slowly, or vice versa. For example, people prefer word processors for editing letters, even though there is evidence that it takes longer to produce a letter on a word processor than on a typewriter [Gould 1981]. Nevertheless, attitude measures are equally as important as performance measures in the evaluation of many systems. If potential users feel that a system is unfriendly, or that it is difficult or stressful to use, they will respond according to these perceptions, regardless of the objective situation.

Information on users' perceptions is easier to obtain than that on performance. The most valid (and thus most useful) attitude questions ask the user for an opinion about the system. Typically, users respond to questions presented either verbally or on paper. The questions may be global ("How easy was it to learn to use this system?") or detailed ("Did you use the UNDELETE function? Was it useful?"). The questions can use rating scales ("On a scale from 1 to 9, with 1 representing very poor and 9 representing very good, please rate. . .") or be completely open-ended. The two open-ended questions that tend to provide the most information are: "What do you like most about the system?" and "What do you like least about the system?"

Questions about users' perceptions are a useful means of documenting users' expectations before they encounter a system ("How long do you expect it will take before you are comfortable using the system?"). Asking such questions both before and after use of a system provides a basis for determining how well the system meets these expectations.

Self-reports assess people's perceptions of their own performance, such as "How good a typist are you?" However, attitude measures in general, and self-reports in particular, are harder to interpret than performance measures because of three potential biases:

- *Halo effect* is the tendency of some people to respond positively (or negatively) to all questions in a set, without giving sufficient consideration to individual questions. We can try to neutralize halo effects by phrasing some questions positively and some negatively.
- *Acquiescence* is the tendency of some to respond in an agreeable, positive way to all questions. Again, mixing the types of questions asked can reduce acquiescence.

- *Cognitive dissonance* is the tendency of everyone not to admit being biased, illogical, or inconsistent as the result of external influences.

In one evaluation we know of, cognitive dissonance obviously played a role. A researcher interviewed the users of an electronic mail system several months after its implementation. One question asked users how they felt their own productivity had changed as a result. The average answer in this self-report was that productivity increased 15 percent. It was clear that subjects had rationalized their responses: if they gave a large percentage, say 50 percent, it would suggest that they had been very lax before the system was installed; if they responded with a very small number, it would suggest that the mail system was not helping them, even though they spent a significant amount of time using it. Obviously the only safe answer was a number large enough to indicate that the system had some benefit, but small enough to suggest they had been operating efficiently to begin with. The users responded with a number that was consistent with their self-image but had no relationship to an objective productivity measure.

When objective information is being sought (such as "how many times a day do you log onto the system?"), human-performance measurement techniques are easier to use and provide more accurate results.

INFORMAL EVALUATIONS

An informal assessment of a user interface can be simple and quick, especially if the person doing the evaluation has some insights into human factors issues. There is a wide range of evaluation techniques available. Before proceeding further, designers should ask themselves the most obvious questions and to answer them honestly:

- In what ways does the system meet and fail to meet the market requirements? What is the impact on users?
- What knowledge am I assuming the user possesses? Is this a reasonable requirement?
- Could someone else learn about the system if he or she didn't know about it?

- What happens if the user does the wrong thing? How hard is it to get back on track?
- What sequences of operations would a typical user want to perform? Does the system support these sequences?
- From the user's perspective, does the system ask for or display any irrelevant information?
- Is the information on the screen organized in a way that the user can understand easily? Is too much displayed, or too little?
- What shortcuts do I know about? Could a new user find them? If not, does the existence of shortcuts suggest that the "official" way is less than reasonably efficient?

Guideline 92. Use the design guidelines to structure an evaluation.

A useful armchair evaluation of a system can be done by using the design guidelines in this book. This approach focuses attention on details of the system that may have been overlooked, but that directly affect the quality of the user interface. An objective early look at the system should yield useful data to factor back into the design.

User Testing

More objective procedures are required, even for informal evaluations. The best by far is testing with real users. Recruiting representative users and having them use the "prototype" will yield indications of what might be confusing or misleading, and thus useful feedback for the next iteration.

One quick way of evaluating a user interface is to simulate the interaction between system and user. This method is mainly applicable to assessing dialogues such as commands, prompts, help, and error messages. In this procedure subjects operate in pairs, one playing the part of the system, the other the part of the user. The "user" says out loud what is being typed in, and the "system" says out loud everything that appears as output on the screen. (Use a sound-proof room if the participants are self-conscious.) Prompts and error messages that might have seemed reasonable when typed in may now sound cryptic, stilted, or awkward. Vocalizing each command or prompt forces our attention clearly on the input and output. We've found that this procedure works very well.

Similar methods can be applied to other types of interface. Forms and other direct-manipulation interfaces can often be simulated with paper forms that subjects fill out in order to carry out the task. Menu interfaces can be mocked-up with sets of cards each showing a menu, manipulated appropriately by the evaluator.

Assessing the reasonableness of a user interface through guideline checking and simulation should uncover many of the major problems. Other procedures are available for more comprehensive analyses of user behavior. All involve having a user sit in front of the system (or a simulation of the system) to do a standard set of tasks, recording the relevant behavior of the system and the user, and then examining these records to uncover patterns of behavior. The three major methods used to record behavior are *manual recording*, *videotaping*, and *protocol analysis*.

In manual analysis, the evaluator passively observes a user performing a standard task and takes notes on important events in the interaction. Such events may include command sequences, errors and error recovery, feature usage, or time required to complete the task.

Videotaping is the second approach. Our experience has been that people do not mind being videotaped. In fact, it's very easy to forget the camera if the experimenter makes little fuss about it. Two cameras—one focused on the user and one on the terminal screen—can record the complete session for later analysis. We have found this approach to be tremendously rewarding. Videotaping is much less prone than manual note-taking to errors of omission or to biases in recording. In addition, these tapes provide convincing evidence of the need for human factors input in interface design. They are useful in convincing management and coworkers that a problem exists. One tape of someone sitting back, looking confused, and saying, "I have no idea what to do," is worth a dozen technical reports on the analysis. Conversely, user success is very convincing on tape.

Protocol analysis is a somewhat more complex method of understanding the user-system interaction. In this procedure, users are asked to verbalize what they are thinking as they attempt to perform a task. The monologue is recorded for later analysis. This method has been used extensively in psychological research, especially in the area of human problem solving, where the vocalizing has provided insights into underlying thought processes [Newell and Simon 1972]. In the evaluation of computer systems, protocol analysis provides insight into the user's conceptual model of the system. In many instances, users uncover the most obvious problems in the system—problems that designers haven't seen because they're too close to it. In one recent case we know of, a user had been searching through a manual for several minutes when she stopped, looked up and stated, "It's curious that the chapter entitled 'Getting Started' is the sixth one, not the first."

If subjects are somewhat reluctant to talk about what they are thinking, a successful variation is to use them in pairs [Brown, Rubinstein, and Burton 1976]. It's helpful if they know each other and are at similar skill levels. Give them a realistic problem to solve. Have one person sit in front of the terminal and the other either read from the manual or simply coach the first one. As the two try to determine how to use the system to solve the problem, their dialogue will usually be filled with both accurate and wrong advice, clear insights and misperceptions, and discussions of ambiguous situations. An added benefit of this approach is that when two people are involved they tend to reinforce the idea that the problems are in the system rather then in themselves. This method gives clear insights into the conceptual models people are building.

Guideline 93. Videotape real users.

Videotaping real users solving realistic problems is the preferred method for obtaining the maximum amount of useful feedback with the minimum of effort. When subjects explain things to each other, their misunderstandings frequently become clear to the observer. Be sure to give the subjects problems to solve that will provoke some discussion. A useful variation is to pair one subject who has had some experience with the system with someone who has not, so that the more experienced user can explain his or her conceptual model to the other. Since subjects seldom understand what it is that they don't understand about a system, monologues almost never provide as much insight as these dialogues.

Keystroke Capturing

Depending on the particular hardware and software configuration being used, it is sometimes feasible to have the system maintain a log of every keystroke that is typed during a session at the terminal. These logs permit the designer to determine which functions and options were used and which were not, and to reconstruct the exact sequence of operations. Thus they provide a record of the steps used in performing particular evaluation tasks. Many designers, however, are reluctant to spend so much time and effort setting up such a logging procedure and analyzing the tens or hundreds of thousands of individual keystrokes to infer why the user typed one sequence rather than another. It's much more direct and accurate to simply ask the user.

In actual user environments, keystroke capturing is a good way to obtain statistics on which features of a system are used and which are not. Analysis of keystroke sequences can also help designers decide upon the details of alternative implementations. By comparing the sequences of steps involved in two alternative implementations, designers can determine which implementation is more efficient.

Documentation in Testing

With any of the methods of recording behavior, the designer must decide whether the users should proceed with or without the help of documentation. If the documentation has been designed along with the system to form part of the whole, evaluating it along with the rest of the system is essential. Do the documentation and the help facility complement each other? Do users find them helpful, or are they contradictory or confusing?

On the other hand, if a goal of the design effort is that the system be self-explanatory, as with some turn-key products, then the documentation should not be used in the test. For the many environments in which users are not expected to read manuals, the general structure of the interface—the prompts, feedback, error messages, and help facility—should itself enable a user to figure out how the system works. Any failure to do so will quickly become evident and can be used to refine the system design. Even when it is not possible to incorporate the results into modifications to the system, such information will be valuable for identifying topics to be emphasized in the documentation or instruction.

Asking someone to try to use the system without any external reference material may seem like stacking the deck against the system, but you'll find that the resulting errors and problems are logical and (in hindsight) predictable. For example, in a recent evaluation of an office automation system [Hersh 1981], we used three pairs of secretaries: two high school clerical and business students, two middle-aged secretaries from a temporary agency, and two somewhat older typing instructors. None had had any experience with word processors or other office automation equipment. When each pair attempted to carry out a set of basic tasks on the system, the bottlenecks and problem areas uncovered by the most experienced pair were virtually the same as those uncovered by the others. The same held true for the tasks that the pairs found it easy to accomplish. The results of such evaluations are surprisingly consistent.

DECISION MAKING

Often designers need data to help them select among alternative strategies for a particular feature. Determining which design to use involves determining not only what the differences are, but whether a difference really matters. If sensitive statistical techniques are needed to reveal a difference, how important can it be?

A range of approaches is available for evaluating alternative design features, depending on the context in which the features will be evaluated. In general, the more abstract the context, the more formal the evaluation needs to be to guarantee adequate reliability and validity. Conversely, the more closely the test context resembles the actual usage context, the more informal the evaluation can be.

The context most closely resembling actual usage would be one in which there are two complete system versions, identical except for the one feature. Representative users could operate each version and show which is more effective. The other extreme would be an evaluation of individual features conducted in isolation in a formal laboratory setting. Most evaluation designs lie between these two end points.

Imagine you are building a text editor and are not sure whether to allow the cursor to be moved freely (up, down, left, and right) or by grammatical entities (by character, word, sentence, paragraph, page, and so on). You could build (or simulate) two variants of the editor, one with free directional keys, and one with grammatical keys, and then give two groups of representative users editing tasks to perform and see which group does better. In a formal, laboratory approach, the cursor and a target position might appear on the CRT screen, and the user would have to move the cursor as fast as possible to the target location. To carry out a study like this and have the results applicable to the editor design, the evaluator would have to make sure that the distances the cursor was to be moved were randomly chosen, that the target locations were representative of actual targets, that the system response times were adequately controlled across the two conditions, that the correct number of subjects were randomly assigned to each condition, and that the user's reaction times could be accurately measured [Card, English, and Burr 1977].

Even if all the other relevant factors are held constant and a significant difference is found, there remains the problem of interpreting the results. In this example, a critical factor may be the time needed to switch between typing text or editing commands and moving the cursor—a factor not evaluated in this study. Moreover, system response time may have a crucial impact on the effectiveness of the alternative approaches. The directional keys might be optimal for fast, predictable system response times, but the grammatical entity keys are optimal for slow or variable response times. In a relatively informal, full-system comparison, these issues become immaterial, because one of the systems being tested will be the final system. In a more abstract feature comparison, holding critical parameters constant and proper interpretation of results become all-important, to allow the results to be accurately generalized.

Command Word Selection

One design decision that is often overlooked but relatively easy to evaluate is the assignment of words in a command language. The following criteria are relevant:

- When a user sees a term in context, he or she should be able to infer what concept (or operation) the term represents.

- When a user has in mind a particular concept (or operation) he or she should be able to guess the appropriate command.
- The term should not have any obvious negative or spurious connotations.

The first two conditions constitute a *semantic association* between an external symbol (the term) and the internal representation (the concept). Fortunately, it is easy to assess the degree of semantic association between a concept and a term long before the system is ever implemented. The procedure involves four steps:

1. Generate the list of concepts (sentences) such as "Create a message" or "Print a copy of the file on the line printer."
2. Write a paragraph or two describing the context for interpretation. This should describe the system in general terms, what the range of operations is. This context is important, for many terms can change meaning dramatically if the context is changed. The word *print,* for example, has very different meanings in a second-grade classroom and a typesetting shop.
3. Get a small group of representative users (not necessarily in the same place or time). Between 10 and 20 people is a reasonable number.
4. Ask the people to read each sentence and (working independently) to write down a word or short phrase that could be used to represent the idea in the sentence.

Tabulation of the responses produces a set of possible terms and phrases. Reversing the process, we create a list of specific terms and phrases, provide the same context, and ask people to write down what they think each term means. If there is a reasonable association between the term and the concept, most people will give similar definitions. When a term or phrase is ambiguous or the definition clearly inappropriate, an alternative should be found.

These two procedures provide a good test for a proposed set of commands. The language forms that are consistently produced from the same concept and consistently suggested by a single concept are the ones to use. However, terms that are optimal in one country, culture, or language may not be in another. If the system will be used cross-culturally, the two term-assessment procedures should be conducted with the entire range of appropriate subjects. Note that terms that prove to be less than optimal can still be used. The important consideration is that problems won't come as a surprise.

The purpose of command-word evaluation is more the elimination of poor words than the finding of the best ones. This approach is consistent with the notion that there probably is no single optimal word for each purpose. If we just produce an entire set of commands with strong semantic associations, we will have done better than most of today's systems. Remember that people learn and adapt. But the less they have to learn and the less they have to adapt, the better the system works for them.

Icon Selection

A variant of the command selection approach can also be used to evaluate icons (formalized pictures). The procedure can be quickly carried out on a CRT, on hard copy, or even in a group setting with a projection-type CRT display.

The procedure requires the set of (verbal) concepts and candidate icons, preferably two or three icons per concept. In the test, the set of icons and the verbal concept appear in the same area on the page or screen. If possible, the pages should be put in a different random order for each subject so as to balance out any effects of subjects seeing the icons in a particular order.

Ten or more people should serve as evaluators, or subjects, for the task. The subjects should be selected and tested in accordance with the guidelines outlined in this chapter. To ensure consistency, it is a good idea to write down a standard set of instructions for each subject to read before beginning the task. The instructions should provide information about the nature of the task, the number of concepts to be judged, and the approximate duration of the session. It is crucial that the instructions adequately describe the context in which the icons will be used; like words, many images can change meaning with changes in context.

Before the subjects begin, be sure they understand the concepts to be evaluated and the procedure, which should be outlined as follows:

1. Read the verbal description or concept.

2. Select the one icon that has the least relation to the verbal description.
3. Select the one icon that most clearly conveys the meaning of the verbal description. Again, one and only one icon should be selected, no matter how similar or dissimilar the candidate set.
4. Finally, rate the "best" icon on a scale from 1 to 5, with 1 meaning that the icon has no relation to the verbal description and 5 that the icon means the same as the verbal description.

Analysis of these data can proceed in a straightforward, two-step process. First, select the best icon candidate for each concept by tabulating the number of times each alternative was selected as the "best." When there is not a clear favorite, use the "worst" selections to determine the least negative candidate.

Second, calculate the mean (average) preference rating for each concept. If a concept's mean rating is 3.0 or greater, then the preferred icon candidate is a promising selection. A mean rating below 3.0 suggests that none of the icon candidates is reasonable. You may want to try again with these concepts, or you may choose to go with the best available. In either case, the decision will be based on evaluative data rather than on speculation.

FORMAL EVALUATIONS

Informal evaluations provide concrete feedback about the strengths and weaknesses of the user interface, and can be carried out quickly by developers themselves during the overall development process. However, when someone besides the developer has an interest in the design and in the outcome of the evaluation, informal procedures are usually not sufficient. This outside interest exists whenever there are significant costs—societal or economic—associated with the system. For example, a formal evaluation is clearly appropriate and necessary for a computer-based control system for a nuclear power plant. Formal evaluation is also necessary when a design is a matter of general scientific interest to technical peers and the designer wants to generalize from a particular system to all systems (say, in an article or book about the system and evaluation).

A formal evaluation reflects a need for solid substantive and methodological expertise, and the issues of reliability and validity become critically important. It is necessary to know which parameters (of the system and of the subjects) to control, which to pay attention to, and which can be safely ignored. Formal procedures, then, require a high level of expertise that you must either acquire yourself or obtain through someone else trained in the relevant disciplines. Issues such as experimental design, statistics, and experimental psychology are beyond the scope of this book, but the bibliography lists several basic references on these topics. Or, you may want to consult someone with training and experience in human-machine system evaluation. An increasing number of human factors specialists are to be found in large development organizations and in some smaller development groups, in consulting services and departments of human factors or (experimental) psychology at local universities, and in departments of industrial engineering and graduate schools of business administration.

EVALUATION OF PEOPLE'S BANK DESIGN

Incorporating our incremental human factors improvements into our initial design for the human interface, our department built a single prototype unit of People's Bank Money Machines, consisting of a conventional ATM and additional hardware for speech output. The bank was clearly anxious to get the machines into production, once the prototype was working and performing according to specifications. We convinced the bank management to let us install the prototype unit in the main branch for testing and evaluation. Our management concurred that an initial positive reception was critical to the success of the Money Machine. At our request, the installation was in a room off the main lobby, rather than in the foyer, allowing us to restrict access for purposes of conducting our tests. The availability of the machines is due to be announced in two months, pending the results of our tests.

Our evaluation had three goals: to identify potential learning and usage problems for both English- and Spanish-speaking customers, to obtain customers' reactions to the design, and to collect data on average transaction times in order to make transactions as efficient as possible.

Because we needed a real context in order to ensure a valid test, we decided to use regular bank customers as subjects and to have them access their own accounts. We selected forty customers at random from those joining the line to conduct business at the teller windows. Thus each subject clearly had one or more transactions to conduct. The tellers asked every tenth customer if he or she would be willing to help us test a new service, explained that the study would take a few extra minutes, and offered the customer a choice of a pen set or a leather check book as a small gift for his or her trouble. We reasoned that a gift was necessary because of the extra time involved, but that too expensive a gift would create too strong an incentive and thus bias the results.

We tried to make the task as natural as possible. A bilingual instructor explained to each customer how to use the machine, much as instructors will do when the machines are implemented bankwide. After explaining that the machines could be used for withdrawing money, making deposits, and getting balances, the instructor gave the customers a plastic identification card, asked them to select an identification code, and then asked them to specify whether they wanted to conduct the transaction in English or in Spanish. After leading the customers through a full cycle for requesting balances, the instructor asked them to conduct the business they had come to the bank to do. After each user completed the transaction (or left the machine for some other reason), the instructor conducted a structured interview. Figure 11-1 shows the form used by the instructor to record the results.

In addition to filling out the questionnaires, the instructors made notes of what happened during each encounter. Videotapes of the first five sessions were also made unobtrusively, but with the subjects' knowledge. Initially we tried to include protocol analysis—that is, customers were asked to describe to the instructor what they were doing—but discarded it because customers got confused trying to accommodate us.

The results of the evaluation provided many reassurances and a few big surprises. Some of the issues affected only a few of the customers, but we reminded ourselves that 4 out of 40 subjects represents 10 percent. An operational system with such a high percentage of problems would be catastrophic.

The evaluation revealed that six people (15 percent) forgot their codes or had trouble choosing one in the first place. The instructor had to suggest a specific category, such as the customer's date of birth, to

PEOPLE'S BANK MONEY MACHINE QUESTIONNAIRE

Note to instructor: Fill in answers to questions 1–4 and 14–16 on the basis of your own observation. For the remaining questions, check only one response and record any comments made.

1. Customer's preferred spoken language
   ______English
   ______Spanish
   ______Other______________

2. Estimated literacy level in preferred language
   ______High
   ______Functional
   ______Marginal

3. Language used on machine
   ______English
   ______Spanish

4. Did customer listen to the handset?
   ______Yes
   ______No

5. How easy was it to learn to use the machine?
   ______Very difficult
   ______Rather difficult
   ______Not bad
   ______Rather easy
   ______Very easy

6. How often does the customer come to People's bank?
   (______times per week)

7. How often would the customer come if always open?
   (______times per week)

8. How often would the customer use the machine instead of going to the teller's window?
   ______Never
   ______Only when bank is closed
   ______Occasionally when bank is open
   ______Frequently
   ______Always

9. Is it faster to use the machine or to do the same thing at the teller's window?
   ______Machine much faster
   ______Machine somewhat faster
   ______About the same
   ______Teller somewhat faster
   ______Teller much faster

Figure 11-1. Post-test interview form

10. In using the machine, did the customer prefer reading or hearing the instructions?
    ______Reading
    ______Hearing
    ______No preference
11. What did the customer like least about the machine?

12. How would the customer improve on the machine?

13. What did the customer like best about the machine?
    (If response is 24-hour access, ask what else.)

14. Approximate age (guess)____________
15. Sex
    ______Male
    ______Female
16. Subject code____________

Figure 11-1 continued

make choosing and remembering easier. This procedure will be carried over into the routine instructional procedure.

The instructor quickly found that it was hard to give instructions relating to the audio because she could not hear what the customers were hearing in the handsets. After testing the first two subjects, we lashed up a second handset for the instructor. Future machines will have an auxiliary jack for instructors to use while they give customers an introduction to or help with the machine.

Four of the subjects walked away from the machine in the middle of the transaction, without taking their cards. Perhaps they didn't have the sense of ownership that most people have with credit and ATM cards because they had just received them. However, leaving the machine in midtransaction presents both security and throughput problems. Someone else could walk up and fraudulently continue the transaction. Once the transaction times out, the machine cannot be used by anyone else until the card is removed. An honest customer would be reluctant to remove another person's card, even with the intention of turning it over to the bank. Therefore, we are investigating the addition of a pressure-sensitive mat or similar device that indicates whether a person is standing at the terminal. If the user leaves in midtransaction, the machine will be instructed to keep the card and recycle to the ready state.

The length of transactions exceeded our throughput goal for the machine, averaging over two minutes. The times were also quite variable. We found that differences in language used did not affect the length of time spent at the machine (English speakers averaged 2.10 minutes, Spanish speakers 2.05), but that those who used the handset took an average of 47 seconds longer than those who used the screen. The comments of the customers and the instructor also indicated that the audio slowed people down. Even when people were familiar with what was on the screen, they tended to listen to the entire audio message rather than "interrupt." The customers did not realize that they could stop the voice and move on to the next step, or perhaps they were being polite.

We may try increasing slightly the length of pauses between the recital of each choice, as a way to encourage early responses. Customers might press the button during the pause (if it's the transaction they want) rather than waiting for the voice to stop. This change calls our attention to the order of items in the menus: the most commonly selected items should come first. This does not matter as much with screen interfaces, but the sequential nature of voice makes it important. As it is, "Savings" comes before "Checking" in the account menus. We need to find out what the correct ordering should be for all menus, something we should have considered before. An additional test will be necessary to validate this approach. We also have to make it clear in the initial instructions that the customer does not need to wait until the voice stops before responding.

We also inferred from customers' experiences with the audio that initial uses of the machine will probably take much longer than later ones. A substantial amount of learning seems to be taking place, and we expect greater speed as people become more comfortable. Because our test involved only first uses, it was biased toward longer times.

A most surprising test result was that two Spanish-speaking customers appeared embarrassed by the instructions given on the screen and in the handset. We discovered that a translation of "Insert the card" into correct Castilian Spanish was considered obscene in one dialect of Latin American Spanish! New translations are being sought in consultation with a university expert on Spanish dialects and idioms.

A significant number of people, about one fourth of the subjects, had trouble of some kind. Our information from the instructor and from the videotapes indicates that most of the problems were due to normal negative reactions to something new. This finding suggests that some form of continuing assistance must be available when the machines are installed on a wider basis, and this help should probably be provided by a person rather than by the machine. We propose that customers be able to ask for help during business hours, and that a helper be stationed near each machine for the first few months after its installation.

In analyzing the interview results, we tried to keep things simple. By using multivariate statistics we could have analyzed the data in hundreds of ways and wrung out every drop of information. But we just wanted some basics. After all, our main goal is to get a quality ATM into service as quickly as possible. First we analyzed the general information provided by the instructor's observations. The results, listed in Table 11-1, confirm that our sample was representative. These numbers will support the validity of our other findings when we present them to the management.

Table 11-1. Subject demographics

Preferred spoken language	
English	22
Spanish	15
French	1
Italian	1
Vietnamese	1
Estimated literacy in preferred language	
High	27
Functional	8
Marginal	5
Language used on machine	
English	27
Spanish	13
Mode selected for transaction	
Screen	24
Handset	16
Sex	
Female	22
Male	18

Next we analyzed the responses to the attitude questions. To get a summary value on the questions involving ratings, such as learning difficulty, we converted the word ratings to numbers 1 to 5 and found the average. For example, on the question "How easy was it to learn to use the machine?" we converted "very difficult" to 1, "rather difficult" to 2, and so on. The average of the 40 responses to this question was 3.6, somewhere between "not bad" and "rather easy." Because 27 customers rated learning either "rather easy" or "very easy" and only one rated it "very difficult," we were pleased with the results.

In the test, 16 customers listened to the handset. The interview showed that 11 preferred the handset, 20 preferred the screen, and that 9 had no preference either way. Five customers (12.5 percent) said the voice capability was the least positive feature of the machine, two (5 percent) that it was the most positive. These figures indicate that although the handset was not highly successful, a sizable proportion of customers did prefer it.

Other feedback suggested that the voice interface needs additional work. Most customers who used the audio said that it was hard to understand or that it had an unnatural accent or quality. One Spanish-speaking man was obviously upset and asked if *that* was how the bank thought Spanish people spoke. We will take these comments back to the voice-synthesizer vendor and rework the phrases to make them sound more natural.

The frequency-of-banking data surprised us a little. Customers' responses on how often they come to the bank ranged from once a month to 10 times per week, with an average of 1.2 times per week. In the question on frequency of use if the bank were always open, the range stayed the same, but the average increased to 1.5 times per week.

The item on machine preference shed some additional light on customers' attitudes. Table 11-2 lists the frequency distribution of responses. On a scale of 1 to 5, the average response was 3.1. This result could be interpreted as occasional usage when the bank is open as well as some usage when the bank is closed. However, 14 customers would always choose a human teller, whereas 21 had a clear preference for the machine. This bimodal distribution suggests that the sample may have comprised two distinct groups: those who accept the machine and those who at best, tolerate it.

Table 11-2. Customers' preferences for machine versus teller

Response	*Number of Customers*
Never	3
Only when bank is closed	11
Occasionally when bank is open	5
Frequently	18
Always	3

The data on perceived speed yielded similar results. (See Table 11-3.) The average (2.8) showed no preference, but again there were two groups: those who perceived the machine as faster and those who perceived tellers as faster. Whether those who think the machine is faster also like it better really doesn't matter to us at this point. It's sufficient for management to recognize that a significant proportion of customers may react positively to the machines while another group may not use them at all, or only if absolutely necessary. These numbers, however, may well change over time as our design improves and as more people become familiar with the machines.

Table 11-3. Perceived speed of machine versus teller

Response	*Number of Customers*
Machine much faster	4
Machine somewhat faster	21
About the same	5
Teller somewhat faster	12
Teller much faster	1

Finally, the questions on likes and dislikes provided some supporting data. When asked what they liked least about the machine, eight customers said that it was impersonal, that they preferred to transact their business with a person. Another three people said that it was initially confusing. We'll attempt to address this problem by providing initial training, making assistance available during normal business hours, and improving the voice output.

Four customers complained that the machines do not permit them to make utility payments, which they said was an important reason for their coming to the bank. If they have to go to the teller's window anyway to pay a bill, why should they use the machine for a withdrawal or deposit? The bank management is now considering adding such a capability to the machines, but we have recommended not doing so, on the grounds that it would complicate the interaction.

There was only one additional suggestion on how to improve the machine: one person thought he should be able to talk to the machine. Since customers are not designers, the lack of further suggestions is not surprising. We can't depend on users to invent or design for us. In any case, customers were clear about what they liked. For 21, the best aspect of the machine was 24-hour access. Another 14 cited its quickness and the fact that it will eliminate waiting in line. Convenience and efficiency! And that's just what we're trying to deliver.

12 Parting Thoughts

"THE BEAUTY OF THIS SYSTEM IS THAT THERE ARE A FEW SMALL ERRORS PROGRAMMED INTO IT, WHICH HELPS TO AVOID TOTAL DEPERSONALIZATION."

Few ideas have borne as much technological fruit as the concept of systems. Virtually all the complicated things that people construct—buildings (structure, plumbing, electricity, communications, transport, fire control); cities (police, fire, public works, revenue, utilities); and of course, computers—rely on collections of relatively independent though interrelated parts. Each part deals with a specific problem or function for the whole. People didn't invent systems, of course; plants and animals display a lot of system character. But the alternative to systems is *synergy*, in which each part is intimately related to each of the others, so that the whole is more than the sum of its parts. Most complicated things exhibit some system and some synergistic character.

Consider the components of an automobile:

- fuel system
- electrical system
- ignition system

Cartoon courtesy of Sidney Harris, Great Neck, New York.

- exhaust system
- engine
- transmission
- suspension system
- braking system
- instrumentation and controls

These subsystems are interdependent—the engine won't run without the electrical system, the battery won't charge if the engine doesn't run, and so on—but the components of each subsystem are largely independent of the components of the others. Thus the synergy is at the subsystem level, not at the component level.

Automobiles have not always been so strongly system oriented. Not long ago, windshield-wiper motors were powered by vacuum created by the engine air intake. If the engine wasn't running, the wipers wouldn't operate, and during acceleration, they would slow or stop. Similarly, Volkswagen bugs for years had no water pump for the windshield cleaner fluid. Instead, the air in the spare tire provided the force to squirt the liquid. This design was a double-edged sword: if there wasn't enough pressure in the tire, the windshield couldn't be cleaned, but the driver in effect checked the spare tire air pressure frequently. A regulator prevented the tire from deflating too much.

The systems idea is powerful because it allows parts of a larger system to be developed independently, according to an interface specification. If the subsystem does what it is supposed to do at the interface, and if it does not have any side effects that are not accounted for, then the larger system will work. It is the side effects—like the loss of windshield wiper power during acceleration—that cause systems to work poorly or fail. Currently, most computer systems have side effects that reduce their usefulness to people. Human engineering frequently deals with issues that span subsystems.

PRINCIPLES OF GOOD HUMAN ENGINEERING

We believe that four principles bear directly on doing good human engineering and should guide all design and development projects:

1. Simplify.

   Of two equally useful designs for a system, choose the simpler. This is the Occam's razor of design. Simple things are easier to build, easier to test, easier to learn, and easier to use.

2. Engineering is compromise.

   Only rarely can a system have the best of everything. The art of engineering is the art of compromise, evaluating tradeoffs on the basis of their relative importance.

3. Think things through.

   There are consequences and side effects of any feature or capability in a system—affecting both system and users. Thoroughness in dealing with these interactions, especially proposed changes, avoids surprises later.

4. The perfect is the enemy of the good.

   It's crucial to stop optimizing at some point, to get out a good product rather than forever seek perfection and never ship anything. There are no perfect designs, so seeking perfection takes a long time.

SUMMARY IDEAS

The following ten ideas summarize the human factors guidelines presented in this book.

1. Know thy user. The user is always right.

   Human factors engineering is user-centered design. By focusing on the user, designers ensure that people's needs drive the technology, rather than the other way around.

2. Develop a use model for the system.

   How people will use the tools determines what those tools should be. Designers are responsible for understanding how users currently solve the problems that the system addresses, and how the system will fit into the user's life. The use model is a sort of user-impact study.

3. Choose a good external myth to influence the way in which users think about the system.

The conceptual models that users develop arise in large part from the behavior of the system. With careful planning and testing, designers can ensure that users' understanding of the system is simple, appropriate, and useful.

4. Use human conversation as a model for dialogues.

   How people behave when they converse with each other provides a rich source of guidance for the design of human interfaces. People are good at interpersonal communication and bring that experience and knowledge to computer interactions.

5. Do documentation as part of design.

   Documentation is as much a part of systems as any of the hardware or programs. Documentation of high quality must be designed along with the rest of a product. Doing the documentation as part of design reveals many flaws while it is still inexpensive to fix them.

6. Build consistent human interfaces.

   Human interface style is a matter of taste and appropriateness to a particular user and system environment. Choose a suitable style and stick with it. Multiple modes representing different styles add complexity but not value to a design.

7. Design the errors in a system.

   Errors happen in the system, not in the user. By attending to the design, engineers can ensure that fewer errors will occur and that users will be better able to recover from those that do.

8. Respond to people in real time.

   What is good response depends on user expectations and on whether delays disrupt the interaction. When the user is involved in a feedback loop, as with typing or graphical input, response must be fast enough to avoid confusion or "stuttering." Variation in response time is at least as important as absolute duration.

9. Use the user's representation for data.

   The computer must accommodate the user, rather than vice versa. Don't force the user to think about data in an unnatural (or just different) way. Allow flexible input representation and provide consistent output representation.

10. You build it, you test it.

    Designers can and must evaluate their systems. User testing is the only means of determining whether a design meets its goals and requirements. Conducting simple evaluations early in the design process eliminates mistakes that would be far more costly to fix at a later time. Testing prototypes with representative users is essential.

There is an old rabbinic saying that goes: "Don't limit a child to your own learning, for he was born in another time." This quotation speaks of children, but a similar thought might well apply to the systems we build. We must allow them to develop in their own worlds, not solely in ours. Our systems are not for us, but for the beneficiaries of our craft.

Appendix
Teaching Human Factors

We believe that the best way to teach human factors is in an interactive setting—one in which students and instructors debate ideas, question precepts, and increase their knowledge together. In a classroom this means that completed assignments are considered in an open forum. It also means that whether an assignment involves a report on an existing system, a critique of a computer-generated bank statement, or a proposal for a command language for use with a telephone, it is likely to be open ended, having no fixed solution or single answer. One valuable strategy in course work involving open-ended assignments is to have the grader (the person who evaluates the work and who gives the final grade) be someone other than the instructor. This arrangement allows students to express and develop ideas, question the instructor, and speak up more freely. It also permits the instructor to relax more in front of the class, hold wider-ranging discussions with students, and stop worrying about grades.

The following selection of sample exercises contains some that can be done in one or two days, and some that may require two or three weeks and may be assigned to a group of two to six students for a collective effort. Most of the exercises can be used either for short assignments whose result will necessarily be incomplete or for two- to three-month projects.

PLAYING A VIDEO GAME

The video games in today's arcades have some fascinating human engineering features. They are used by children and adults without any special training or documentation. That they are successful is without question. The knobs, pushbuttons, displays, toggle switches, and scrolling are all important to their operation.

Pick a video game and play it several times. Then write a report evaluating the aspects of the game that seem to be important to its ease-of-use. Include in your discussion both those features that work well and those that don't.

RIDING AN ELEVATOR

Some people hate riding in elevators, and this exercise may shed light on why. An elevator can actually be quite complicated to understand. In what sequence does it visit floors? What is the effect of pressing the "close door" button? Are you afraid to press the "emergency stop" button? Does repetitive pressing of the button for your floor speed things up? How do adjacent elevators interact in the task that they share?

Ride an elevator and write a report evaluating its human interface.

EVALUATING YOUR COMPUTER

Write a human factors evaluation of the computer you are most familiar with and the things needed to use it. Here are some possible questions to answer:

- Is there an introductory document describing the use of your computer in general terms? If so, is it helpful? What kind of information does it contain?
- Is there a user's guide or some other collection of documents to help you operate the system? Describe the guide or other documents in relation to the system.
- Are the documents describing the operations clear, complete, and enjoyable to read? Is there a good index? Are there many examples?
- Does the keyboard have many special-purpose keys? Do you understand what the keys mean? Do you often forget what the keys mean?
- Can you understand what is written on the screen? Is it obvious to most users how to use it?
- Is the language of operation transparent? Are there some simple and clear rules for creating instructions?
- Are the messages that the system gives simple and clear? Are they full of computer jargon?
- Is there a clear external myth for the system? Describe it.

Now prepare a report at least five pages long for use by a person or company considering the purchase of the computer. Describe critically all aspects of the system affecting ease of use, and provide definite conclusions.

MOVING THE CURSOR

On most video terminals, the computer displays a cursor that indicates a place on the screen, such as a character in a document or a choice in a list of menu items. A cursor is said to be "free moving" if you can move it to virtually any point on the screen's work area. A free moving cursor is more like running your finger over the screen, with no constraints arising from what is on the screen. A bound cursor is limited in its motion to the field, window, or region in which it is contained. Certain operations move a bound cursor from one area to another. On many systems, actual use of the cursor may be some combination of the two. For example, when you choose menu items the cursor may hop from one item to the next, but when you edit tables the cursor may be positioned anywhere, even between columns.

Write a paper explaining why one method of cursor movement is superior to another. The best explanation would articulate principles of cursor movement that relate to human behavior. If you decide that one is better than the other only in certain circumstances, describe the relevant circumstances in detail.

DESIGNING A SCROLLING EDITOR

Imagine that you are editing a file of text and that the line you are editing is highlighted on the screen. Let us call this the "current line."

In one type of editing environment, the text is presented on the screen in units. Each unit fills the work area of the screen. For example, if your screen is the size of a full page and your document is five pages long, you will view the text as five separate pages. To edit a particular line you make it the current line. If you want a line on the next page, you ask the computer to display the next page and move the current line to the correct position. Let us call this a "fixed-page" editor.

In another scenario, imagine that the text of your document is presented as an endless scroll of paper. You place text on the screen and, in effect, roll the window of the screen around the document. In such a system, the current line itself is fixed, say somewhere near the middle of the screen.

To edit the text, you scroll the text until the material you seek is on the current line. This is called a "scrolling" editor.

Write a paper explaining why one method is superior to the other.

DESIGNING A SIMPLE COMMAND LANGUAGE

Imagine that the climate control on your new car comes equipped with voice input. You can speak command words, numbers, or short phrases (such as "defrost," "heat 70 degrees," or "off") to the control unit. Such a language might have 10 or 15 commands, each expressed by a single word or number. To be a bit more specific, imagine the following commands:

CLIMATE	Introduces a climate control command.
HEAT	Sets the climate control to generate heat.
COOL	Sets the climate control to air conditioning.
FAN ON	Causes the built-in fan to be operated. The fan has three speeds, low, medium, and high.
FAN OFF	Stops the fan.

Devise a suitable command language and write a user reference manual. The manual must describe the complete action of the climate control under any possible sequence of words in a command. You may assume that if a word is spoken that is not one of the command words, no attempt is made to understand it, but that its presence is known. You should keep your system as simple as possible and yet conceivably useful. Be prepared to justify your design.

CREATING ERROR MESSAGES

The error messages generated by a computer tend to be cryptic, couched in jargon, and apparently unconnected to the user's problem. Human-engineered systems should provide clear, understandable error messages.

List 10 error messages that you encounter in your everyday work on a system, preferably 10 that are more or less related to the same task, such as manipulating files. Then prepare a five-page report discussing them and a list of specific recommendations for improvement. You might consider backup messages (an amplification of the existing message, to be given if a help command is issued). Comment also on the attitude taken toward the user and the style of language used.

STARTING UP

On large interactive systems a user logs in and enters a password. On stand-alone computers, the user may have to turn on the machine, load a floppy disk, and press some special keys in order to start work. Either of these scenarios constitutes a start-up sequence.

Prepare a one- or two-page list of instructions for the start-up sequence of a system you know well. Then redesign the start-up sequence with better human engineering. Prepare a second list of instructions to accomplish the same end. To do this, imagine the best of possible worlds, in which consideration of the user is paramount, while also taking into account any reasonable constraints imposed by the hardware or software you are using. For example, if you are using a large interactive system, it will be difficult or impossible to dispense with a password although you may call it by a different name. On a stand-alone computer the load media (floppy disk or tape) may be indispensable.

DETERMINING APPROPRIATE RESPONSE TIME

Call someone on the telephone, preferably an understanding friend. In the middle of the conversation, stop and see how long it takes for the other person to comment on it. Try changing your partner's expectations and repeating the test. For example, you might say, "Give me a second to write this down and I will be right with you." Write down how long it is before the person loses patience or checks to see that the telephone connection is still okay. The goal of this exercise is to determine how many seconds elapse before your subject becomes unhappy. Repeat the experiment with at least three other people.

Write a report analyzing the data you've collected. In your report try to discuss why a longer response time is appropriate in certain situations. Explain whether or not these data are relevant to response time in computer dialogues.

ANALYZING OUTPUT

First find three different items that are examples of outstanding human engineering (charts, graphs, bills, or other pieces of output). Copies of *Time* or *Newsweek* magazines might provide especially clear examples. The items need not be actually computer generated but should be at least suggestive of computer output. Next, find three varied items that are deficient in comprehensibility, and indicate by what criteria you have judged them so.

Write a small report containing the examples, with annotations.

IMPROVING THE FORMAT OF YOUR BANK STATEMENT

Take your bank statement and redesign it so that it is better human engineered. To make a fair comparison, prepare old and new statements the same way, say, on a typewriter or word processor. Then give them to a friend or classmate without identifying which is which. Evaluate the results in an objective way.

Write a report discussing the changes you made to the statement and the results from the evaluation.

BE A FIRST-TIME USER

In the hands of an expert or salesperson, any system may look easy to use. To determine the true ease of use of a system, go to a computer store and ask for a demonstration of a product that you are unfamiliar with.

When you get to the computer store, choose a product that can be demonstrated live. Ask the salesperson to give you a run-through of the things it does. While you are talking with the salesperson, try to probe as deeply as you can. Ask to use the system yourself, even if the sales person has to tell you which keys to press. Notice whether the commands appear to be consistent or not, what the displays are like, and what kind of conceptual model you are asked to develop. If possible, examine a copy of the complete user's guide.

Write a four- or five-page report describing your experience.

REDESIGNING THE TELEPHONE

In addition to digits, a pushbutton telephone has two additional keys, * and #, that enhance its capabilities.

Consider things you might do with the telephone, such as setting up conference calls (calls with at least three parties on the line), transfers (switching to another number on the same exchange), call forwarding (having calls automatically referred to another number for a specified time), and Queueing (entering busy numbers in the telephone's memory for automatic redialing). You may even be using some of these and similar features already, but the current design of the telephone "keyboard" is inadequate for all these applications. Redesign the standard telephone keyboard and its underlying control logic so that the keyboard can be easily used for such applications. Keep in mind that you are redesigning a telephone, not building a new computer. Prepare a ten-to-thirty-page design, complete with an illustration of the keyboard and a small user's manual. The design should include a thorough evaluation of human factors, expandability to new uses, and the cost of the final product. Also consider whether it should look like the existing telephone keyboard so as to gain acceptance by the public.

WRITING A USER'S GUIDE

Choose a small part of a system you are familiar with, such as a five-key editor or the commands to save and retrieve files—any part whose function is clear and discrete. (For example, it doesn't make any sense to edit files without saving them.) Then write a complete, easy-to-read, full-of-examples, nicely formatted, and otherwise high-quality user's guide. If you have chosen your system function well, five pages may be enough.

Acknowledgments

Many special people did special things to aid us, including helping us realize that in designing a product for someone else's use, no two people have the market cornered on insight and good ideas.

In the time it took us to create one book, Barbara Rubinstein gave birth to two babies. She must know something we don't. During the same time period Sandy Hersh finished a business degree and progressed from a part-time secretary to general manager of a corporation. Our productivity pales in comparison to both these wonderful women. In addition to their own work, each glued her husband back together on a daily basis so that our work could go on.

Emily and Adam Hersh helped their dad in many ways. Their many hugs and kisses gave him the energy to sit in the basement in front of the computer terminal, typing away into the night.

Adam Rubinstein learned to say "no" as the final draft was going to the printer. His father finds this inspiring, and is trying to emulate him. Beth Rubinstein has the patience of extreme youth. Her patience and many smiles have been an example for her father.

Larry Samberg is a believer. He was our manager during much of the writing, and created an environment in which we could both learn and write. Without his support, The Human Factor could scarcely have happened.

Charles Abernethy provided valuable conversation, ideas, and good will during the book's gestation.

David Fanger was the guinea pig upon whom the ideas in "The Other Kind of Software" chapter were tested. His perspective as a writer of user documentation helped us greatly. He also graciously offered to review the whole book, to good effect.

Kenneth Lodding fashioned the original errorless design on which the one in Chapter 9 is based. It's his no-fault. Thank you to Austin

Henderson whose ideas on command scanners are embedded in the Hermes message system, and reflected in Chapter 8.

Branko Gerovac, whose name is pronounced "Gerr-o-vahts," as best we can transliterate it, reviewed the book and provided many useful comments and suggestions. Peter Christy, Dan Kalikow, Bob Levy, Ben Shniederman, and John C. Thomas read, critiqued, and thus helped us improve successive drafts of the book.

Glossary

Human factors, like other fields, has its own jargon and terminology. Here are brief definitions of the terms used in this book, as well as a few related terms from psychology and statistics.

ANTHROPOMETRIC: Referring to the measure of man; the division of human factors dealing with physical characteristics and capabilities of people.

ANTHROPOMORPHIC: Resembling man, especially giving human characteristics to nonhuman things.

ATTRIBUTES: Characteristics that can be used to differentiate otherwise similar things.

CHUNKING: Combining of parts into larger conceptual elements.

CLOSURE: The feeling of having finished some task. Closure feels good.

COGNITION: Thinking; in psychology, the study of how people process information.

COGNITIVE STYLE: The way an individual processes information. There are various qualitatively different styles.

CONCEPTUAL MODEL: The understanding that a user has of the system he or she uses.

CONTROL (EXPERIMENTAL): A subject in an experiment who does the task in the normal way instead of in the way being tested.

DIN: West German Standards Association, *Deutsche Industrie Normen.*

EASE OF USE: A catchall phrase for the goodness of a human interface. An easy-to-use system causes the user few troubles.

EXTERNAL MYTH: The consistent external behavior of a system.

FORCE-DISPLACEMENT CURVE: The relationship between pressure and how far down a keyboard key is depressed.

FORMAL LANGUAGE: A created language or notation, often defined explicitly. Examples are Boolean algebra, musical notation, and FORTRAN.

GESTALT: Overall impression or understanding, often attained without instruction or rational analysis; an integrated whole.

HUMAN INTERFACE: Everything that the user sees, touches, or otherwise senses and interacts with in a computer (or other) system.

LEARNING CURVE: The amount of a skill that has been learned over a period of time.

LONG-TERM MEMORY: Memory that humans keep after their attention has shifted. This memory is potentially unlimited in extent and duration.

MEAN: The average of a group of numbers, that is, the sum of the numbers divided by how many there are in the group.

MEDIAN: A number in a group chosen so that half of the numbers in the group are larger, and half are smaller.

MODE (HUMAN INTERFACE): A state or condition that affects the interpretation of user actions.

MODE (STATISTICS): The most frequent value in a set of numbers.

NATURAL LANGUAGE: A language that has evolved through usage rather than been invented. Examples are French, English, and Japanese.

PROMPT: Text printed by a computer to indicate that input is required or permitted and to suggest the kind of input that may be entered.

SEMANTICS: The meaning associated with a statement in some language, as opposed to its form or syntax.

SHORT-TERM MEMORY: Memory that lasts only a short while and is limited to 7 ± 2 items.

SIGNIFICANCE LEVEL: The likelihood that a positive experimental result happened by chance. A significant level of 0.05 means that 5 out of 100 times a false-positive result will be obtained.

SYNTAX: The form of a statement in a language, as opposed to its meaning or semantics.

TASK ANALYSIS: The process of determining what potential users of a system currently do or would do with the system to accomplish their goals. Task analysis is analysis of behavior and goals, not of the system to be designed.

USE MODEL: The ways in which a system is used in an environment, an environmental impact statement.

VARIANCE OF THE MEAN: A measure of the spread of a set of values, that is, how much they differ from each other.

Bibliography

[Abelson 1976]
Robert P. Abelson
Script Processing in Attitude Formation and Decision Making, in J. S. Carroll and J. W. Payne (eds.), *Cognition and Social Behavior.*
Hillsdale, NJ: Lawrence Earlbaum Associates, 1976.

[Anderson and Bower 1974]
John R. Anderson and Gordon H. Bower
Human Associative Memory.
New York: Halsted Press, 1974.

[Bandura and Walters 1963]
A. Bandura and R. H. Walters
Social Learning and Personality Development
New York: Hold, Rinehart, and Winston, 1963.

[Boies 1982]
Stephen J. Boies
ADS—Audio Distribution System
Presented at Probe Seminar on Voice Processing, New York, September 15–16, 1982.

[Brooks 1975]
Frederick P. Brooks, Jr.
The Mythical Man-Month
Reading, MA: Addison-Wesley, 1975.

[Brown 1983]
John S. Brown
The Pragmatics of AI Methodology—Where the High Road Meets the Low Road
Conference on "The Reality of Artificial Intelligence"
Cambridge, MA: Massachusetts Institute of Technology, March 23, 1983.

[Brown et al 1974]
John S. Brown, Richard R. Burton, and Alan G. Bell
SOPHIE: A Sophisticated Instructional Environment for Teaching Electronic Troubleshooting (An Example of AI in CAI).
BBN Report No. 2790, 1 March 1974.
Cambridge, MA: Bolt Beranek and Newman Inc.

[Brown et al 1976]
John Seely Brown, Richard Rubinstein, and Richard Burton
Reactive Learning Environment for Computer Assisted Electronics Instruction
BBN Report No. 3314; ICAI Report No. 1
Cambridge, MA: Bolt Beranek and Newman Inc., October 1976.

[Byte 1982]
Byte Magazine, August 1982, p. 449.

[Campbell and Stanley 1963]
Donald T. Campbell and Julian C. Stanley
Experimental and Quasi-experimental Designs for Research
Chicago: Rand McNally College Publishing Company, 1963.

[Card et al 1977]
Stuart K. Card, William K. English, and B. Burr
Evaluation of Mouse, Rate-Controlled Isometric Joystick, Step Keys, and Text Keys for Text Selection on a CRT.
Technical Report SSL-77-1
Xerox Palo Alto Research Center, April, 1977.

[Card et al 1980]
Stuart K. Card, Thomas P. Moran, and Allen Newell
Computer Text-Editing: An Information-Processing Analysis of a Routine Cognitive Skill
Cognitive Psychology, 1980, vol. 12, pp. 32–74.
(Also available as PARC Report No. P76-00082, Xerox Palo Alto Research Center, December, 1976.)

[Chapanis 1965]
Alfonse Chapanis
On the Allocation of Functions between Men and Machines
Occupational Psychology, 1965, vol. 39, pp. 1–11.

[Chapanis 1975]
Alfonse Chapanis (ed.)
Ethnic Variables in Human Factors Engineering.
Baltimore: The Johns Hopkins Press, 1975.

[Chomsky 1957]
Noam Chomsky
Syntactic Structures.
The Hague: Mouton, 1957.

[Cox 1958]
D. R. Cox
Planning of Experiments
New York: John Wiley & Sons, Inc., 1958.

[Datamation 1983]
Datamation, August 1983, p. 229.

[Davis 1982]
Randy Davis
Expert Systems: Where are we? and where do we go from here?
A.I. Memo No. 665, Artificial Intelligence Laboratory,
Massacusetts Institute of Technology, June, 1982.

[Dean 1982]
Morris Dean
How a Computer Should Talk to People
IBM System Journal, 1982, vol. 21, no. 4, pp. 424–453.

[Engel and Granda 1975]
Stephen E. Engel and Richard E. Granada
Guidelines for Man/Display Interfaces
IBM Technical Report no. TR 00.2720, December 19, 1975.

[Geller et al 1974]
Daniel M. Geller, Lynne Goodstein, Maury Silver, and Wendy C. Sternberg
On Being Ignored: The effects of the violation of implicit rules of social interaction.
Sociometry, 1974, vol. 37, no. 4, pp. 541–556.

[Gould 1981]
John D. Gould
Composing Letters with Computer-Based Text Editors
Human Factors, 1981, vol. 23, no. 5, pp. 593–606.

[Gould 1982]
John D. Gould
Writing and Speaking Letters and Messages
International Journal of Man-Machine Studies, 1982, vol. 16, pp. 147–171.

[Gould and Ascher 1974]
John D. Gould and Robert N. Ascher
Query by Non-programmer
Paper presented at the 82nd Annual Convention of the American Psychological Association, New Orleans, August 30 to September 3, 1974.

[Gould et al 1982]
John D. Gould, John Conti, and Todd Hovanyecz
Composing Letters with a Simulated Listening Typewriter
Proceedings from Conference on Human Factors in Computer Systems, Gaithersburg, Maryland, March 15–17, 1982, pp. 367–370.

[Grice 1975]
H. P. Grice
Logic and Conversation
In P. Cole & J. Morgan, *Syntax & Semantics, Vol. 3: Speech Acts.*
New York: Academic Press, 1975.

[Halasz and Moran 1982]
Frank Halasz and Thomas P. Moran
Analogy Considered Harmful.
Proceedings from Conference on Human Factors in Computer Systems, Gaithersburg, Maryland, March 15–17, 1982, pp. 383–386.

[Hannyngton 1871]
Major-General Hannyngton
The Journal of the Institute of Actuaries and Assurance Magazine, 1871, vol. 26, p. 244.

[Harris 1977]
Larry R. Harris
ROBOT: A High Performance Natural Language Interface for Data Base Query
Technical Report 11-1, Mathematics Department, Dartmouth College, 1977.

[Hersh 1981]
Harry M. Hersh
EMS/VMS Learning Analysis
Internal Technical Report, Corporate Research Group, Digital Equipment Corporation, July 31, 1981.

[Hersh 1982a]
Harry M. Hersh
DECgraph Icon Assessment
Internal Technical Report, User Research Group, Digital Equipment Corporation, 1982.

[Hersh 1982b]
Harry M. Hersh
Electronic Mail Usage Analysis
Proceedings from Conference on Human Factors in Computer Systems, Gaithersberg, Maryland, March 15–17, 1982, pp. 278–280.

[Hyman 1982]
Anthony Hyman
Charles Babbage: Pioneer of the Computer
Princeton, NJ: Princeton University Press, 1982.

[Kahneman 1973]
Daniel Kahneman
Attention and Effort
Englewood Cliffs, NJ: Prentice-Hall, Inc., 1973.

[Ledgard et al 1980]
Henry Ledgard, John A. Whiteside, Andrew Singer, and William Seymour
The Natural Language of Interactive Systems
Communications of the ACM, 1980, vol. 23, no. 10, pp. 556–563.

[Levy 1982]
Robert Levy
Individual Differences
Internal Technical Report, Corporate Research Group, Digital Equipment Corporation, 1982.

[Lindsay and Norman 1977]
Peter H. Lindsay and Donald A. Norman
Human Information Processing: An Introduction to Psychology, Second Edition
New York: Academic Press, 1977.

[Mason and Carey 1983]
R. E. A. Mason and T. T. Carey
Prototyping Interactive Information Systems
Communications of the ACM, 1983, vol. 26, no. 5, pp. 347–354.

[Miller and Isard 1963]
George A. Miller and S. Isard
Some Perceptual Consequences of Linguistic Rules
Journal of Verbal Learning and Verbal Behavior, 1963, vol. 2, pp. 217–228.

[Miller and Selfridge 1950]
George A. Miller and J. A. Selfridge
Verbal Context and the Recall of Meaningful Material
American Journal of Psychology, 1950, vol. 63, pp. 176–185.

[Miller 1974]
Lance A. Miller
Programming by Non-programmers
International Journal of Man-Machine Studies, 1974, vol. 6, pp. 237–260.

[Miller and Becker 1974]
Lance A. Miller and C. Becker
Programming in Natural English
IBM Technical Report RC5137, November 1974.

[Miller 1968]
Robert B. Miller
Response Time in Man-Computer Conversational Transactions
American Federation of Information Processing Societies Conference Proceedings, Fall 1968, vol. 33 (pt. 1), pp. 267–277.

[Mooers 1983]
Charlotte D. Mooers
Changes that Users Demanded in the Human Interface to the Hermes Message System
Proceedings of CHI'83 Human Factors in Computing Systems, Boston, December 12–15, 1983
New York: Association for Computer Machinery, 1983.

[Moran 1981]
Thomas P. Moran
The Command Language Grammar: A representation for the user interface of interactive computer systems.
International Journal of Man-Machine Studies, 1981, vol. 15, pp. 3–50.

[Myer et al 1973]
Theodore H. Myer, revised by William W. Plummer
TENEX Executive Language: Manual for users
NIC No. 16874
Cambridge, MA: Bolt Beranek and Newman, Inc., April 1973.

[Myers 1972]
Jerome L. Myers
Fundamentals of Experimental Design, Second Edition
Boston: Allyn and Bacon, Inc., 1972.

[NBS 1982]
National Bureau of Standards
National Bureau of Standards Workshop on Standardization for Speech I/O Technology
Gaithersberg, Maryland, March 18–19, 1982.

[Neisser 1967]
Ulrich Neisser
Cognitive Psychology,
New York: Appleton-Century-Crofts, 1967.

[Nelson 1980]
Ted Nelson
Interactive Systems and the Design of Virtuality
Creative Computing, November and December, 1980.

[NET 1982]
New England Telephone
Can Computers Understand a 'Downeast Twang?'
Mainelines, June 1982, pp. 1–2.

[Newell and Simon 1972]
Allen Newell and Herbert A. Simon
Human Problem Solving
Englewood Cliffs, NJ: Prentice-Hall, 1972.

[Norman 1982]
Donald A. Norman
Steps toward a Cognitive Engineering: Design rules based on analyses of human error.
Proceedings from Conference on Human Factors in Computer Systems, Gaithersberg, Maryland, March 15–17, 1982, pp. 378–382.

[Ochsman and Chapanis 1974]
Robert B. Ochsman and Alfonse Chapanis
The Effects of 10 Communictaion Modes on the Behavior of Teams During Co-operative Problem-Solving
International Journal of Man-Machine Study, 1974, vol. 6, pp. 579–619.

[Papert 1980]
Seymore Papert
Mindstorms: Children, Computers, and Powerful Ideas
New York: Basic Books, 1980.

[Peterson 1980]
James L. Peterson
Computer Programs for Detecting and Correcting Spelling Errors
Communications of the ACM, 1980, vol. 23, no. 12, pp. 676–687.

[Pisoni 1982]
David B. Pisoni
Perception of Synthetic Speech: Some contributions by the human listener
Speech Technology, 1982, vol. 1, no. 2, pp. 10–23.

[Probe 1982]
Probe Seminar on Voice Processing, New York, September 15–16, 1982.

[Ramsey et al 1978]
H. Rudy Ramsey, Michael E. Atwood, and Priscilla J. Kirshbaum
A Critically Annotated Bibliography of the Literature on Human Factors in Computer Systems
Technical Report SAI-78-070-DEN, Science Applications, Inc., May 1978.
(Also available as Manuscript 1822 from Journal Supplement Abstract Service, American Psychological Association.)

[Ramsey and Atwood 1979]
H. Rudy Ramsey and Micheal E. Atwood
Human Factors in Computer Systems: A review of the literature
Technical Report SAI-79-111-DED, Science Applications, Inc., September 1979.

[Reisner 1977]
Phyllis Reisner
Use of Psychological Experimentation as an Aid to Development of a Query Language
IEEE Transactions on Software Engineering, vol. SE-3, no. 3, May 1977.

[Rooney 1981]
Andrew A. Rooney
A Few Minutes with Andy Rooney
New York: Warner Books, 1981.

[Rosenthal 1978]
Robert Rosenthal
How Often Are Our Numbers Wrong?
American Psychologist, November 1978, pp. 1005–1008.

[Rude et al 1979]
Richard V. Rude, Deborah L. Melone, and Charlotte D. Mooers
The Hermes Message System: Integrated Communications Management (Level I: Basic Communications)
Cambridge, MA: Bolt Beranek and Newman, Inc., 1979.

[Shneiderman 1982]
Ben Shneiderman
The Future of Interactive Systems and the Emergence of Direct Manipulation
Behavior and Information Technology, 1982, vol. 1, no. 3, pp. 237–256.

[Sinaiko 1975]
H. Wallace Sinaiko
Verbal Factors in Human Engineering: Some cultural and psychological data.
In A. Chapanis (ed.), *Ethnic Variables in Human Factors Engineering*
Baltimore: Johns Hopkins Press, 1975.

[Singer, Ledgard, and Hueras 1980]
The Annotated Assistant: A step towards human engineering
IEEE Transactions on Software Engineering, 1981, vol. SE-7, no. 4, pp. 353–374.
Cognitive Psychology, 1980, vol. 12, pp. 32–74.

[Stern 1981]
Nancy Stern
From ENIAC to UNIVAC: An appraisal of the Eckert-Mauchly computers
Bedford, MA: Digital Press, 1981.

[Strunk and White 1979]
William Strunk & E. B. White
The Elements of Style.
New York: Macmillan, 1979.

[Sutherland 1980]
Ivan E. Sutherland
Sketchpad: A man-machine graphical communication system
New York: Garland Publishing, 1980.

[Teitelman 1974]
Warren Teitelman
Interlisp Reference Manual
Xerox Palo Alto Research Center, 1974.

[Thomas 1976]
John C. Thomas
Quantifiers and Question-Asking
Research Report RC5866, IBM Watson Research Center, February 18, 1976.

[Thomas and Carroll 1981]
John C. Thomas and John M. Carroll
Human Factors in Communication
IBM Systems Journal, 1981, vol. 20, no. 2, pp. 237–263.

[Thomas and Gould 1975]
John C. Thomas and John D. Gould
A Psychological Study of Query by Example
AFIPS Conference Proceedings, 1975, vol. 44, pp. 439–445.

[Weizenbaum 1966]
Joseph Weizenbaum
ELIZA—A Computer Program for the Study of Natural Language Communication Between Man and Machine
Communications of the ACM, 1966, vol. 9, no. 1, pp. 36–45.

[Whiteside et al 1982]
John Whiteside, Norman Archer, Dennis Wixon, and Michael Good
How Do People Really Use Text Editors?
SIGOA Newsletter, 1982, vol. 3, nos. 1 and 2, pp. 29–40.

[Wilpon and Rabiner 1983]
Jay B. Wilpon and Lawrence R. Rabiner
On the Recognition of Isolated Digits from a Large Telephone Customer Population
The Bell System Technical Journal, 1983, vol. 62, no. 7, pp. 1977–2000.

[Woods et al 1972]
William A. Woods, R. M. Kaplan, and Bonnie Nash-Webber
The Lunar Sciences Natural Language Information System: Final Report
BBN Report No. 2378
Cambridge, MA: Bolt, Beranek and Newman, Inc., June, 1972.

Index